Parables From Nature

Parables From Nature
by Mrs. Alfred Gatty

©2008 Wilder Publications

This book is a product of its time and does not reflect the same values as it would if it were written today. Parents might wish to discuss with their children how views on race have changed before allowing them to read this classic work.

All rights reserved. Printed in the United States of America. No part of this book may be used or reproduced in any manner without written permission except for brief quotations for review purposes only.

Wilder Publications, LLC.
PO Box 3005
Radford VA 24143-3005

ISBN 10: 1-60459-621-X
ISBN 13: 978-1-60459-621-2

A Lesson of Faith

"If a man die, shall he live again?
All the days of my appointed time will I wait, till my change come."
—JOB xiv. 14.

"Let me hire you as a nurse for my poor children," said a Butterfly to a quiet Caterpillar, who was strolling along a cabbage-leaf in her odd lumbering way. "See these little eggs," continued the Butterfly; "I don't know how long it will be before they come to life, and I feel very sick and poorly, and if I should die, who will take care of my baby butterflies when I am gone? Will you, kind, mild, green Caterpillar? But you must mind what you give them to eat, Caterpillar!—they cannot, of course, live on your rough food. You must give them early dew, and honey from the flowers; and you must let them fly about only a little way at first; for, of course, one can't expect them to use their wings properly all at once. Dear me! it is a sad pity you cannot fly yourself. But I have no time to look for another nurse now, so you will do your best, I hope. Dear! dear! I cannot think what made me come and lay my eggs on a cabbage-leaf! What a place for young butterflies to be born upon! Still you will be kind, will you not, to the poor little ones? Here, take this gold-dust from my wings as a reward. Oh, how dizzy I am! Caterpillar! you will remember about the food—"

And with these words the Butterfly closed her eyes and died; and the green Caterpillar who had not had the opportunity of even saying Yes or No to the request, was left standing alone by the side of the Butterfly's eggs.

"A pretty nurse she has chosen, indeed, poor lady!" exclaimed she, "and a pretty business I have in hand! Why, her senses must have left her, or she never would have asked a poor crawling creature like me to bring up her dainty little ones! Much they'll mind me, truly, when they feel the gay wings on their backs, and can fly away out of my sight whenever they choose! Ah! how silly some people are, in spite of their painted clothes and the gold-dust on their wings!"

However, the poor Butterfly was dead, and there lay the eggs on the cabbage-leaf; and the green Caterpillar had a kind heart, so she resolved to do her best. But she got no sleep that night, she was so very anxious. She made her back quite ache with walking all night long round her little charges, for fear any harm should happen to them; and in the morning says she to herself—

"Two heads are better than one. I will consult some wise animal upon the matter, and get advice. How should a poor crawling creature like me know what to do without asking my betters?"

But still there was a difficulty—whom should the Caterpillar consult? There was the shaggy Dog who sometimes came into the garden. But he was so rough!—he would most likely whisk all the eggs off the cabbage-leaf with one brush of his tail, if she called him near to talk to her, and then she should never forgive herself. There was the Tom Cat, to be sure, who would sometimes sit at the foot of the apple-tree, basking himself and warming his fur in the sunshine; but he was so selfish and indifferent!—there was no hope of his giving himself the trouble to think about butterflies' eggs.

"I wonder which is the wisest of all the animals I know," sighed the Caterpillar, in great distress; and then she thought, and thought, till at last she thought of the Lark; and she fancied that because he went up so high, and nobody knew where he went to, he must be very clever, and know a great deal; for to go up very high (which she could never do) was the Caterpillar's idea of perfect glory.

Now, in the neighbouring corn-field there lived a Lark, and the Caterpillar sent a message to him, to beg him to come and talk to her; and when he came she told him all her difficulties, and asked him what she was to do, to feed and rear the little creatures so different from herself.

"Perhaps you will be able to inquire and hear something about it next time you go up high," observed the Caterpillar timidly.

The Lark said, "Perhaps he should;" but he did not satisfy her curiosity any further. Soon afterwards, however, he went singing upwards into the bright, blue sky. By degrees his voice died away in the distance, till the green Caterpillar could not hear a sound.

It is nothing to say she could not see him; for, poor thing! she never could see far at any time and had a difficulty in looking upwards at all, even when she reared herself up most carefully, which she did now; but it was of no use, so she dropped upon her legs again, and resumed her walk round the Butterfly's eggs, nibbling a bit of the cabbage-leaf now and then as she moved along.

"What a time the Lark has been gone!" she cried, at last. "I wonder where he is just now! I would give all my legs to know! He must have flown up higher than usual this time, I do think! How I should like to know where it is that he goes to, and what he hears in that curious blue sky! He always sings in going up and coming down, but he never lets any secret out. He is very, very close!"

And the green Caterpillar took another turn round the Butterfly's eggs.

At last the Lark's voice began to be heard again. The Caterpillar almost jumped for joy and it was not long before she saw her friend descend with hushed note to the cabbage bed.

"New, news, glorious news, friend Caterpillar!" sang the Lark; "but the worst of it is, you won't believe me!"

"I believe everything I am told," observed the Caterpillar hastily.

"Well, then, first of all, I will tell you what these little creatures are to eat"—and the Lark nodded his beak towards the eggs. "What do you think it is to be? Guess!"

"Dew, and the honey out of flowers, I am afraid," sighed the Caterpillar.

"No such thing, old lady! Something simpler than that. Something that you can get at quite easily."

"I can get at nothing quite easily but cabbage-leaves," murmured the Caterpillar, in distress.

"Excellent! my good friend," cried the Lark exultingly; "you have found it out. You are to feed them with cabbage-leaves."

"Never!" said the Caterpillar indignantly. "It was their dying mother's last request that I should do no such thing."

"Their dying mother knew nothing about the matter," persisted the Lark; "but why do you ask me, and then disbelieve what I say? You have neither faith nor trust."

"Oh, I believe everything I am told," said the Caterpillar.

"Nay, but you do not," replied the Lark; "you won't believe me even about the food, and yet that is but a beginning of what I have to tell you. Why, Caterpillar, what do you think those little eggs will turn out to be?"

"Butterflies, to be sure," said the Caterpillar.

"Caterpillars!" sang the Lark; "and you'll find it out in time;" and the Lark flew away, for he did not want to stay and contest the point with his friend.

"I thought the Lark had been wise and kind," observed the mild green Caterpillar, once more beginning to walk round the eggs, "but I find that he is foolish and saucy instead. Perhaps he went up too high this time. Ah, it's a pity when people who soar so high are silly and rude nevertheless! Dear! I still wonder whom he sees, and what he does up yonder."

"I would tell you, if you would believe me," sang the Lark, descending once more.

"I believe everything I am told," reiterated the Caterpillar, with as grave a face as if it were a fact.

"Then I'll tell you something else," cried the Lark; "for the best of my news remains behind. You will one day be a Butterfly yourself."

"Wretched bird!" exclaimed the Caterpillar, "you jest with my inferiority—now you are cruel as well as foolish. Go away! I will ask your advice no more."

"I told you you would not believe me," cried the Lark, nettled in his turn.

"I believe everything that I am told," persisted the Caterpillar; "that is"—and she hesitated,—"everything that it is reasonable to believe. But to tell me that butterflies' eggs are caterpillars, and that caterpillars leave off crawling and get wings, and become butterflies!—Lark! you are too wise to believe such nonsense yourself, for you know it is impossible."

"I know no such thing," said the Lark, warmly. "Whether I hover over the corn-fields of earth, or go up into the depths of the sky, I see so many wonderful things, I know no reason why there should not be more. Oh, Caterpillar! it is because you crawl, because you never get beyond your cabbage-leaf, that you call any thing impossible."

"Nonsense!" shouted the Caterpillar. "I know what's possible, and what's not possible, according to my experience and capacity, as well as you do. Look at my long green body and these endless legs, and then talk to me about having wings and a painted feathery coat! Fool!—"

"And fool you! you would-be-wise Caterpillar!" cried the indignant lark. "Fool, to attempt to reason about what you cannot understand! Do you not hear how my song swells with rejoicing as I soar upwards to the mysterious wonder-world above? Oh, Caterpillar! what comes to you from thence, receive, as I do, upon trust."

"That is what you call—"

"Faith," interrupted the Lark.

"How am I to learn Faith?" asked the Caterpillar.

At that moment she felt something at her side. She looked round—eight or ten little green caterpillars were moving about, and had already made a show of a hole in the cabbage-leaf. They had broken from the Butterfly's eggs!

Shame and amazement filled our green friend's heart, but joy soon followed; for, as the first wonder was possible, the second might be so too. "Teach me your lesson, Lark!" she would say; and the Lark sang to her of the wonders of the earth below, and of the heaven above. And the Caterpillar talked all the rest of her life to her relations of the time when she should be a Butterfly.

But none of them believed her. She nevertheless had learnt the Lark's lesson of faith, and when she was going into her chrysalis grave, she said—"I shall be a Butterfly some day!"

But her relations thought her head was wandering, and they said, "Poor thing!"

And when she was a Butterfly, and was going to die again, she said—

"I have known many wonders—I have faith—I can trust even now for what shall come next!"

The Law of Authority and Obedience

"Who made thee a ruler and a judge over us?"
—ACTS vii. 27.

A fine young Working-bee left his hive, one lovely summer's morning, to gather honey from the flowers. The sun shone so brightly, and the air felt so warm, that he flew a long, long distance, till he came to some gardens that were very beautiful and gay; and there having roamed about, in and out of the flowers, buzzing in great delight, till he had so loaded himself with treasures that he could carry no more, he bethought himself of returning home. But, just as he was beginning his journey, he accidentally flew through the open window of a country-house, and found himself in a large dining-room.

There was a great deal of noise and confusion, for it was dinner-time, and the guests were talking rather loudly, so that the Bee got quite frightened. Still he tried to taste some rich sweetmeats that lay temptingly in a dish on the table, when all at once he heard a child exclaim with a shout, "Oh, there's a bee, let me catch him!" on which he rushed hastily back to (as he thought) the open air. But, alas! poor fellow, in another second he found that he had flung himself against a hard transparent wall! In other words, he had flown against the glass panes of the window, being quite unable, in his alarm and confusion, to distinguish the glass from the opening by which he had entered.

This unexpected blow annoyed him much; and having wearied himself in vain attempts to find the entrance, he began to walk slowly and quietly up and down the wooden frame at the bottom of the panes, hoping to recover both his strength and composure.

Presently, as he was walking along, his attention was attracted by hearing the soft half-whispering voices of two children, who were kneeling down and looking at him.

Said the one to the other, "This is a working-bee, Sister; I see the wax-bags under his thighs. Nice fellow! how busy he has been!"

"Does he make the wax and honey himself?" whispered the Girl.

"Yes, he gets them from the insides of the flowers. Don't you remember how we watched the bees once dodging in and out of the crocuses, how we laughed at them, they were so busy and fussy, and their dark coats looked so handsome against the yellow leaves? I wish I had seen this fellow loading himself to-day.

But he does more than that. He builds the honeycomb, and does pretty nearly everything. He's a working-bee, poor wretch!"

"What is a working-bee? and why do you call him 'Poor wretch,' Brother?"

"Why, don't you know, Uncle Collins says, all people are poor wretches who work for other people who don't work for themselves? And that is just what this bee does. There is the queen-bee in the hive, who does nothing at all but sit at home, give orders, and coddle the little ones; and all the bees wait upon her, and obey her. Then there are the drones—lazy fellows, who lounge all their time away. And then there are the working-bees, like this one here, and they do all the work for everybody. How Uncle Collins would laugh at them, if he knew!"

"Doesn't Uncle Collins know about bees?"

"No, I think not. It was the gardener who told me. And, besides, I think Uncle Collins would never have done talking about them and quizzing them, if he once knew they couldn't do without a queen. I heard him say yesterday, that kings and queens were against Nature, for that Nature never makes one man a king and another a cobbler, but makes them all alike; and so he says, kings and queens are very unjust things."

"Bees have not the sense to know anything about that," observed the little Girl, softly.

"Of course not! Only fancy how angry these working fellows would be, if they knew what the gardener told me!"

"What was that?"

"Why, that the working-bees are just the same as the queen when they are first born, just exactly the same, and that it is only the food that is given them, and the shape of the house they live in, that makes the difference. The bee-nurses manage that; they give some one sort of food, and some another, and they make the cells different shapes, and so some turn out queens, and the rest working-bees. It's just what Uncle Collins says about kings and cobblers—Nature makes them all alike. But, look! the dinner's over—we must go."

"Wait till I let the Bee out, Brother," said the little Girl, taking him gently up in a soft handkerchief; and then she looked at him kindly and said, "Poor fellow! so you might have been a queen if they had only given you the right food, and put you into a right-shaped house! What a shame they didn't! As it is, my good friend," (and here her voice took a childish mocking tone)—"As it is, my good friend, you must go and drudge away all your life long, making honey and wax. Well, get along with you! Good luck to your labours!" And with these words she fluttered her handkerchief through the open window, and the Bee found himself once more floating in the air.

Oh, what a fine evening it was! But the liberated Bee did not think so. The sun still shone beautifully though lower in the sky, and though the light was softer, and the shadows were longer; and as to the flowers, they were more fragrant than ever; yet the poor Bee felt as if there were a dark heavy cloud over his own heart, for he had become discontented and ambitious, and he rebelled against the authority under which he had been born.

At last he reached his home—the hive which he had left with such a happy heart in the morning—and, after dashing in, in a hurried and angry manner, he began to unload the bags under his thighs of their precious contents, and as he did so he exclaimed, "I am the most wretched of creatures!"

"What is the matter? what have you done?" cried an old Relation who was at work near him; "have you been eating the poisonous kalmia flowers, or have you discovered that the mischievous honey-moth has laid her eggs in our combs?"

"Oh, neither, neither!" answered the Bee, impatiently; "only I have travelled a long way, and have heard a great deal about myself that I never knew before, and I know now that we are a set of wretched creatures!"

"And, pray, what wise animal has been persuading you of that, against your own experience?" asked the old Relation.

"I have learnt a truth," answered the Bee, in an indignant tone, "and it matters not who taught it me."

"Certainly not; but it matters very much that you should not fancy yourself wretched merely because some foolish creature has told you you are so; you know very well that you never were wretched till you were told you were so. I call that very silly; but I shall say no more to you." And the old Relation turned himself round to his work, singing very pleasantly all the time.

But the Traveller-bee would not be laughed out of his wretchedness; so he collected some of his young companions around him, and told them what he had heard in the large dining-room of the country-house; and all were astonished, and most of them vexed. Then he grew so much pleased at finding himself able to create such excitement and interest, that he became sillier every minute, and made a long speech on the injustice of there being such things as queens, and talked of Nature making them all equal and alike, with an energy that would have delighted Uncle Collins himself.

When the Bee had finished his speech, there was first a silence and then a few buzzes of anger, and then a murmured expression of plans and wishes. It must be admitted, their ideas of how to remedy the evil now for the first time suggested to them, were very confused.

Some wished Uncle Collins would come and manage all the beehives in the country, for they were sure he would let all the bees be queens, and then what a jolly time they should have! And when the old Relation popped his head round the corner of the cell he was building, just to inquire, "What would be the fun of being queens, if there were no working-bees to wait on one?" the little coterie of rebels buzzed very loud, and told him he was a fool, for, of course, Uncle Collins would take care that the tyrant who had so long been queen, and the royal children, now ripening in their nurse-cells, should be made to wait on them while they lasted.

"And when they are finished?" persisted the old Relation, with a laugh.

"Buzz, buzz," was the answer; and the old Relation held his tongue.

Then another Bee suggested that it would, after all, be very awkward for them all to be queens; for who would make the honey and wax, and build the honeycombs, and nurse the children? Would it not be best, therefore, that there should be no queens whatever, but that they should all be working-bees?

But then the tiresome old Relation popped his head round the corner again, and said, he did not quite see how that change would benefit them, for were they not all working-bees already?—on which an indignant buzz was poured into his ear, and he retreated again to his work.

It was well that night at last came on, and the time arrived when the labours of the day were over, and sleep and silence must reign in the hive. With the dawn of the morning, however, the troubled thoughts unluckily returned, and the Traveller-bee and his companions kept occasionally clustering together in little groups, to talk over their wrongs and a remedy.

Meantime, the rest of the hive were too busy to pay much attention to them, and so their idleness was not detected. But, at last, a few hot-headed youngsters grew so violent in their different opinions, that they lost all self-control, and a noisy quarrel would have broken out, but that the Traveller-bee flew to them, and suggested that, as they were grown up now, and could not all be turned into queens, they had best sally forth and try the republican experiment of all being working-bees without any queen whatever.

With so charming an idea in view, he easily persuaded them to leave the hive; and a very nice swarm they looked as they emerged into the open air, and dispersed about the garden to enjoy the early breeze. But a swarm of bees, without a queen to lead them, proved only a helpless crowd, after all. The first thing they attempted, when they had recollected to consult, was, to fix on the sort of place in which they should settle for a home.

"A garden, of course," says one. "A field," says another. "There is nothing like a hollow tree," remarked a third. "The roof of a good outhouse is best protected from wet," thought a fourth. "The branch of a tree leaves us most at liberty," cried a fifth. "I won't give up to anybody," shouted all.

They were in a prosperous way to settle, were they not?

"I am very angry with you," cried the Traveller-bee, at last; "half the morning is gone already, and here we are as unsettled as when we left the hive!"

"One would think you were going to be queen over us, to hear you talk," exclaimed the disputants. "If we choose to spend our time in quarrelling, what is that to you? Go and do as you please yourself!"

And he did; for he was ashamed and unhappy; and he flew to the further extremity of the garden to hide his vexation; where, seeing a clump of beautiful jonquils, he dived at once into a flower to soothe himself by honey-gathering. Oh, how he enjoyed it! He loved the flowers and the honey-gathering more than ever, and began his accustomed murmur of delight, and had serious thoughts of going back at once to the hive as usual, when as he was coming out of one of the golden cups, he met his old Relation coming out of another.

"Who would have thought to find you here alone?" said the old Relation. "Where are your companions?"

"I scarcely know; I left them outside the garden."

"What are they doing?"

". . . Quarrelling . . ." murmured the Traveller-bee.

"What about?"

"What they are to do."

"What a pleasant occupation for bees on a sunshiny morning!" said the old Relation, with a sly expression.

"Don't laugh at me, but tell me what to do," said the puzzled Traveller. "What Uncle Collins says about Nature and our all being alike, sounds very true, and yet somehow we do nothing but quarrel when we try to be all alike and equal."

"How old are you?" asked the old Relation.

"Seven days," answered the Traveller, in all the sauciness of youth and strength.

"And how old am I?"

"Many months, I am afraid."

"You are right, I am an oldish bee. Now, my dear friend, let us fight!"

"Not for the world. I am the stronger, and should hurt you."

"I wonder what makes you ask advice of a creature so much weaker than yourself?"

"Oh, what can your weakness have to do with your wisdom, my good old Relation? I consult you because I know you are wise; and I am humbled myself, and feel that I am foolish."

"Old and young—strong and weak—wise and foolish—what has become of our being alike and equal? But never mind, we can manage. Now let us agree to live together."

"With all my heart. But where shall we live?"

"Tell me first which of us is to decide, if we differ in opinion?"

"You shall; for you are wise."

"Good! And who shall collect honey for food?"

"I will; for I am strong."

"Very well; and now you have made me a queen, and yourself a working-bee! Ah! you foolish fellow, won't the old home and the old queen do? Don't you see that if even two people live together, there must be a head to lead and hands to follow? How much more in the case of a multitude!"

Gay was the song of the Traveller-bee as he wheeled over the flowers, joyously assenting to the truth of what he heard.

"Now to my companions," he cried at last. And the two flew away together and sought the knot of discontented youngsters outside the garden wall.

They were still quarrelling, but no energy was left them. They were hungry and confused, and many had flown away to work and go home as usual.

And very soon afterwards a cluster of happy buzzing bees, headed by the old Relation and the Traveller, were seen returning with wax-laden thighs to their hive.

As they were going to enter, they were stopped by one of the little sentinels who watch the doorway.

"Wait," cried he; "a royal corpse is passing out!"

And so it was;—a dead queen soon appeared in sight, dragged along by working-bees on each side; who, having borne her to the edge of the hive-stand, threw her over for interment.

"How is this? what has happened?" asked the Traveller-bee, in a tone of deep anxiety and emotion: "Surely our queen is not dead?"

"Oh, no!" answered the sentinel; "but there has been some accidental confusion in the hive this morning. Some of the cell-keepers were unluckily absent, and a young queen-bee burst through her cell, which ought to have been blocked up for a few days longer. Of course the two queens fought till one was dead; and, of course, the weaker one was killed. We shall not be able to send off a swarm quite so soon as usual this year; but these accidents can't be helped."

"But this one might have been helped," thought the Traveller-bee to himself, as with a pang of remorse he remembered that he had been the cause of the mischievous confusion.

"You see," buzzed the old Relation, nudging up against him,—"You see even queens are not equal! and that there can be but one ruler at once!"

And the Traveller-bee murmured a heart-wrung "Yes."

And thus the instincts of Nature confirm the reasoning conclusions of man.

The Unknown Land

"But now they desire a better country."
—HEBREWS xi. 16.

It mattered not to the Sedge Warbler whether it were night or day!

She built her nest down among the willows, and reeds, and long thick herbage that bordered the great river's side, and in her sheltered covert she sang songs of mirth and rejoicing both by night and day.

"Where does the great river go to?" asked the little ones, as they peered out of their nest one lovely summer night, and saw the moonbeams dancing on the waters as they hurried along.

Now, the Sedge Warbler could not tell her children where the great river went to; so she laughed, and said they must ask the Sparrow who chattered so fast, or the Swallow who travelled so far, next time one or other came to perch on the willow-tree to rest.

"And then," said she, "you will hear all such stories as these!"—and thereupon the Sedge Warbler tuned her voice to the Sparrow's note, and the little ones almost thought the Sparrow was there, the song was so like his—all about towns, and houses, and gardens and fruit-trees, and cats, and guns; only the Sedge Warbler made the account quite confused, for she had never had the patience to sit and listen to the Sparrow, so as really to understand what he said about these matters.

But imperfect as the tale was, it amused the little ones very much, and they tried then to sing like it, and sang till they fell asleep; and when they awoke, they burst into singing again; for, behold! the eastern sky was red with the dawn, and they knew the warm sunbeams would soon send beautiful streaks of light in among the reeds and flags that sheltered their happy home.

Now, the Mother-bird would sometimes leave the little ones below, and go up into the willow-branches to sing alone; and as the season advanced she did this oftener and oftener; and her song was plaintive and tender then, for she used to sing to the tide of the river, as it swept along she knew not whither, and think that some day she and her husband and children should all be hurrying so onward as the river hurried,—she knew not whither also,—to the Unknown Land whence she had come. Yes! I may call it the Unknown Land; for only faint images remained upon her mind of the country whence she had flown.

At first she used to sing these ditties only when alone, but by degrees she began to let her little ones hear them now and then—for were they not going to accompany her? and was it not as well, therefore, to accustom them gradually to think about it?

Then the little ones asked her where the Unknown Land was. But she smiled, and said she could not tell them, for she did not know.

"Perhaps the great river is travelling there all along," thought the eldest child. But he was wrong. The great river was rolling on hurriedly to a mighty city, where it was to stream through the arches of many bridges, and bear on its bosom the traffic of many nations; restless and crowded by day; gloomy, dark, and dangerous by night! Ah! what a contrast were the day and night of the mighty city to the day and night of the Sedge Warbler's home, where the twenty-four hours of changes God has appointed to Nature were but so many changes of beauty!

"Mother, why do you sing songs about another land?" asked a young tender-hearted fledgling one day. "Why should we leave the reed-beds and the willow-trees? Cannot we all build nests here, and live here always? Mother, do not let us go away anywhere else. I want no other land, and no other home but this. There are all the aits in the great river to choose from, where we shall each settle; there can be nothing in the Unknown Land more pleasant than the reed-beds and the willow-trees here. I am so happy!—Leave off those dreadful songs!"

Then the Mother's breast heaved with many a varied thought, and she made no reply. So the little one went on—

"Think of the red glow in the morning sky, Mother, and the soft haze—and then the beautiful rays of warm light across the waters! Think of the grand noonday glare, when the broad flags and reeds are all burnished over with heat. Think of these evenings, Mother, when we can sit about in the branches—here, there, anywhere—and watch the great sun go down behind the sky or fly to the aits of the great river, and sing in the long green herbage there, and then come home by moonlight and sing till we fall asleep; and wake singing again, if any noise disturb us, if a boat chance to paddle by, or some of those strange bright lights shoot up with a noise into the sky from distant gardens. Think, even when the rain comes down, how we enjoy ourselves, for then how sweet it is to huddle into the soft warm nest together, and listen to the drops pattering upon the flags and leaves overhead! Oh, I love this dear, dear home so much!—Sing those dreadful songs about another land no more!"

Then the Mother said—

"Listen to me, my child, and I will sing you another song."

And the Sedge Warbler changed her note, and sang to her tender little one of her own young days, when she was as happy and as gay as now, though not here among the reed-beds; and how, after she had lived and rejoiced in her happiness many pleasant months, a voice seemed to rise within her that said—"This is not your Rest!" and how she wondered, and tried not to listen, and tried to stop where she was, and be happy there still. But the voice came oftener and oftener, and louder and louder; and how the dear partner she had chosen heard and felt the same; and how at last they left their home together, and came and settled down among the reed-beds of the great river. And, oh, how happy she had been!

"And where is the place you came from, Mother?" asked the little one. "Is it anywhere near, that we may go and see it?"

"My child," answered the Sedge Warbler, "it is the Unknown Land! Far, far away, I know: but where, I do not know. Only the voice that called me thence is beginning to call again. And, as I was obedient and hopeful once, shall I be less obedient and hopeful now—now that I have been so happy? No, my little one, let us go forth to the Unknown Land, wherever it may be, in joyful trust."

"You will be with me;—so I will," murmured the little Sedge Warbler in reply; and before she went to sleep she joined her young voice with her mother's in the song of the Unknown Land.

One day afterwards, when the parent birds had gone off to the sedgy banks of a neighbouring stream, another of the young ones flew to the topmost branches of some willow-trees, and, delighted with his position, began to sing merrily, as he swung backwards and forwards on a bough. Many were the songs he tried, and well enough he succeeded for his age, and at last he tried the song of the Unknown Land.

"A pretty tune, and a pretty voice, and a pretty singer!" remarked a Magpie, who unluckily was crossing the country at the time, and whose mischievous spirit made him stop to amuse himself, by showing off to the young one his superior wisdom, as he thought it.

"I have been in many places, and even once was domesticated about the house of a human creature, so that I am a pretty good judge of singing," continued Mr. Mag, with a cock of his tail, as he balanced himself on a branch near the Sedge Warbler; "but, upon my word, I have seldom heard a prettier song than yours—only I wish you would tell me what it is all about."

"It is about the Unknown Land," answered the young Warbler, with modest pleasure, and very innocently.

"Do I hear you right, my little friend?" inquired the Magpie with mock solemnity—"The Unknown Land, did you say? Dear, dear! to think of finding such abstruse philosophy among the marshes and ditches! It is quite a treat! And pray, now, what is there that you can tell an odd old fellow like me, who am always anxious to improve myself, about this Unknown Land?"

"I don't know, except that we are going there some day," answered the Sedge Warbler, rather confused by the Magpie's manner.

"Now, that is excellent!" returned the Magpie, chuckling with laughter. "How I love simplicity, and, really, you are a choice specimen of it, Mr. Sedge Warbler. So you are thinking of a journey to this Unknown Land, always supposing, of course, my sweet little friend, that you can find the way to it, which, between you and me, I think there must naturally be some doubt about, under the circumstances of the place itself being unknown! Good evening to you, pretty Mr. Sedge Warbler. I wish you a pleasant journey!"

"Oh, stop, stop!" cried the young bird, now quite distressed by the Magpie's ridicule; "don't go just yet, pray. Tell me what you think yourself about the Unknown Land."

"Oh, you little wiseacre, are you laughing at me? Why, what can any body, even so clever a creature as yourself think about an unknown thing? You can guess, I admit, anything you please about it, and so could I, if I thought it worth while to waste my time so foolishly. But you will never get beyond guessing in such a case—at all events, I confess my poor abilities can't pretend to do anything more."

"Then you are not going there yourself?" murmured the overpowered youngster.

"Certainly not. In the first place, I am quite contented where I am; and, in the second place, I am not quite so easy of belief as you seem to be. How do I know there is such a place as this Unknown Land at all?"

"My father and mother told me that," answered the Sedge Warbler, with more confidence.

"Oh, your father and mother told you, did they?" sneered the Magpie, scornfully. "And you're a good little bird, and believe everything your father and mother tell you. And if they were to tell you you were going to live up in the moon, you would believe them, I suppose?"

"They never deceived me yet!" cried the young Sedge Warbler firmly, his feathers ruffling with indignation as he spoke.

"Hoity, toity! what's the matter now, my dainty little cock? Who said your father and mother had ever deceived you? But, without being a bit deceitful,

I take the liberty to inform you that they may be extremely ignorant. And I shall leave you to decide which of the two, yourself; for, I declare, one gets nothing but annoyance by trying to be good-natured to you countrified young fellows. You are not fit to converse with a bird of any experience and wisdom. So, once for all, good-bye to you!"

And the Magpie flapped his wings, and was gone before the Sedge Warbler had half recovered from his fit of vexation.

There was a decided change in the weather that evening, for the summer was now far advanced, and a sudden storm had brought cooler breezes and more rain than usual, and the young birds wondered, and were sad, when they saw the dark sky, and the swollen river, and felt that there was no warm sunshine to dry the wet, as was usual after a mid-day shower.

"Why is the sky so cloudy and lowering, and why is the river so thick and gloomy, and why is there no sunshine, I wonder?" said one.

"The sun will shine again to-morrow, I dare say," was the Mother's answer; "but the days are shortening fast; and the storm has made this one very short; and the sun will not get through the clouds this evening. Never mind! the wet has not hurt the inside of our nest. Get into it, my dear ones, and keep warm, while I sing to you about our journey. Silly children, did you expect the sunshine to last here for ever?"

"I hoped it might, and thought it would, once, but lately I have seen a change," answered the young one who had talked to her mother so much before. "And I do not mind now, Mother. When the sunshine goes, and the wet comes, and the river looks dark and the sky black, I think about the Unknown Land."

Then the Mother was pleased, and, perched upon a tall flag outside the nest, she sang a hopeful song of the Unknown Land; and the father and children joined—all but one! He, poor fellow, would not, could not sing; but when the voices ceased, he murmured to his brothers and sisters in the nest—

"This would be all very pleasant and nice, if we could know anything about the Land we talk about."

"If we were to know too much, perhaps we should never be satisfied here," laughed the tender little one, who had formerly been so much distressed about going.

"But we know nothing," rejoined the other bird; "indeed, how do we know there is such a place as the Unknown Land at all?"

"We feel that there is, at any rate," answered the Sister-bird. "I have heard the call our mother tells about, and so must you have done."

"You fancy you have heard it, that is to say," cried the Brother; "because she told you. It is all fancy, all guess-work; no knowledge! I could fancy I heard it too, only I will not be so weak and silly; I will neither think about going, nor will I go."

"This is not your Rest," sang the Mother, in a loud clear voice, outside; and "This is not your Rest," echoed the others in sweet unison; and "This is not your Rest," sounded in the depths of the poor little Sedge Warbler's own heart.

"This is not our Rest!" repeated the Mother. "The river is rushing forward; the clouds are hurrying onward; the winds are sweeping past, because here is not their Rest. Ask the river, ask the clouds, ask the winds, where they go to:—Another Land! Ask the great sun, as he descends away out of sight, where he goes to:—Another Land! And when the appointed time shall come, let us also arise and go hence."

"Oh! Mother, Mother, would that I could believe you! Where is that other Land?" Thus cried the distressed doubter in the nest. And then he opened his troubled heart, and told what the Magpie had said, and the parent birds listened in silence, and when he ceased—

"Listen to me, my son," exclaimed the Mother, "and I will sing you another song."

Whereupon she spoke once more of the land she had left before; but now the burden of her story was, that she had left it without knowing why. She "went out not knowing whither,"—in blind obedience, faith, and hope. As she traversed the wide waste of waters, there was no one to give her reasons for her flight, or tell her, "This and this will be your lot." Could the Magpie have told her, had he met her there? But had she been deceived? No! The secret voice which had called and led her forth, had been one of Kindness.

When she came to the reed-beds she knew all about it. For then arose the strong desire to settle. Then she and her dear partner lived together. And then came the thought that she must build a nest. Ah! had the Magpie seen her then, building a home for children yet unborn, how he would have mocked at her! What could she know, he would have asked, about the future? Was it not all guess-work, fancy, folly? But had she been deceived! No! It was that voice of Kindness that had told her what to do. For did she not become the happy mother of children? And was she not now able to comfort and advise her little ones in their troubles? For, let the Magpie say what he would, was it likely that the voice of Kindness would deceive them at last?

"No!" cried she; "in joyful trust let us obey the call, though now we know not why. When obedience and faith are made perfect, it may be that knowledge and explanation shall be given." So ended the Mother's strain, and no sad misgivings ever clouded the Sedge Warbler's home again.

Several weeks of changing autumn weather followed after this, and the chilly mornings and evenings caused the songs of departure to sound louder and more cheerily than ever in the reed-beds. They knew, they felt, they had confidence, that there was joy for them in the Unknown Land.

But one dark morning, when all were busy in various directions, a sudden loud sound startled the young ones from their sports, and in terror and confusion they hurried home. The old nest looked looser and more untidy than ever that day, for some water had oozed in through the half-worn bottom. But they huddled together into it, as of old, for safety. Soon, however, it was discovered that neither Father nor Mother were there; and after waiting in vain some time for their return, the frightened young ones flew off again to seek them.

Oh! weary, weary search for the missing ones we love! It may be doubted whether the sad reality, when they came upon it, exceeded the agony of that hour's suspense.

It ended, however, at last! On a patch of long rank herbage which covered a mud bank, so wet that the cruel sportsman could not follow to secure his prey, lay the stricken parent birds. One was already dead, but the Mother still lived, and as her children's wail of sorrow sounded in her ear, she murmured out a last gentle strain of hope and comfort.

"Away, away, my darlings, to the Unknown Land. The voice that has called to all our race before, and never but for kindness, is calling to you now! Obey! Go forth in joyful trust! Quick! Quick! There's no time to be lost!"

"But my Father—you—oh, my Mother!" cried the young ones.

"Hush, sweet ones, hush! We cannot be with you there. But there may be some other Unknown Land which this may lead to;" and the Mother laid her head against her wounded side and died.

Long before the sunbeams could pierce the heavy haze of the next autumn morning, the young Sedge Warblers rose for the last time o'er their much loved reed-beds, and took flight—"they knew not whither."

Dim and undefined hope, perhaps, they had that they might find their parents again in the Unknown Land. And if one pang of grief struck them when these hopes ended, it was but for a moment, for, said the Brother-Bird—

"There may be some other Unknown Land, better even than this, to which they may be gone."

Knowledge Not the Limit of Belief

"Canst thou by searching find out God?"
    —JOB xi. 7.

It was but the banging of the door, blown to by a current of wind from the open window, that made that great noise, and shook the room so much!

The room was a Naturalist's library, and it was a pity that some folio books of specimens had been left so near the edge of the great table, for, when the door clapt to, they fell down, and many plants, sea-weeds, etc., were scattered on the floor.

And, "Do we meet once again?" said a zoophyte to a seaweed in whose company he had been thrown ashore,—"Do we meet once again? This is a real pleasure. What strange adventures we have gone through since the waves flung us on the sands together!"

"Ay, indeed," replied the Seaweed, "and what a queer place we have come to at last! Well, well—but let me first ask you how you are this morning, after all the washing, and drying, and squeezing, and gumming, we have undergone?"

Zoophyte. "Oh, pretty well in health, Seaweed, but very, very sad. You know there is a great difference between you and me. You have little or no cause to be sad. You are just the same now that you ever were, excepting that you can never grow any more. But I! ah, I am only the skeleton of what I once was! All the merry little creatures that inhabited me are dead and dried up. They died by hundreds at a time soon after I left the sea; and even if they had survived longer, the nasty fresh water we were soaked in by the horrid being who picked us up, would have killed them at once. What are you smiling at?"

Seaweed. "I am smiling at your calling our new master a horrid being, and also at your speaking so positively about the little creatures that inhabited you."

"And why may I not speak positively of what I know so well?" asked the other.

Seaweed. "Oh, of what you know, by all means! But I wonder what we do know! People get very obstinate over what they think they know, and then, lo and behold! it turns out to be a mistake."

Zoophyte. "What makes you say this?"

Seaweed. "I have learnt it from a very curious creature I have made acquaintance with here—a bookworm. He walks through all the books in this library just as he pleases, and picks up a quantity of information, and knows a great deal. And he's a mere nothing, he says, compared to the creature who picked us up—the 'horrid being,' as you call him. Why, my dear friend, the Bookworm tells me that he who found us is a man, and that a man is the most wonderful creature in all the world; that there is nothing in the least like him. And this particular one here is a naturalist; that is, he knows all about living creatures, and plants, and stones, and I don't know what besides. Now, wouldn't you say that it was a great honour to belong to him, and to have made acquaintance with his friend the Bookworm?"

Zoophyte. "Of course I should, and do."

Seaweed. "Very well, I know you would; and yet I can tell you that this naturalist and his bookworm are just instances of what I have been saying. They fancy that betwixt them they know nearly everything, and get as obstinate as possible over the most ridiculous mistakes."

Zoophyte. "My good friend, are you a competent judge in such matters as these?"

"Oh, am I not!" the Seaweed rejoined. "Why now, for instance, what do you think the Bookworm and I have been quarrelling about half the morning? Actually as to whether I am an animal or a vegetable. He declares that I am an animal full of little living creatures like yours, and that there is a long account of all this written on the page opposite the one on which I am gummed!"

"Of all the nonsense I ever listened to!" began the Zoophyte, angrily, yet amused—but he was interrupted by the Seaweed—

"And as for you—I am almost ashamed to tell you—that you and all your family and connexions were, for generations and generations, considered as vegetables. It is only lately that these naturalists found out that you were an animal. May I not well say that people get very obstinate about what they think they know, and after all it turns out to be a mistake? As for me, I am quite confused with these blunders."

"O dear, how disappointed I am!" murmured the Zoophyte. "I thought we had really fallen into the hands of some very interesting creatures. I am very, very sorry! It seemed so nice that there should be wonderful, wise beings, who spend their time in finding out all about animals, and plants, and such things, and keep us all in these beautiful books so carefully. I liked it so much and now I find the wonderfully wise creatures are wonderfully stupid ones instead."

"Very much so," laughed the Seaweed, "though our learned friend, the Bookworm, would tell you quite otherwise; but he gets quite muddled when he talks about them, poor fellow!"

"It is very easy to ridicule your betters," said a strange voice; and the Bookworm, who had just then eaten his way through the back of Lord Bacon's Advancement of Learning, appeared sitting outside, listening to the conversation. "I shall be very sorry that I have told you anything, if you make such a bad use of the little bit of knowledge you have acquired."

"Oh, I beg your pardon, dear friend!" cried the Seaweed. "I meant no harm. You see it is quite new to us to learn anything; and, really, if I laughed, you must excuse me. I meant no harm—only I do happen to know—really for a fact—that I never was alive with little creatures like my friend the Zoophyte; and he happens to know—really for a fact—that he never was a vegetable; and so you see it made us smile to think of your wonderful creature, man, making such wonderfully odd mistakes."

At this the Bookworm smiled; but he soon shook his head gravely, and said—"All the mistakes man makes, man can discover and correct—I mean, of course, all the mistakes he makes about creatures inferior to himself, whom he learns to know from his own observation. He may not observe quite carefully enough one day, but he may put all right when he looks next time. I never give up a statement when I know it is true: and so I tell you again—laugh as much as you please—that, in spite of all his mistakes, man is, without exception, the most wonderful and the most clever of all the creatures upon earth!"

"You will be a clever creature yourself if you can prove it!" cried both the Zoophyte and Seaweed at once.

"The idea of taking me with my hundreds of living inhabitants for a vegetable!" sneered the Zoophyte.

"And me with my vegetable inside, covered over with lime, for an animal!" smiled the Seaweed.

Bookworm. "Ah! have your laugh out, and then listen. But, my good friends, if you had worked your way through as many wise books as I have done, you would laugh less and know more."

Zoophyte. "Nay, don't be angry, Bookworm."

Bookworm. "Oh, I am not angry a bit. I know too well the cause of all the folly you are talking, so I excuse you. And I am now puzzling my head to find out how I am to prove what I have said about the superiority of man, so as to make you understand it."

Seaweed. "Then you admit there is a little difficulty in proving it? Even you confess it to be rather puzzling."

Bookworm. "I do; but the difficulty does not lie where you think it does. I am sorry to say it—but the only thing that prevents your understanding the superiority of man, is your own immeasurable inferiority to him! However many mistakes he may make about you, he can correct them all by a little closer or more patient observation. But no observation can make you understand what man is. You are quite within the grasp of his powers, but he is quite beyond the reach of yours."

Seaweed. "You are not over-civil, with all your learning, Mr. Bookworm."

Bookworm. "I do not mean to be rude, I assure you. You are both of you very beautiful creatures, and, I dare say, very useful too. But you should not fancy either that you do know everything, or that you are able to know everything. And, above all, you should not dispute the superiority and powers of other creatures merely because you cannot understand them."

Seaweed. "And am I then to believe all the long stories anybody may choose to come and tell me about the wonderful powers of other creatures?—and, when I inquire what those wonderful powers are, am I to be told that I can't understand them, but am to believe them all the same as if I did?"

Bookworm. "Certainly not, unless the wonderful powers are proved by wonderful results; but if they are, I advise you to believe in them, whether you understand them or not."

Seaweed. "I should like to know how I am to believe what I don't understand."

Bookworm. "Very well, then, don't! and remain an ignorant fool all your life. Of course, you can't really understand anything but what is within the narrow limits of your own powers; so, if you choose to make those powers the limits of your belief, I wish you joy, for you certainly won't be overburdened with knowledge."

Seaweed. "I will retort upon you that it is very easy to be contemptuous to your inferiors, Mr. Bookworm. You would do much better to try and explain to me those wonderful powers themselves, and so remove all the difficulties that stand in the way of my belief."

Bookworm. "If I were to try ever so much, I should not succeed. You can't understand even my superiority."

Seaweed. "Oh, Bookworm! now you are growing conceited."

Bookworm. "Indeed I am not; but you shall judge for yourself. I can do many things you can't do; among others, I can see."

Seaweed. "What is that?"

Bookworm. "There, now! I knew I should puzzle you directly! Why, seeing is something that I do with a very curious machine in my head, called an eye. But as you have not got an eye, and therefore cannot see, how am I to make you understand what seeing is?"

Seaweed. "Why, you can tell us, to be sure."

Bookworm. "Tell you what? I can tell you I see. I can say, Now I see, now I see, as I walk over you and see the little bits of you that fall under my small eye. Indeed, I can also tell you what I see; but how will that teach you what seeing is? You have got no eye, and therefore you can't see, and therefore also you can never know what seeing is."

Zoophyte. "Then why need we believe there is such a thing as seeing?"

Bookworm. "Oh, pray, don't believe it! I don't know why you should, I am sure! There's no harm at all in being ignorant and narrow-minded. I am sure I had much rather you took no further trouble in the matter; for you are, both of you, very testy and tiresome. It is from nothing but pride and vanity, too, after all. You want to be in a higher place in creation than you are put in, and no good ever comes of that. If you'd be content to learn wonderful things in the only way that is open to you, I should have a great deal of pleasure in telling you more."

Zoophyte. "And pray what way is that?"

Bookworm. "Why, from the effects produced by them. As I said before, even where you cannot understand the wonderful powers themselves, you may have the grace to believe in their existence, from their wonderful results."

Seaweed. "And the results of what you call 'seeing' are—"

"In man," interrupted the Bookworm, "that he gets to know everything about you, and all the creatures, and plants, and stones he looks at; so that he knows your shape, and growth, and colour, and all about the cells of the little creatures that live in you—how many feelers they have, what they live upon, how they catch their food, how the eggs come out of the egg-cells, where you live, where you are to be found, what other zoophytes are related to you, which are most like you—in short, the most minute particulars;—so that he puts you into his collections, not among strange creatures, but near to those you are nearest related to; and he describes you, and makes pictures of you, and gives you a name so that you are known for the same creature, wherever you are found, all over the world. And now, I'm quite out of breath with telling you all these wonderful results of seeing."

"But he once took me for a vegetable," mused the Zoophyte.

"Yes; as I said before, he had not observed quite close enough, nor had he then invented a curious instrument which enables his great big eye to see such little fellows as your inhabitants are. But when he made that instrument, and looked very carefully, he saw all about you."

"Ay, but he still calls me an animal," observed the Seaweed.

"I know he does, but I am certain he will not do so long! If you are a vegetable, I will warrant him to find it out when he examines you a little more."

"You expect us to believe strange things, Bookworm," observed the Zoophyte.

"To be sure, because there is no end of strange things for you to believe! And what you can't find out for yourself, you must take upon trust from your betters," laughed the Bookworm. "It's the only plan. Observation and Revelation are the sole means of acquiring knowledge."

Just at that moment the door opened, and two gentlemen entered the room.

"Ah, my new specimens on the floor!" observed the Naturalist; "but never mind," added he, as he picked them up; "here is the very one we wanted; it will serve admirably for our purpose. I shall only sacrifice a small branch of it, though."

And the Naturalist cut off a little piece of the Seaweed and laid it in a saucer, and poured upon it some liquid from a bottle, and an effervescence began to take place forthwith, and the Seaweed's limy coat began to give way; and the two gentlemen sat watching the result.

"Now," whispered the Bookworm to the Zoophyte, "those two men are looking closely at your Seaweed friend, and trying what they call experiments, that they may find out what he is; and if they do not succeed, I will give up all my arguments in despair."

But they did succeed!

The gentlemen watched on till all the lime was dissolved, and there was nothing left in the saucer but a delicate red branch with little round things upon it, that looked like tiny apples.

"This is the fruit decidedly," remarked the Naturalist; "and now we will proceed to examine it through the microscope."

And they did so.

And an hour or more passed, and a sort of sleepy forgetfulness came over the Bookworm and his two friends; for they had waited till they were tired for further remarks from the Naturalist. And, therefore, it was with a start they were aroused at last by hearing him exclaim, "It is impossible to entertain the slightest doubt. If I ever had any, I have none now; and the Corallinas must be removed back once more to their position among vegetables!"

The Naturalist laughed as he loosened the gum from the specimen, which he placed on a fresh paper, and classed among Red Seaweeds. And soon after, the two gentlemen left the room once more.

"So he has really found our friend out!" cried the Zoophyte; "and he was right about the fruit, too! Oh, Bookworm, Bookworm! would that I could know what seeing is!"

"Oh, Zoophyte, Zoophyte! I wish you would not waste your time in struggling after the unattainable! You know what feeling is. Well, I would tell you that seeing is something of the same sort as feeling, only that it is quite different. Will that do?"

"It sounds like nonsense."

"It is nonsense. There can be no answer but nonsense, if you want to understand 'really for a fact,' as you call it, powers that are above you. Explain to the rock on which you grow, what feeling is!"

"How could I?" said the Zoophyte; "it has no sensation."

"No more than you have sight," rejoined the Bookworm.

"That is true indeed," cried the Zoophyte. "Bookworm! I am satisfied—humbled, I must confess, but satisfied. And now I will rejoice in our position here, glory in our new master, and admire his wonderful powers, even while I cannot understand them."

"I am proud of my disciple," returned the Bookworm kindly.

"I also am one of them," murmured the Seaweed; "but tell me now, are there any other strange powers in man?"

"Several," was the Bookworm's answer; "but to be really known they must be possessed. A lower power cannot compass the full understanding of a higher. But to limit one's belief to the bounds of one's own small powers, would be to tie oneself down to the foot of a tree, and deny the existence of its upper branches."

"There are no powers beyond those that man possesses, I suppose," mused the Zoophyte.

"I am far from saying that," replied the Bookworm; "on the contrary—"

But what he would have said further no one knows, for once more the door opened, and the Naturalist, who now returned alone, spent his evening in putting by the specimens in their separate volumes on the shelves. And it was a long, long time before the Bookworm saw them again; for the volumes in which they were kept were bound in Russia leather, to the smell of which he had a particular dislike, so that he could never make his way to them for a friendly chat again.

Training and Restraining

"Train up a child in the way he should go."
—PROVERBS. xxii. 6.

"What a fuss is made about you, my dear little friends!" murmured the Wind, one day, to the flowers in a pretty villa garden. "I am really quite surprised at your submitting so patiently and meekly to all the troublesome things that are done to you! I have been watching your friend the Gardener for some time to-day; and now that he is gone at last, I am quite curious to hear what you think and feel about your unnatural bringing up."

"Is it unnatural?" inquired a beautiful Convolvulus Major, from the top of a tapering fir-pole, up which she had crept, and from which her velvet flowers hung suspended like purple gems.

"I smile at your question," was the answer of the Wind. "You surely cannot suppose that in a natural state you would be forced to climb regularly up one tall bare stick such as I see you upon now. Oh dear, no! Your cousin, the wild Convolvulus, whom I left in the fields this morning, does no such thing, I assure you. She runs along and climbs about, just as the whim takes her. Sometimes she takes a turn upon the ground; sometimes she enters a hedge, and plays at bo-peep with the birds in the thorn and nut-trees—twisting here, curling there, and at last, perhaps coming out at the top, and overhanging the hedge with a canopy of green leaves and pretty white flowers. A very different sort of life from yours, with a Gardener always after you, trimming you in one place, fastening up a stray tendril in another, and fidgeting you all along—a sort of perpetual 'mustn't go here'—'mustn't go there.' Poor thing! I quite feel for you! Still I must say you make me smile; for you look so proud and self-conscious of beauty all the time, that one would think you did not know in what a ridiculous and dependent position you are placed."

Now the Convolvulus was quite abashed by the words of the Wind, for she was conscious of feeling very conceited that morning, in consequence of having heard the Gardener say something very flattering about her beauty; so she hung down her rich bellflowers rather lower than usual, and made no reply.

But the Carnation put in her word: "What you say about the Convolvulus may be true enough, but it cannot apply to me. I am not aware that I have any poor relations in this country, and I myself certainly require all the care that is bestowed upon me. This climate is both too cold and too damp for me. My young plants require heat, or they would not live; and the pots we are kept in protect us from those cruel wire-worms who delight to destroy our roots."

"Oh!" cried the Wind, "our friend the Carnation is quite profound and learned in her remarks, and I admit the justice of all she says about damp and cold, and wire-worms; but,"—and here the Wind gave a low-toned whistle as he took a turn round the flower-bed—"but what I maintain, my dear, is that when you are once strong enough and old enough to be placed in the soil, those gardeners ought to let you grow and flourish as Nature prompts, and as you would do were you left alone. But no! forsooth, they must always be clipping, and trimming, and twisting up every leaf that strays aside out of the trim pattern they have chosen for you to grow in. Why not allow your silver tufts to luxuriate in a natural manner? Why must every single flower be tied up by its delicate neck to a stick, the moment it begins to open? Really, with your natural grace and beauty, I think you might be trusted to yourself a little more!"

And the Carnation began to think so too; and her colour turned deeper as a feeling of indignation arose within her at the childish treatment to which she had been subjected. "With my natural grace and beauty," repeated she to herself, "they might certainly trust me to myself a little more!"

Still the Rose-tree stood out that there must be some great advantages in a Gardener's care; for she could not pretend to be ignorant of her own superiority to all her wild relations in the woods. What a difference in size, in colour, and in fragrance!

Then the Wind assured the Rose he never meant to dispute the advantage of her living in a rich-soiled garden; only there was a natural way of growing, even in a garden; and he thought it a great shame for the gardeners to force the Rose-tree into an unnatural way, curtailing all the energies of her nature. What could be more outrageous, for example, than to see one rose growing in the shape of a bush on the top of the stem of another?

"Think of all the pruning necessary," cried he, "to keep the poor thing in the round shape so much admired. And what is the matter with the beautiful straggling branches, that they are to be cut off as fast as they appear? Why not allow the healthy Rose-tree its free and glorious growth? Why thwart its graceful droopings or its high aspirings? Can it be too large or too luxuriant? Can its flowers be too numerous? Oh, Rose-tree, you know your own surpassing merits too well to make you think this possible!"

And so she did, and a new light seemed to dawn upon her as she recollected the spring and autumnal prunings she regularly underwent, and the quantities of little branches that were yearly cut from her sides, and carried away in a wheel-barrow. "It is a cruel and a monstrous system, I fear," said she.

Then the Wind took another frolic round the garden, and made up to the large white Lily, into whose refined ear he whispered a doubt as to the necessity or advantage of her thick powerful stem being propped up against a stupid, ugly stick! He really grieved to see it! Did that lovely creature suppose that Nature, who had done so much for her that the fame of her beauty extended throughout the world, had yet left her so weak and feeble that she could not support herself in the position most calculated to give her ease and pleasure?

"Always this tying up and restraint!" pursued the Wind, with an angry puff. "Perhaps I am prejudiced; but as to be deprived of freedom would be to me absolute death, so my soul revolts from every shape and phase of slavery!"

"Not more than mine does!" cried the proud white Lily, leaning as heavily as she could against the strip of matting that tied her to her stick. But it was of no use—she could not get free; and the Wind only shook his sides and laughed spitefully as he left her, and then rambled away to talk the same shallow philosophy to the Honeysuckle that was trained up against a wall.

Indeed, not a flower escaped his mischievous suggestions. He murmured among them all—laughed the trim-cut Box-edges to scorn—maliciously hoped the Sweet-peas enjoyed growing in a circle, and running up a quantity of crooked sticks—and told the flowers, generally, that he should report their unheard-of submission and meek obedience wherever he went.

Then the white Lily called out to him in great wrath, and told him he mistook their characters altogether. They only submitted to these degrading restraints because they could not help themselves; but if he would lend them his powerful aid, they might free themselves from at least a part of the unnatural bonds which enthralled them.

To which the wicked Wind, seeing that his temptations had succeeded, replied, in great glee, that he would do his best; and so he went away, chuckling at the discontent he had caused.

All that night the pretty silly flowers bewailed their slavish condition, and longed for release and freedom; and at last they began to be afraid that the Wind had only been jesting with them, and that he would never come to help them, as he had promised. However, they were mistaken; for, at the edge of the dawn, there began to be a sighing and a moaning in the distant woods, and by the time the sun was up, the clouds were driving fast along the sky, and the trees were bending about in all directions; for the Wind had returned—only now he had come in his roughest and wildest mood—knocking over everything before him.

"Now is your time, pretty flowers!" shouted he, as he approached the garden; and "Now is our time!" echoed the flowers tremulously, as, with a sort of fearful pleasure, they awaited his approach.

He managed the affair very cleverly, it must be confessed. Making a sort of eddying circuit round the garden, he knocked over the Convolvulus-pole, tore the strips of bast from the stick that held up the white Lily, loosed all the Carnation flowers from their fastenings, broke the Rose-tree down, and levelled the Sweet-peas to the ground. In short, in one half-hour he desolated the pretty garden; and when his work was accomplished, he flew off to rave about his deed of destruction in other countries.

Meanwhile, how fared it with the flowers? The Wind was scarcely gone before a sudden and heavy rain followed, so that all was confusion for some time. But towards the evening the weather cleared up, and our friends began to look around them.

The white Lily still stood somewhat upright, though no friendly pole supported her juicy stem; but, alas! it was only by a painful effort she could hold herself in that position. The Wind and the weight of rain had bent her forward once, beyond her strength, and there was a slight crack in one part of the stalk, which told that she must soon double over and trail upon the ground.

The Convolvulus fared still worse. The garden-beds sloped towards the south; and when our friend was laid on the earth—her pole having fallen—her lovely flowers were choked up by the wet soil which drained towards her. She felt the muddy weight as it soaked into her beautiful velvet bells, and could have cried for grief: she could never free herself from this nuisance. O that she were once more climbing up the friendly fir-pole!

The Honeysuckle escaped no better; and the Carnation was ready to die of vexation, at finding that her coveted freedom had levelled her to the dirt.

Before the day closed, the Gardener came whistling from his farm work, to look over his pretty charges. He expected to see a few drooping flowers, and to find that one or two fastenings had given way. But for the sight that awaited him he was not prepared at all. Struck dumb with astonishment, he never spoke at first, but kept lifting up the heads of the trailing, dirtied flowers in succession. Then at last he broke out into words of absolute sorrow:—

"And to think of my mistress and the young lady coming home so soon, and that nothing can be done to these poor things for a fortnight, because of the corn harvest! It's all over with them, I fear;" and the Gardener went his way.

Alas! what he said was true; and before many days had passed, the shattered Carnations were rotted with lying in the wet and dirt on the ground. The white Lily was languishing discoloured on its broken stalk; the Convolvulus flowers could no longer be recognised, they were so coated over with mud stains; the Honeysuckle was trailing along among battered Sweet-peas, who never could succeed in shaking the soil from their fragrant heads; and though the Rose-tree had sent out a few straggling branches, she soon discovered that they were far too weak to bear flowers—nay, almost to support themselves—so that they added neither to her beauty nor her comfort. Weeds meanwhile sprang up, and a dreary confusion reigned in the once orderly and brilliant little garden.

At length, one day before the fortnight was over, the house-dog was heard to bark his noisy welcome, and servants bustled to and fro. The mistress had returned; and the young lady was with her, and hurried at once to her favourite garden. She came bounding towards the well-known spot with a song of joyous delight; but, on reaching it, suddenly stopped short, and in a minute after burst into a flood of tears! Presently, with sorrowing steps, she bent her way round the flower-beds, weeping afresh at every one she looked at; and then she sat down upon the lawn, and hid her face in her hands. In this position she remained, until a gentle hand was laid upon her shoulder.

"This is a sad spectacle, indeed, my darling," said her mother's voice.

"Never mind about the garden, mamma," replied the young girl, lifting up her tearful face; "we can plant new flowers, and tie up even some of these afresh. But what I have been thinking is, that now, at last, I quite understand what you have so often said about the necessity of training, and restraint, and culture, for us as well as for flowers, in a fallen world. The wind has torn away these poor things from their fastenings, and they are growing wild whichever way they please. I know I should once have argued that if it were their natural mode of growing it must therefore be the best. But I cannot say so, now that I see the result. They are doing whatever they like, unrestrained and the end is, that my beautiful GARDEN is turned into a WILDERNESS."

The Light of Truth

"We know that all things work together for good."
—ROM. viii. 28.

"Detestable phantom!" cried the traveller, as his horse sank with him into the morass; "to what a miserable end have you lured me by your treacherous light!"

"The same old story for ever!" muttered the Will-o'-the-Wisp in reply. "Always throwing blame on others for troubles you have brought upon yourself. What more could have been done for you, unhappy creature, than I have done? All the weary night through have I danced on the edge of this morass, to save you and others from ruin. If you have rushed in further and further, like a headstrong fool, in spite of my warning light, who is to blame but yourself?"

"I am an unhappy creature, indeed," rejoined the traveller: "I took your light for a friendly lamp, but have been deceived to my destruction."

"Yet not by me," cried the Will-o'-the-Wisp, anxiously. "I work out my appointed business carefully and ceaselessly. My light is ever a friendly lamp to the wise. It misleads none but the headstrong and ignorant."

"Headstrong! ignorant!" exclaimed the Statesman, for such the traveller was. "How little do you know to whom you are speaking! Trusted by my King—honoured by my country—the leader of her councils—ah, my country, my poor country, who will take my place and guide you when I am gone?"

"A guide who cannot guide himself! Misjudging, misled, and—though wise, perhaps, in the imperfect laws of society—ignorant in the glorious laws of Nature and of Truth—who will miss you, presumptuous being? You have mistaken the light that warned you of danger for the star that was to guide you to safety. Alas for your country, if no better leader than you can be found!"

The Statesman never spoke again, and the Will-o'-the-Wisp danced back to the edge of the black morass; and as he flickered up and down, he mourned his luckless fate—always trying to do good—so often vilified and misjudged. "Yet," said he to himself, as he sent out his beams through the cheerless night, "I will not cease to try; who knows but that I may save somebody yet! But what an ignorant world I live in!"

"Cruel monster!" shrieked the beautiful Girl in wild despair, as her feet plunged into the swamp, and she struggled in vain to find firmer ground, "you have betrayed me to my death!"

"Ay, ay, I said so! It is always some one else who is to blame, and never yourself, when pretty fools like you deceive themselves. You call me 'monster'—why did you follow a 'monster' into a swamp?" cried the poor Will-o'-the-Wisp angrily.

"I thought my betrothed had come out to meet me. I mistook your hateful light for his. Oh, cruel fiend, I know you now! Must I die so young, so fair? Must I be torn from life, and happiness, and love? Ay, dance! dance on in your savage joy."

"Fool as you are, it is no joy to me to see you perish," answered the Will-o'-the-Wisp. "It is my appointed law to warn and save those who will be warned. It is my appointed sorrow, I suppose, that the recklessness and ignorance of such as you, persist in disregarding that law, and turning good into evil. I shone bright and brighter before you as you advanced, entreating you, as it were, to be warned. But, in wilfulness, you pursued me to your ruin. What cruel mother brought you up, and did not teach you to distinguish the steady beam that guides to happiness, from the wandering brilliancy that bodes destruction?"

"My poor mother!" wept the Maiden; "what words are these you speak of her? But you, in your savage life, know nothing of what she has done for me, her only child. Mistress of every accomplishment that can adorn and delight society, my lightest word, my very smile, is a law to the world we move in."

"Even so! Accomplished in fleeting and fantastic arts that leave no memorial behind them—unacquainted with the beauty and purposes of the realities around you, which work from age to age in silent mercy for gracious ends, and put to shame the toil that has no aim or end. Oh that you had but known the law by which I live!"

The Maiden spoke no more, and then she ceased to struggle. The Will-o'-the-Wisp danced back yet another time to the edge of the black morass: "For," said he, "I may save somebody yet. But what a foolish world I live in!"

"The old Squire should mend these here roads," observed Hobbinoll the Farmer to his son Colin, as they drove slowly home from market in a crazy old cart which shook about with such jerks, that little Colin tried in vain to keep curled up in a corner. It was hard to say whether the fault was most in the roads,—though they were rather rutty, it must be owned,—or in the stumbling old pony who went from side to side, or in the not very sober driver, who seemed unable at times to distinguish the reins apart, so that he gave sudden pulls, first one way and then the other. But through all these troubles it comforted the Farmer's heart to lay all the blame on the Squire for the bad roads that led across the boggy moor.

Colin, however, took but little interest in the matter; but at length, when a more violent jerk than usual threw him almost sprawling on the bottom of the cart, he jumped up, laid hold of the side planks, and began to look around him with his half-sleepy eyes, trying to find out where they were. At last he said, "She's coming, father."

"Who's coming?" shouted Hobbinoll.

"T' mother," answered Colin.

"What's she coming for, I wonder," said Hobbinoll; "we've enough in the cart without her."

"But you're going away from her, father," expostulated Colin, half crying. "I see her with the lanthorn, and she'll light us home. You can't see, father; let me have the reins." But Hobbinoll refused to give up the reins, though he was not very fit to drive. In the struggle, however, he caught sight of the light which Colin took for his mother's lanthorn.

"And is that the fool's errand you'd be going after?" cried he, pointing with his whip to the light. "It's lucky for you, young one, you have not had the driving of us home to-night, though you think you can do anything, I know. A precious home it would have been at the bottom of the sludgy pool yonder, for that's where you'd have got us to at last. Yon light is the Will-o'-the-Wisp, that's always trying to mislead folks. Bad luck befall him! I got halfway to him once when I was a young 'un, but an old neighbour who'd once been in himself was going by just then, and called me back. He's a villain is that sham-faced Will-o'-the-Wisp."

With these words the Farmer struck the pony so harshly with his heavy whip, twitching the reins convulsively at the same time, at the mere memory of his adventure in the bog, that little Colin was thrown up and down like a ball, and the cart rolled forward in and out of the ruts at such a pace, that Hobbinoll got home to his wife sooner than she ever dared to hope for on market evenings.

"They are safe," observed the Will-o'-the-Wisp, as the cart moved on, "and that is the great point gained! Nevertheless, such wisdom is mere brute experience. In their ignorance they would have struck the hand that helped them. Nevertheless, I will try again, for I may yet save some one else. But what a rude and ungrateful world I live in!"

"I see a light at last, papa!" shouted a little Boy on a Shetland pony, as he rode by his Father's side along the moor. "I am so glad! There is either a cottage or a friendly man with a lanthorn who will help us to find our way. Let me go after him; I can soon overtake him." And the little boy touched his pony with a whip, and in another minute would have been cantering along after the light, but that his Father laid a sudden and a heavy hand upon the bridle.

"Not a step further in that direction, at any rate, if you please, my darling."

"Oh, papa!" expostulated the child, pointing with his hand to the light.

And, "Oh, my son, I see!" cried the Father, smiling; "and well is it for you that I not only see, but know the meaning of what I see at the same time. That light is neither the gleam from a cottage, nor yet a friendly man with a lanthorn, as you think, though, for the matter of that, the light is friendly enough to those who understand it. It shines there to warn us from the dangerous part of the bog. Kind old Will-o'-the-Wisp!" pursued the Father, raising his voice, as if calling through the darkness into the distance—"Kind old Will-o'-the-Wisp, we know what you mean; we will not come near your deathly swamps. The Old Naturalist knows you well—good-night, and thank you for the warning."

So saying, the Naturalist turned the reins of his son's pony the other way, and they both trotted along, keeping the beaten road as well as they could by the imperfect light.

"After all, it was more like a lanthorn than those pictures of the nasty Will-o'-the-Wisp, papa," murmured the little Boy, reluctantly urging his pony on.

"Our friend is not much indebted to you for the pretty name you have called him," laughed the Father. "You are of the same mind as the poet, who, with the licence of his craft, said—

'Yonder phantom only flies
To lure thee to thy doom.'"

"Yes, papa, and so he does," interposed the Boy.

"But, indeed, he does no such thing, my dear—on the contrary, he spends all his life in shining brightly to warn travellers of the most dangerous parts of the swamp."

"But the shining seems as if he was inviting them to go after him, papa."

"Only because you choose to think so, my dear, and do not inquire. Does the sailor think the shining of the lighthouse invites him to approach the dangerous rocks on which it is built?"

"Oh, no, papa, because he knows it is put there on purpose to warn him away."

"He only knows by teaching and inquiry, Arthur; and so you also, by teaching and inquiry will learn to know that this Will-o'-the-Wisp is made to shine for us in swamps and marshes as a land-beacon of danger. The laws of Nature, which are the acted will of God, work together in this case, as in all others, for a good end. And it is given to us as both a privilege and a pleasure to search them out, and to avail ourselves of the mercies, whilst we admire the wonders of the great Creator. Can you think of a better employment?"

The fire was very bright, and the tea was warm and good, that greeted the travellers, Father and Son, on their arrival at home that night. Many a joke, too, passed with Mamma as to the sort of tea they should have tasted, and the kind of bed they should have laid down in, had they only gone after the Will-o'-the-Wisp, as young Arthur had so much wished to do.

And for just a few days after these events—not more, for children's wisdom seldom does, or ought to, last much longer—Arthur had every now and then a wise and philosophical fit, and on the principle, that, however much appearances might be to the contrary, the laws of Nature were always working to some good and beneficent end, he sagely and gravely reproved his little sister for crying when a shower of hailstones fell; "For surely," said he, "though we cannot go out to-day, the storm is doing good to something or somebody somewhere."

It was a blessed creed! though it cost him a struggle to adhere to it, when the lightning flashed round him, and the thunder roared in the distance, and he saw from the windows dark clouds hanging over the landscape. When someone said the storm had been very grand, he thought—yes, but it was grander still to think that all these laws of Nature, as they are called,—this acted will of God—was for ever working night and day, in darkness and in light, recognised or unheeded, for some wise and beneficent end.

Yes! when he was older he would try and trace out these ends—a better employment could not be found. And it may be, that in long after years, when the storms and the clouds that gathered round him were harder yet to look through, because they were mental troubles—it may be, that then, from amidst the tender recollections of his infancy, the gleaming of the Will-o'-the-Wisp would suddenly rise and shine before him with comfort. For the Student of

Nature who had traced so many blessed ends out of dark and mysterious beginnings, held fast to the humility and faith of childhood; and where his mind was unable to penetrate, his heart was contented to believe.

Meanwhile the Will-o'-the-Wisp had heard the kind good-night that greeted him as the travellers passed by on that dark evening. And his light shone brighter than ever, as he said: "I am happy now. I have saved the life of one who not only is thankful for it, but knows the hand that saved him." With these words he cheerily danced back again to his appointed post.

Waiting

"It is good that a man should both hope and quietly wait."
—LAM. iii. 26

It was, doubtless, a very sorry life the House Cricket led, before houses were built and fires were kindled. There was no comfortable kitchen-hearth then, in the warm nooks and corners of which he might sit and sing his cheerful song, coming out every now and then to bask himself in the glow of the blazing light. On the contrary, he, so fond of heat, had no place to shelter in but holes in hollow trees, or crevices in rocks and stones, or some equally dull and damp abode. Besides which, he had to bear the incessant taunts and ridicule of creatures who were perfectly comfortable themselves, and so had no fellow-feeling for his want of cheerfulness.

"Why don't you go and spring about, and sing in the fields with your cousin, the Grasshopper?" was the ill-natured question of the Spider, as she twisted her web in one of the refuge-holes the Cricket had crept into; "I am sure your legs are long enough, if you would only take the trouble to undouble them. It's nothing but a sulky, discontented feeling that keeps you and all your family moping in these out-of-the-way corners, when you ought to be using your limbs in jumping about and enjoying yourself. And I dare say, too, that you could sing a great deal louder if you chose."

The Cricket thought perhaps he could—but he must feel very differently to what he did then, before it would be possible to try. Something was so very very wrong with him, but what that something was he did not know. All the other beasts and birds and insects seemed easy and happy enough. The Spider, for instance, was quite at home and gay in the hole he found so dismal.

And it was not the Spider only who was contented: the Flies—the Bees—the Ants—the very Mole, who sometimes came up from burrowing, and told wonderful stories of his underground delights—the birds with their merry songs—the huge beasts, who walked about like giants in the fields—all—all were satisfied with their condition, and happy in themselves. Every one had the home he liked, and no one envied the other.

But with him it was quite otherwise: he never felt at home! on the contrary, it always seemed to him that he was looking out for something that was not there, some place that could never be found, some state where he could rise out of the depression and uneasiness which here seemed to clog him down, though he could not understand why.

Poor fellow! as things were now, he felt for ever driven to hide in holes, although he knew that his limbs were built for energy; and few ever heard his voice, though he possessed one fitted for something much better than doleful complaints.

Sometimes a set of House Crickets would meet and talk the matter over. They looked at their long folded-up legs, and could not but see how exactly they were like those of the Grasshopper. And yet the idea of following the Grasshopper into the cool grass, and jumping about all day, was odious to them. Once, indeed, a Cricket of great self-denial offered to go into the fields and find one of his green cousins, and ask his opinion on the subject, and whether he could give any reason why the grasshopper life should be so distasteful to such near relations.

And he actually went; and when the Grasshopper could be persuaded to stand quiet for a few seconds, and listen, he was so much concerned for the Crickets (for he had a tender heart, from living so much in the grass, and being so musical), that he said he would himself visit his cousins, and see what could be done for them. Perhaps it was some little accidental ailment, or it might be a chronic affection in the family, owing to mismanagement when they were young, but which a little judicious treatment would correct.

With these views he started for the hollow tree in which the Crickets had taken shelter, and soon reached it, for he travelled the whole way in bounds. And the last bound took him fairly into the midst of the family circle, in which indeed he alighted with more vivacity than politeness, for his cousins did not like such startling gaiety.

However, he steadied himself carefully, and then began to examine the legs and knees of all the Crickets assembled. He drew them out, and looked them well over; for, thought he, "there is perhaps some blunder or flaw in the way the joints are put together." But he could find nothing amiss. There sat the Crickets with legs and bodies as nicely made as his own, only with no energy for exertion.

What he might have thought, or what he might have said, after this puzzling discovery, no one can tell; for at the end of his examination he was seized with the fidgets, and, "Excuse me, my dear friends," cried he, "I have the cramp in my left leg—I must jump!" And jump he did—once, twice, thrice—and the last jump carried him out of the tree; and either on purpose, or from forgetfulness, he sprang singing away, and returned to his cousins the Crickets no more.

Oh, this yearning after some other better state that lies unrevealed in the indefinite future—how restless and disheartening a sensation! Oh, this painful contrast of perfection in all created things around, to the lonely meditator on so much happiness, who is the solitary exception to the rule—how trying the position! How cruel, how almost overwhelming the struggle between the iron chain of reality and the soaring wing of aspiration!

But, "What is the use, my poor good friends," expostulated a plodding old Mole one day, after coming out to see how the upper world went on, and hearing the Cricket's complaints—"what is the use of all this groaning and conjecturing? You admit that every other creature but yourself is perfect in its way, and quite happy. Well, then, I will tell you that you ought to be quite sure you are perfect in your way too, though you have not found it out yet; and that you will be happy one day or other, although it may not be the case just now. Do you suppose this fine scheme of things we live in is to be soiled with one speck of dirt, as it were for the sake of teasing such a little insignificant creature as yourself! Don't think it for a moment, for it is not at all likely! But you must not suppose that everything goes right at first even with the best of us. I have had some small experience, and I know. But everything fits in at last. Of that I am quite sure. For instance, now, I do not suppose it ever occurred to you to think what a trial it must be to a young Mole when he first begins to burrow in the earth. Do you imagine that he knows what he is doing it for, or what will be the result? No such thing. It is a complete working in the dark, not knowing in the least where he is going. Dear me! if one had once stopped to conjecture and puzzle, what a hardship it would have seemed to drive one's nose by the hour together into unknown ground, for some unexplained reason that did not come out for some time afterwards, and that one had no certainty would ever come out at all! But everything fits in at last. And so it did with us. I remember it quite well in my own case. We drove the earth away and outwards, till the space so cleared proved an absolute palace! By the bye, I must try and get you down into our splendid abode—it will cheer you up, and teach you a useful lesson. Well, so you see we found out at last what all the grubbing had been for—"

"Ah! but," interrupted the Cricket, "you were labouring for some purpose all the time, and if I had to labour I could hope. The difficulty is, to sit moping with nothing to do but wait."

"It is nonsense to talk of nothing to do," answered the Mole; "every creature has something to do. You, for instance, have always to watch for the sun. You know you like the beams and warmth he sends out better than anything else in the world, so you should get into the way of them as much as you can. And after the sun has set, you must hunt up the snuggest holes you can find, and so make the best of things as they are; and for the rest, you must wait. And waiting answers sometimes as well as working, I can assure you. There was the young Ox in the plains near here. As soon as he could run about at all, he began driving his clumsy head against everything he met. No one could tell why; but he fidgeted and butted about all day long, and many of his friends and acquaintances were very much offended by his manners. Others laughed. The dogs, indeed, were particularly amused, and used to bark at him constantly—even close to his nose sometimes, as he lowered his head after them. Well, at last, out came the secret. Two fine horns grew out from our friend's head, and people soon understood the meaning of all the butting; and one of the saucy curs who was playing the old barking game with him one day got finely tossed for his pains. Everything fits in at last, my friends! No cravings are given in vain. There is always something in store to account for them, you may be quite sure. You may have to wait a bit—some of you a shorter, some a longer time; but do wait—and everything will fit in and be perfect at last."

It was a most fortunate circumstance for the Crickets that the Mole happened to give them this good advice; for a malicious Ape had lately been suggesting to them, whether, as they were totally useless and very unhappy, it would not be a good thing for them all, to starve themselves to death, or in some other way, to rid the world of their whole race.

But the Mole's good sense gave a different turn to their ideas; and hope is so natural and pleasant a feeling, that when once they ventured to encourage it, it flourished and grew in their hearts till it created a sort of happiness of itself. In short, they determined to wait and meantime to watch for the sun, as their friend had advised.

There are not many records of the early history of the House Cricket; but it is supposed that they travelled about a good deal—preferring always the hottest countries; and rumours of a few straggling families, who had discovered a sort of Cricket Elysium at the mouth of volcanoes, were afloat at one time. But the truth of the report was never ascertained: and as, doubtless, if ever they got there, they were sure to be swept away to destruction by the first eruption that took place, it is no wonder that the fact has never been thoroughly established.

Meanwhile several generations died off; and things remained much as they were. But the words of the Mole were carried down from father to son, and became a by-word of comfort among them:—"Everything would fit in at last!

no cravings are given in vain. There is always something in store to account for them. Wait—and everything will fit in, and be perfect at last."

Gleams of hope, indeed, were not wanting to our poor little friends, during this time of probation. Wherever fires were kindled by human hands, whether by wanderers in the depths of forests, or sojourners in tents, a stir of excitement and rapturous expectation was caused among such Crickets as were near enough to know and enjoy the circumstance. But, alas! when the travellers journeyed onwards, or the tents were removed elsewhere, the disappointment that ensued was bitter in proportion.

Many an evil hint, too, had they on such occasions from the mischief-making creatures which are to be found in all grades of life, that such, and no better, would be their fate for ever. Rays of joy, beaming only to be extinguished in cruel mockery of their feelings—such was to be their perpetual portion!

"But we will not believe it," cried the Crickets, heart-broken as they were. "Everything will be perfect at last," sang they as loudly as they could. "No cravings are given in vain." And as they always sang this same song, the mischief-makers got tired of listening at last, and left them to sing and weep alone. Ah! it required no small strength of mind to resist, as they did, such plausible insinuations, supported as they were by present appearances.

But, truly, though it tarried, the day of deliverance and joy did come! The first fire that ever warmed the hearthstone that flagged the grand old chimney-arch of ancient times, ended for ever the mystery of the House Crickets' wants and cravings; and when it commonly blazed every winter night in men's dwellings, all the doubts and woes of Cricket life were over.

These seemed to have passed away like the dreams of a disturbed night, which had been succeeded by daylight and reality. And oh, what ecstasy of joy the Crickets felt! How loud they shouted, and how high they sprang! "We knew it would be so! The good old Mole was right! The grumbling beasts were wrong! Everything is perfect now, and no one is so happy as we are."

"Grandmother, what creature is it that I hear singing so loudly in the corner by the fire?" inquires the little one of the good old dame who sits musing on the oaken settle.

"I do not hear it, my child, and I do not know," answers the deaf and blind old crone. "But if it be singing, love, it is happy, and enjoys these blessed fires as much as I do. 'Let everything that hath breath praise the Lord.' "

Ah! it was no wonder that amidst the many merry voices that then shouted, and still shout, round those warm and friendly fires, no voice is louder, no joy more grateful, than that of the patient Cricket.

He has "waited" through fear and shadows—has hoped through darkness and ignorance—and his abode now glows with warmth and light. And, if he received a lesson of wisdom from a creature more humble and seemingly more blind than himself, it is at least not the only instance in which instruction has been so obtained.

And now we know the reason why the Crickets come by troops into our houses, and live and thrive about our cheering fires, and sing so loud and long that the housewives sometimes (I grieve to say) get weary of the noise, and try to lessen the number of their lively visitors.

But yet there is a strange old notion of good fortune attending the presence of these little chirping creatures. They are welcomed as bringing "good luck" to the family about whose hearth they settle. And so they do! They bring with them a tale of promises made good. They sing a song of hope fulfilled; and though in that glad music there be neither speech nor language which we can recognise as such, there is yet a voice to be heard among them by all who love to listen, with reverent delight, to the sweet harmonies and deep analogies of Nature.

A Lesson of Hope

"Oh, yet we trust that, somehow, good
Will be the final goal of ill!"
From TENNYSON'S In Memoriam.

"How the rising blast is driving through the ancient forest! What a dismal roaring there is among the pine-trees! What a sharp clattering among the half-dried poplar-leaves! What a sighing among the beeches! A wild mysterious hour, and full of strange fantastic types of mortal life!"

It was thus I spoke, when, having wandered out one gloomy autumn night to muse on Nature and her laws, I found myself contemplating, in the deep recesses of a wood, the progress of a violent storm. And as I paused, I leant back, in sad reflections lost, against an oak, and, looking upwards to the sky, tried to gaze into the depths of those black vapoury masses that had arisen, one knew not how or whence, to darken over the expanse of heaven; when, all at once there shone down upon me, from an opening in the clouds, the full rays of a bright October moon.

The light was sudden, and a sudden revulsion took place within my heart. I had been thinking that, like the cruel storm, and like the heavy clouds, were the troubles and the trials of human existence: and now, when that sweet radiance broke upon my eyes, I heard a voice exclaim, as if in echo to my thoughts—"It is the moon that shone in Paradise!" It was the Bird of Night, quite near me, in the hollow of a tree. Looking to see from whence the sound had come, I met his large, grave, meditative eyes fixed on my moonlit face, and then I heard the voice exclaim again—"The moon that shone in Paradise!"

Oh, what a thought to come across the tumult of that hour! The moon that shone in Paradise!—up to whose radiant orb the eyes of countless generations have been turned—from the first glance of spotless innocence, to the last yearning gaze of sorrow-stricken manhood! And why?—but that in that calm unchanging glory there shines forth a promise of eternal, everlasting peace.

But now another voice was heard, despite the howling of the storm. It was a croaking Raven, swinging on a branch beside me. He came between me and the light, and ever and anon his coal-black wings seemed spreading for a flight.

"Deluded fool," he muttered, "with your endless myths! This comes of living in the dark all day, and spending all your time in guess-work! See! your precious moon is gone!"

"Not gone, though hidden," was the answer.

But I heard no more than this, for here the frightful wind grew louder still. He roared in fury all around, scattering the last leaves from the bending trees, as if he hated the very relics of the gentle summer. And many bowed their heads, and others moaned in grief.

"Hast thou come with mighty news from distant lands," shouted the Pine-tree scornfully, as he tossed his branches to the storm, "that thou bringest such confusion in thy path? Ambassador of evil, who hast sent thee here?"

"Cannot yonder moon teach thee milder thoughts?" cried the Elm-tree, as he stood majestic in his sorrow and despair.

"Our hour is come," exclaimed the softer Beech. "My leaves lie scattered all around. Our life is closing fast. Naked and forlorn we stand amid the ruins of the past."

"What mockery of existence," stormed the black-leaved Poplar in his wrath, "to be placed here, and clothed in such sweet beauty, nurtured by gentle dews and tender sunshine, and then be left at last the victims of reckless fury, with all our glories torn by force away! Would I had never risen from the ground!"

"Oh, my aspiring friend," the ill-mouthed Raven cried, "the few months' splendour does not satisfy your heart! You aim too high, methinks. Well, well! aspiring thoughts are very fine; but were I you, I would accommodate myself to facts. A short spring, a shorter summer, and then to perish. Ha! here you are again, my ancient worthy friend!"

And then another gust broke in with savage fury on the forest, and many a stalwart branch crashed down upon the ground. The wailings of afflicted Nature rose amidst the storm.

"Is there no refuge from this end?" enquired the Oak. "Why have I lived at all?"

"Because destruction is the law of life," the Raven uttered, with his fiercest croak. "Where would destruction be, were there no life to be destroyed? It is a glorious law."

"No law, but only an exception," cried the Bird of Night.

And as he spoke there streamed once more from out the clouds that type of peace that passeth not away—the moon that shone in Paradise. Oh, what a silver mantle she let fall upon the disrobed branches of those trees! Wet as they were with rain-drops, and waving in the gale, it seemed as if they shone in robes of starlight glory. What gracious promises seemed streaming down with that sweet light!

"Lift up your heads, ye forest trees, once more!" so sang the mild-eyed Bird of Night. "Fury is short-lived—love alone enduring. All that destroys is transitory, but order is everlasting. The unbridled powers of cruelty may rage—it is but for a time! And ye may darken over the blue heavens, ye vapoury masses in the sky. It matters not! Beyond the howling of that wrath, beyond the blackness of those clouds, there shines, unaltered and serene, the moon that shone in Paradise."

"Your myth again, detested Bird of Night! Here to the rescue, ancient friend!"

And louder then than ever came that cruel, cruel wind.

"It matters not," once more the Owl exclaimed. "The stormy winds must cease, the clouds must pass away, and yonder sails the light that tells of harmony restored."

"Infatuated fool, to live on hope, with death around you and before you!" groaned the Raven—and then a crash like thunder rent the air. The Oak had fallen to the ground. I started at the shock.

"Will the day ever come," I cried aloud, as if addressing some mysterious friend, "will the day ever come when storms and woe shall cease? Order and peace seem meant, but death and ruin come to pass."

"Oh, miserable doubter, do you ask? Must the brute beasts and mute creation rise to give an answer to your fears? Look in the heaven above, and in the earth below, and in the water deep beneath the earth. One only law is given—the law of order, harmony, and joy."

"Alas, how often broken!" I exclaimed.

"Ay, but disturbance is no law, and therefore cannot last. Disorder, death, and destruction:—by their own nature they are transitory—rebellious powers that struggle for a time, and frustrate here and there the gracious purposes ordained. But they exist not of themselves; have neither law nor being in themselves; exist but as disturbers of a scheme whose deep foundations cannot be overthrown. Life, order, harmony, and peace; means duly fitting ends; the object, universal joy. This is the law. Believe in it, and live!"

And as the voice grew silent, from the sky beamed over all the scene the placid moon once more. The wind had lulled or passed away to other regions of the earth, and over all the forest streamed the brilliant light. Once more the lit-up trees shone spangled o'er with rays; and happy murmurs broke upon my ear, instead of loud complaints.

"We have been wild and foolish, gracious moon!" exclaimed the tender Beech. "We doubted all the promises and hopes that you shed so freely down. In pity to the terrors of the night, forgive us once again!"

"You have said right, my sister," said the Oak. "That heavenly power, whom neither winds nor storms can reach, will view with tenderness our troubled lot, who live amid the tempests of the earth. She will forgive, she hath forgiven us all. Hath she not clothed us now with robes more brilliant than the summer ones we love?"

"The robes of hope and promise," wept the Poplar, as he spoke, for all his branches trembled with delight, and stars seemed dropping all around.

"I mourn my dark despair," bewailed the Elm. "I should have called the past to memory! We never are deserted in our need. The winter tempests rage, and terrible they are; but always the bright moon from time to time returns, to shed down rays of hope and promises of glory on our heads; and still we doubt and fear, and still the patient moon repeats her tale. And then the spring and summer time return, and life, and joy, and all our beauteous robes. Oh, what weak tremblers we must be!"

And so, through all the rest of that strange night, murmurs of comfort sounded through the wood, and I returned at last to the poor lonely cottage that I called my home, and wept mixed tears of sorrow and of joy. Father and mother lost, swept suddenly away, and I, with straitened means, left alone to struggle through the world! Did I not stand before my desolate hearth, like one awakened from a dream, a vision—(surely such it was!)—exclaiming in despair, as did the weeping Beech, "Naked and forlorn I stand amid the ruins of the past." But through the casement glided in on me, me also, as I stood, the blessed rays of that eternal moon—the moon that shone in Paradise—the moon that promises a Paradise restored.

And ever and anon, throughout the struggle of my life, I would return for wisdom and for hope to the old forest where I dreamt the dream. As time passed on, and winter snows came down, a cold, unmeaning sleep seemed to bind up the trees—but still, at her appointed time, the moon came out, and lit up even snow with robes of light and hope.

And then the spring-time burst the cruel bonds that held all Nature in a stagnant state. Verdure and beauty came again; and, as I listened to the gales that breathed soft music through the trees, I thought, "If I could dream again, I should hear songs of exquisite delight." But that was not to be. Still, I could revel in the comfort of the sight, and watch the moonbeams glittering in triumphant joy through the now verdant bowers of those woods, playing in happy sport amid the shadows of the leaves.

And to me also came a spring! From me, too, passed away the winter and its chill! And now I take the children of my love, and the sweet mother who has borne them, to those woods; and ever and anon we tell long tales of Nature and her ways, and how the poor trees moan, when storms and tempests come; and how the wise Owl talks to heedless ears his deep philosophy of law, of order that must one day certainly prevail, and how the patient moon is never weary of her task of shedding rays of hope and promise on the world; and even while we speak, the children clap their hands for joy, and say they never will despair for anything that comes, for, lo! above their heads there suddenly shines out—THE MOON THAT SHONE IN PARADISE!

The Circle of Blessing

"Freely ye have received, freely give."
—MATTHEW x. 8.

"Come back to me, my children let us not part," murmured the sea to the Vapours, which rose from its surface, drawn upwards by the heat of the tropical sun. "Return to my bosom, and contribute your share to the preservation of my greatness and strength."

"There is no lasting greatness, but in distributed good," replied the Vapours; "behold we carry your cooling influence to the heated air around. Let us alone, oh Sea! The work is good."

"But carried on at my expense," murmured the Sea. "Is the air your parent, and not I, that you are so careful of its interests and so neglectful of mine? Why are you thus ungrateful to me, from whom your very existence springs? O foolish children! by diminishing my power you are sapping the foundations of your own life. Your very being depends on mine."

"Small and great, great and small, we all depend on each other," sang the Vapours as they hovered in the air. "Mighty Ocean, give us of your abundance for those that need. It is but little that we ask."

"Divided interests are the ruin of fools," muttered the angry Sea.

"But extended ones the glory of the wise," replied the Vapours, as they still continued to rise. "See, now, have we not done ourselves, what we would have you also do? Behold, we have left our salts in your bosom for those that need them."

"And I have cast them as a useless burden to my lowest depths," exclaimed the Sea, indignantly. "Have I not enough, already? Superfluous bounties deserve but little thanks, methinks."

"Yet in those depths, perchance they may be as welcome as we to the air above," persisted the Vapours. "It is ever thus: and all will be made good at last. Small and great, great and small, we are dependent on each other evermore."

"Begone, then," moaned the Sea. "You, who are willing to sacrifice a certain good for an uncertain fancy, begone, and be yourselves the first victims of your folly. The breezes, that are now driving you forward across my surface, will rise to fury, and blow you into nothingness as you proceed. Lost among the stormy gusts, where will be your use to others or my recompense for your loss? You will not even exist to repent of this mad desertion of your home. Adieu! for ever and for ever, adieu!"

"Adieu, but not for ever," answered the Vapours, as they dispersed before the wind.

It was not a satisfactory parting, perhaps; for, often as their race had made the journey round the earth, it had never fallen within the power of any portion of them to explain the course of their career, to the surface sea, which had originally grudged their departure.

However, the Vapours had now commenced their circuit, and were carried onward by the steady south-east trade-winds to the regions of equatorial calms, that wonderful belt of heat and accumulation, where they were met by breezes which in like manner were travelling from the north, and here this meeting caused for a while a lingering in the career of both. But these opposing winds, laden with vapours from the two hemispheres, had each their mission, and worked under an appointed law.

It was their province to carry the exhalations from north and south into the cooler upper sky where once more their course was free to travel round the world. Lifted up thus, however, no sooner had the Vapours entered a more temperate atmosphere, than their particles expanded, and a portion of them clung together in drops, which, whilst under the influence of excessive heat, was never the case. They thus became much heavier than before; so heavy, indeed, that the winds were not able to bear them aloft.

"You cannot carry us all," said the Vapours to their struggling supporters. "Some of us will, therefore, return with a message of comfort to the mighty Sea, to tell him all is well."

But even when they came down in torrents of rain to his bosom, the Sea grumbled still. "It is well that a part, at least, of what was lost, returns," said he. But he neither knew nor cared what became of the rest.

The rest, however, fared happily and well; for high above earth and sea—so high, indeed, that they in no way interfered with the winds that swept below—they were borne along by the upper currents of air which were travelling to the north, and carried them forward on their journey of beneficence, and never-ceasing good.

Surely, it must have been a sweet sensation to be drifted along by a never-varying breeze through the higher regions of the sky, undisturbed by care, in a dream of delicious idleness and ease. But this was but a portion of the career of the Vapours from the Sea.

At the next meeting, at the outskirts of the tropics, with travellers like themselves coming in the opposite direction, there was a fresh pressure of opposing breezes, a temporary lingering, and then a descent, by which they left those higher regions for ever. Henceforth, they were to be dispersed by surface winds on their course of usefulness to man.

And if, when cradled in that blissful passage high over the Tropics, those Vapours had for a time forgotten their mission, there was no possibility of forgetting it henceforth. Taken up with triumphant delight by all the varying breezes that sport over the northern hemisphere, there was no direction in which they were not to be found. A portion was wanted here, another portion there; the snows of Iceland, and the vineyards of Italy, the orange groves of Spain, and the river which pours over the mighty rocks at Niagara, must all be fed at their appointed seasons, and the food was travelling to them now.

But the eye would weary which strove to look sympathisingly round the vast expanse of the globe. It is enough if we can follow the Vapours through some stages of their journey of love.

On the summit of a mountain, over whose sides the gorse and heather were wont to flower together in bright profusion, and with their lovely intermixture of hues, all the ground was parched and dry. A burning sun by day, rarely followed by dewy nights; a summer drought, in fact, had ruled for weeks over the spot, and the shrunken flower-buds and parched leaves bore painful witness to the fact. The little mountain tarn below was almost dry, and the Sundew plants by its sides, which were wont to revel in the damp surrounding moss, had lost their nature altogether, and never now offered their coronet of sparkling drops to the admiration of those that passed.

The pretty tumbling waterfall lower down, too, which travellers used to delight to visit, and which was fed by streams from the hills, was reduced to a miserable trickle. Cottage children were sent to fetch water from distances so great that they sat down and wept by the road-side on their errand; and farmers wore a gloomy, anxious look, which told of a thousand fears about their crops and cattle.

But, while they were thus troubled and careful, lo, the rescue was coming from afar! yea, travelling towards them upon the wings of the wind. Vapours from tropical seas, Vapours which had left behind them their no-longer-needed salt, were coming accumulated as clouds, to fall as gracious rain and dews upon the thirsty regions of the North.

They are variable and fantastic winds, perhaps, that course over the northern hemisphere. Not steady and uniform in their direction, like the trade-winds in the Tropics; nor like those upper currents far above the trade-winds, which carry the Vapours to the second belts of calms. No! variable and fantastic they certainly are, and, therefore, we cannot reckon on their arrival to a day,—nay, not to a month; but on their arrival at last, we may always surely depend, and perhaps, in this trial of patient expectation, a lesson of quiet faith is intended to be learnt.

And so, just as farmers, and cottage children, and the earth, and its flowers, and leaves, and springs of water, had all sunk into a state of dismal distrust and discomfort, the deliverance came to them as they slept!

Slight variations in the wind had been observed for more than a day; but still no change of weather took place, until one night a steady breeze from the south-west set in, and prevailed for hours. And presently there was a gathering up of clouds all over the sky, though in the darkness of the night their arrival passed unobserved.

Gracious clouds! they were the Vapours of the Sea, which, after many wanderings, had found their way here, at last, on their mission of love. And lo! the sound of waters was heard once more on the dried-up hills, and sweet, heavy showers dropped down on the delighted earth. All night long it continued, and all night long the earth was streaming tears of joy; and another day and another night succeeded, during which more or less of rain or dew continued to descend.

"Welcome, welcome, oh ye Showers and Dew!" were the Earth's first words; and, "Leave me now no more," her constant after-cry.

"Poor Earth, poor Earth!" murmured the Vapours, which, condensed into rain-drops, were trembling, like diamonds on the leaves and flowers in the sunshine of the second dawn. "Poor Earth, poor Earth! you too refuse to learn the law which brought us here. What you have received so freely, will you not freely give?"

"Nay; but linger with me yet," expostulated the Earth; "and let me rather store you up for my own use hereafter. What do I know of the future, and what it may bring forth? How can I be sure that the fitful winds will supply me again in time of need? I cannot afford to think of others. Leave me, leave me not."

"None must store against an uncertain future evil, when so many are suffering under a present one," replied the Vapours; "nevertheless, a message of comfort will come to you, after we are gone."

And so, when the sun shone out in his heat and glory, the diamond rain-drops were drawn upwards from the flowers and leaves into the air once more. Only the little Sundews kept their coronets of crystal beads throughout the day, as was their custom: though how they managed it, it would be hard to say.

Perhaps as their own natural juices are so thick and clammy, these, mingling with the Vapours as they exuded, held them longer fast.

"You are our prisoners," was the triumphant cry of the Sundew leaves, as they glistened in their liquid gems.

"Nay, but why would you detain us, selfish flowers?" exclaimed the Vapours.

"Oh, you shall go, you shall go; but only gradually, as the moisture courses through our veins to re-supply your place. This is our way of life. But we must hear all from you first. All! all! all! and most of all, why you have tarried so long, till we had almost perished in the dreadful drought?"

It was a long story the Vapours had then to tell, of their irregular passage to the Polar Seas; and how, after their chilly sojourn there as snow, they had passed southwards once more on the summits of drifting icebergs, and again been exhaled, and given back to the ministry of the wandering winds.

"Surely," said they, "we have touched no place in all our wild journeyings where we have not left some blessing behind. Here and there, indeed, folks think they have had too much of us, and here and there too little; but, oh, my delicate friends, believe us, we are faithful and true to our mission all over the world. Behold, we pour into the earth as rain, or slide into it as moisture; and lo, the soil gives its gases into our care, and the roots of the plants draw us and them up together, and feeding on them, expand and flourish, and grow; and when the useful deed is done, and the sun shines down on our labour, up we ascend again to its absorbing rays, to be carried forward again and again, to other gracious deeds. Blame us not therefore, if, in turning aside to some other case of need, we have come a little late to your hills. Own that you have not been forgotten!"

"It is true," murmured the Sundews in return; "but remember, we pine and die without your presence."

"Dear little Sundews, there is not a plant in all the boggy heaths that is so dear to us as you are. See now, we linger with you yet; there is moisture in your mossy bed around this tarn to last for many weeks; and ever as a portion of us steals away, its place shall be supplied from below, so that your leaves shall never miss their sparkling diadem of gems."

The Sundews had no need to tremble after that; but as the exhalations went up from the surface-ground, and the moisture sank lower and lower down into it, a fear stole over the Earth, that another thought might arise, for she knew not that all would return to her again in due season. But, when in the cool of the evening the Vapours descended upon her bosom, as refreshing mist and dew, she received a portion of comfort. Nevertheless, like the Sea, she grumbled on. "It is well that a part, at least, of what was lost, returns!" she remarked in her greedy anxiety, as the Sea had done before; and, like him, she neither knew nor cared what became of the rest.

There was a mission for every portion, however, and through the now saturated ground the rain-drops sank together, amidst roots, and stones, and soil, moistening all before them as they went, and replenishing the springs that ran among the hills.

The tumbling Waterfall had, by this time, well nigh given up hope. The mournful trickle with which it fell, was an absolute mockery of its former precipitous haste;—when lo! some sudden influence is at work, a rush of vigour flows into the exhausted veins; there is a swelling in the distant springs, nearer and nearer it comes, and now over the rocky ledge there is a heavier flow: a little more, and yet a little more: and then, at last, a rush of water full and fresh is heard!

"Welcome, welcome! oh, ye Springs and Floods," cried the Waterfall, as once more it rolled in its beauty along its precipitous course, scattering foam and spray upon the moss and flowers that graced its edge. "Stay in the mountains always, that I may thirst no more; leave me, leave me not again!"

"You too, who live by giving and receiving," cried the Vapours as they flushed the stream—"you too, wishing to stop the gracious course of good? Oh shame, shame, shame!"

And then, as if in mockery of the request, a playful gust blew off from the waterfall as it descended, some of its glittering spray, and tossed it to the sunshiny air, where it dispersed once more in smoky mist—but only to return again in time of need.

Down in the lower country, where stately houses, enclosed in noble parks, adorned the land, a beautiful lake lay stretched under the noon-day sun. It was fed by the stream which, at some miles' distance, received the tumbling waterfall into its course, and then ran through the lake's broad sheet, escaping at the further end in a quick-flowing rill. On the placid mirror-like surface majestic swans swept proudly by, not unsusceptible of the freshening in the water from the filling of the springs above.

A little pleasure-boat was floating lazily about, impelled occasionally forward by the stroke of an oar from a youth, who with one companion of his own age, and an elderly man who sat abstractedly reading a book, formed the passengers of this tiny bark.

The rower's young companion was lounging in a half-sitting, half-reclining posture in the bows of the boat, and both were gazing at the old Baronial Hall, which, with its quaint turrets, long terraces, and picturesque gardens, faced the lake at a slightly distant elevation, where it stood embosomed in trees.

"Well! if the place were to be mine," observed the lounger, with his eyes fixed upon it, "I know exactly what I should do. I would throw all your agricultural and educational, and endless improvement schemes overboard at once; leave them for those whose business it is to look after them; and enjoy myself, and live like a prince while I had the chance."

"And die worse than a beggar at last," cried the other youth, as he rested on his oars and looked at his cousin who had spoken—"I mean without a friend! You cannot secure even enjoyment, in stagnation," added he. "The very pond here is kept pure by giving out through a stream at one end, what it receives through a stream at the other."

"And the stream from which it receives," said the old man, looking up from his book, "is a type of God Himself; and the stream to which it gives, is a type of the human race. Those who receive from the fountain, without giving to the stream, work equally against the laws of Nature and of God."

A few strokes of the oar here carried the boat away. Well it is with those who in the secrets of Nature read the wisdom of God!

Softly did that summer evening sink upon the park and the old Baronial Hall, and heavy were the mists and dews that hung over the woods, and gardens, and flowers, and great was the rejoicing in the country round, when after a time, they were followed by fertilizing rains. Fertilizing rains!—the words are easily spoken, but who knows their full meaning, save he who has watched over corn-fields or vineyards, threatened with ill-timed drought?

We take a great deal for granted in this world, and expect that everything as a matter of course ought to fit into our humours, and wishes, and wants; and it is often only when danger threatens, that we awake to the discovery, that the guiding reins are held by One whom we had well-nigh forgotten in our careless ease.

"If it had not thundered, the peasant had not made the sign of the cross," is the rude proverb of a distant land; and peasant and king are alike implicated in its meaning.

"It is all right now," observed the farmer, as he returned home in the evening, after contemplating the goodly acres drenched and dripping with rain.

And it was all right indeed, for, long after the farmer had forgotten his previous anxieties in sleep, the circle of blessing was at work in the length and breadth of his fields. There, the condensed vapours sank into the willing soil, which gave to them her gases and her salts.

There, the fibres of the roots of corn and grass sucked up the welcome food which brought strength and power into the juices of the plant; and then, by slow but sure degrees, the stunted ears began to fill, and men said the harvest would be good.

"Stay with us for ever," asked the Corn-ears of the Vapours, as they felt themselves swell under the delicious influence.

The Vapours made no answer, for they did not like to speak of death; but they dealt gently with the corn, and did not leave it till it had ripened gradually for the harvest, and no longer needed their aid; and then they exhaled once more into the air, to follow out their mission elsewhere.

A curly-headed urchin stood by a pump, looking disconsolately at the huge heavy handle, which he could not lift. A little watering-pot was grasped in his hands, and it was easy to see what he wanted. Some one passing by observed him, and with a smile gave him help. A very few strokes of the handle brought up the water from below, the little watering-pot was filled, and the child ran away.

He had a garden of his own: a garden in which a few kidney-beans in one place, and sweet-peas in another, with scatterings of mustard and cress, formed a not very usual mixture; but it served its purpose of giving employment and pleasure to the child.

The kidney-beans which he hoped to eat one day at dinner, were evidently the objects of his most attentive care, for he soaked them again and again with the water from his pot, tossing only a few drops of it over the flowers.

Little guessed he of the long long journey the Vapours of the Sea had made before they helped to fill the springs which fed the well over which the pump was built. Little guessed he either of what would become of them when, after helping to fill his kidney-beans with delicate juices, they returned back to the ministry of the winds.

When he touched his pinafore, after he had finished his work, he found it soaked with wet; and when, soon after, he saw it hung in front of the fire to dry, he sat down and amused himself by watching the steam as it rose from the linen, under the influence of heat.

Trifling it seems to tell;—an every-day occurrence of life, not worth a record: yet there was a law even for the vapour that rose from the infant's pinafore in front of the nursery fire. Nothing shall be lost of that which God has ordained to good; and the Vapours were soon on their mission again. Through chimney or window they escaped to the cooler air, and returned to their ceaseless work.

"Give us of your salts," was at last their request, as they percolated through the lower ground to join the mighty rivers which ran into the Sea. "Give us of your salts, and lime, and mineral virtues, oh thou Earth! that we may bear them with us to the Sea from whence we came."

"Is not the Sea sufficient to itself?" enquired the jealous Earth.

"None are sufficient to themselves, oh, careful Mother!" answered the Vapours as they streamed in water along their way. "Small and great, great and small, we all depend on each other. How shall the Shells, and Coral Reefs, and Zoophytes of the deep continue to grow and live, if you refuse them the virtues of your soil? Give us of your salts, and lime, and the mineral deposits of your bosom, oh, Mother Earth! that they may live and rejoice."

"Have you nothing to offer in return?" asked the still-hesitating Earth.

"Do you not know that we have left a blessing behind us wherever we have been?" exclaimed the Vapours. "But no matter for the past. See, we will do ourselves as we would have you do. We will bind ourselves in beauty in the caves of your kingdom, and live with you for ever."

So, as they passed on their way, loading themselves with the virtues of the Earth, some turned aside, and sinking to the subterranean depths, oozed with their limy burden through the roofs of caverns and sides of rocks, and hung suspended in graceful stalactites, or shone out in many-sided crystal forms.

"Now I am satisfied," observed the Earth. "What I see I know. They have left me something behind for what they have taken away."

"And now we are satisfied," cried the rest of the Vapours, as they poured into the rivers and were carried out into the Sea. "Have we not returned with a blessing and treasures in our hand?"

And thus, from age to age, ever since the primary mists went up from the earth and watered the whole face of the ground, the mighty work has gone on, and still continues its course. For not to inactivity and idleness did the Vapours now return, but only to recommence afresh their labours of love.

Yes! evermore rejoicing on their way, through all varieties of accident, of climate, and of place, whether as Snow or Hail, as Showers or Dews, as Floods or Springs, as Rivers or as Seas, the waters are still obediently fulfilling His word who called them into being, and are carrying the everlasting Circle of Blessing round the world.

Oh, ye Showers and Dew; oh, ye Winds of God; oh, ye Ice and Snow; oh, ye Seas and Floods; verily, even when man is mute and forgetful, ye bless the Lord, ye praise Him and magnify Him for ever!

The Law of the Wood

"Let every one of us please his neighbour for his good."
—ROM. xv. 2.

"Never!"

What a word to be heard in a wood on an early summer morning, before the sun had quite struggled through the mists, and before the dew had left the flowers; and while all Nature was passing through the changes that separate night from day, adapting herself gently to the necessities of the hour.

"Never!"

What a word to come from a young creature, which knew very little more of what had gone before, than of what was coming after, and who could not, therefore, be qualified to pronounce a very positive judgment upon anything.

But, somehow or other, it is always the young and inexperienced, who are most apt to be positive and self-willed in their opinions; and so, the young Spruce-fir, thinking neither of the lessons which Nature was teaching, nor of his own limited means of judging, stuck out his branches all round him in everybody's face, right and left, and said—

"Never!"

It so startled a squirrel, who was sitting in a neighbouring tree, pleasantly picking out the seeds of a fir cone, that he dropped his treasured dainty to the ground; and springing from branch to branch, got up as high as he could, and then, looking down, remarked timidly to himself, "What can be the matter with the Spruce-firs?"

Nothing was the matter with the Spruce-firs, exactly; but the history of their excitement was as follows:—They, and a number of other trees, were growing together in a pretty wood. There were oaks, and elms, and beeches, and larches, and firs of many sorts; and here and there, there was a silver-barked Birch. And there was one silver-barked Birch in particular, who had been observing the spruce-firs all that spring; noticing how fast they were growing, and what a stupid habit (as he thought) they had, of always getting into everybody's way, and never bending to accommodate the convenience of others.

He might have seen the same thing for some years before, if he had looked; but he was not naturally of an inquisitive disposition, and did not trouble himself with other people's affairs: so that it was only when the Spruce-fir next him had come so close that its branches fridged off little pieces of his delicate paper-like bark, when the wind was high, that his attention was attracted to the subject.

People usually become observant when their own comfort is interfered with, and this was the case here. However little the Birch might have cared for the Spruce-fir's behaviour generally, there was no doubt that it was very disagreeable to be scratched in the face; and this he sensibly felt, and came to his own conclusions accordingly.

At first, indeed, he tried to sidle and get out of the Fir's way, being himself of a yielding, good-natured character, but the attempt was a quite hopeless one. He could not move on one side a hundredth part as fast as the fir branches grew; so that, do what he would, they came pushing up against him, and teased him all day.

It was quite natural, therefore, that the poor Birch should begin to look round him, and examine into the justice and propriety of such a proceeding on the part of the Spruce-firs; and the result was, that he considered their conduct objectionable in every way.

"For," said he, (noticing that there was a little grove of them growing close together just there,) "if they all go on, shooting out their branches in that manner, how hot and stuffy they will get! Not a breath of air will be able to blow through them soon, and that will be very bad for their health; besides which, they are absolute pests to society, with their unaccommodating ways. I must really, for their own sakes, as well as my own, give them some good advice."

And accordingly, one morning,—that very early summer morning before described,—the Birch, having had his silvery bark a little more scratched than usual, opened his mind to his friends.

"If you would but give way a little, and not stick out your branches in such a very stiff manner on all sides, I think you would find it a great deal more comfortable for yourselves, and it would certainly be more agreeable to your neighbours. Do try!"

"You are wonderfully ready in giving unasked advice!" remarked the young Spruce-fir next the Birch, in a very saucy manner. "We are quite comfortable as we are, I fancy; and as to giving way, as you call it, what, or whom are we called upon to give way to, I should like to know?"

"To me, and to all your neighbours," cried the Birch, a little heated by the dispute.

On which the Spruce-fir next the Birch cried "Never!" in the most decided manner possible; and those beyond him cried "Never!" too; till at last, all the Spruce-firs, with one accord, cried, "Never!" "Never!" "Never!" and half frightened the poor squirrel to death. Every hair on his beautiful tail trembled with fright, as he peeped down from the top of the tree, wondering what could be the matter with the Spruce-firs.

And certainly, there was one thing the matter with them, for they were very obstinate; and as nobody can be very obstinate without being very selfish, there was more the matter with them than they themselves suspected, for obstinacy and selfishness are very bad qualities to possess.

But, so ignorant were they of their real character, that they thought it quite a fine thing to answer the Birch-tree's mild suggestion in such a saucy manner. Indeed, they actually gave themselves credit for the display of a firm, independent spirit; and so, while they shouted "Never!" they held out their branches as stiffly as possible towards each other, till they crossed, and recrossed, and plaited together. On which they remarked—

"What a beautiful pattern this makes! How neatly we fit in one with the other! How pretty we shall look when we come out green all over! Surely the Wood-pigeons would have been quite glad to have built their nests here if they had known. What a pity they did not, poor things! I hear them cooing in the elm-tree yonder, at a very inconvenient height, and very much exposed."

"Don't trouble yourselves about us," cooed the Wood-pigeons from their nest in the elm. "We are much happier where we are. We want more breeze, and more leafy shade, than you can give us in your close thick-growing branches."

"Every one to his taste," exclaimed the young Spruce-fir, a little nettled by the Wood-pigeons' cool remarks; "if you prefer wind and rain to shelter, you are certainly best where you are. But you must not talk about leafy shade, because every one knows that you can have nothing of it where you are, to what you will find here, when we come out green all over."

"But when will that be?" asked the Wood-pigeons in a gentle voice. "Dear friends, do you not know that the spring is over, and the early summer has begun, and all the buds in the forest are turned to leaves? And you yourselves are green everywhere outside, not only with your evergreen hue, but with the young summer's shoots. I sadly fear, however, that it is not so in your inner bowers."

"Perhaps, because we are evergreens, our sprouting may not go on so regularly as with the other trees," suggested one. But he felt very nervous at his foolish remark. It was welcomed, however, as conclusive by his friends, who were delighted to catch at any explanation of a fact which had begun to puzzle them.

So they cried out, "Of course!" with the utmost assurance, and one of them added, "Our outer branches have been green and growing for some time, and doubtless we shall be green all over soon!"

"Doubtless!" echoed every Spruce-fir in the neighbourhood, for they held fast by each other's opinions, and prided themselves on their family attachment.

"We cannot argue," cooed the Wood-pigeons in return. "The days are too short, even for love; how can there ever be time for quarrelling?"

So things went on in the old way, and many weeks passed over; but still the interlaced branches of the Spruce-firs were no greener than before. But beautiful little cones hung along the outermost ones; and, judging by its outside appearance, the grove of firs looked to be in a most flourishing state.

Alas! however, all within was brown and dry; and the brownness and dryness spread further and further, instead of diminishing, and, no wonder, for the summer was a very sultry one, and the confined air in the Fir-grove became close and unhealthy; and after heavy rains, an ill-conditioned vapour rose up from the earth, and was never dispersed by the fresh breezes of heaven.

Nevertheless, the Spruce-firs remained obstinate as ever. They grew on in their old way, and tried hard to believe that all was right.

"What can it matter," argued they, "whether we are green or not, inside? We are blooming and well everywhere else, and these dry branches don't signify much that I can see. Still, I do wonder what can be the reason of one part being more green than another."

"It is absurd for you to wonder about it," exclaimed the Birch, who became more irritated every day. "There is not a tree in the world that could thrive and prosper, if it persisted in growing as you do. But it is of no use talking! You must feel and know that you are in each other's way every time you move; and in everybody else's way too. In mine, most particularly."

"My dear friend," retorted the Spruce-fir, "your temper makes you most absurdly unjust. Why, we make a point of never interfering with each other, or with anybody else! Our rule is to go our own way, and let everybody else do the same. Thus much we claim as a right."

"Thus much we claim as a right!" echoed the Spruce-fir grove.

"Oh, nonsense about a right," persisted the Birch. "Where is the good of having a right to make both yourself and your neighbours miserable? If we each of us lived in a field by ourselves, it would be all very well. Every one might go his own way then undisturbed. But mutual accommodation is the law of the wood, or we should all be wretched together."

"My friend," rejoined the Spruce-fir, "you are one of the many who mistake weakness for amiability, and make a merit of a failing. We are of a different temper, I confess! We are, in the first place, capable of having ideas, and forming opinions of our own, which everybody is not; and, in the second place, the plans and habits we have laid down to ourselves, and which are not wrong in themselves, we are courageous enough to persist in, even to the death."

The Spruce-fir bristled all over with stiffness, as he refreshed himself by this remark.

"Even," enquired the Birch, in an ironical tone; "even at the sacrifice of your own comfort, and that of all around you?"

"You are suggesting an impossible absurdity," answered the vexed Spruce-fir, evasively. "What is neither wrong nor unreasonable in itself can do no harm to anybody, and I shall never condescend to truckle to other people's whims as to my line of conduct. But there are plenty, who, to get credit for complaisance to their neighbours, would sacrifice their dearest principles without a scruple!"

"Come, come!" persisted the Birch; "let us descend from these heights. There are plenty of other people my friend, who would fain shelter the most stupid obstinacy, and the meanest selfishness, behind the mask of firmness of character or principle,—or what not. Now what principle, I should like to know, is involved in your persisting in your stiff unaccommodating way of growing, except the principle of doing what you please at the expense of the feelings of other people?"

"Insolent!" cried the Spruce-fir; "we grow in the way which Nature dictates; and our right to do so must therefore be unquestionable. We possess, too, a character of our own, and are not like those who can trim their behaviour into an unmeaning tameness, to curry favour with their neighbours."

"I ought to be silent," cried the Birch; "for I perceive my words are useless. And yet, I would like you to listen to me a little longer. Does the Beech-tree sacrifice her character, do you think, when she bends away her graceful branches to allow room for the friend at her side to flourish too? Look, how magnificently she grows, stretching protectingly as it were, among other trees; and yet, who so accommodating and yielding in their habits as she is?"

"It is her nature to be subservient, it is ours to be firm!" cried the Spruce-fir.

"It is her nature to throw out branches all round her, as it is that of every other tree," insisted the friendly Birch; "but she regulates the indulgence of her nature by the comfort and convenience of others."

"I scorn the example you would set me," cried the Spruce-fir; "it is that of the weakest and most supple of forest trees. Nay, I absolutely disapprove of the tameness you prize so highly. Never, I hope, will you see us bending feebly about, and belying our character, even for the sake of flourishing in a wood!"

It was all in vain, evidently; so the Birch resolved to pursue the matter no further, but he muttered to himself—

"Well, you will see the result."

On which the Spruce-fir became curious, and listened for more. The Birch, however, was silent, and at last, the Spruce-fir made a sort of answer in a haughty, indifferent tone—

"I do not know what you mean by the result."

"You will know some day," muttered the Birch, very testily, (for the fir branches were fridging his bark cruelly—the wind having risen—) "and even I shall be released from your annoyance, before long!"

"I will thank you to explain yourself in intelligible language," cried the Spruce-fir, getting uneasy.

"Oh! in plain words, then, if you prefer it," replied the Birch. "You are all of you dying."

"Never!" exclaimed the Spruce-fir; but he shook all over with fright as he uttered it. And when the other Spruce-firs, according to custom, echoed the word, they were as tremulous as himself.

"Very well, we shall see," continued the Birch. "Every one is blind to his own defects, of course; and it is not pleasant to tell home truths to obstinate people. But there is not a bird that hops about the wood, who has not noticed that your branches are all turning into dry sticks; and before many years are over, there will be no more green outside than in. The flies and midges that swarm about in the close air round you, know it as well as we do. Ask the Squirrel what he thinks of your brown crackly branches, which would break under his leaps. And as to the Wood-pigeons, they gave you a hint of your condition long ago. But you are beyond a hint. Indeed, you are, I believe, beyond a cure."

They were, indeed; but a shudder passed through the Fir-grove at these words, and they tried very hard to disbelieve them. Nay, when the winter came, they did disbelieve them altogether; for, when all the trees were covered with snow, no one could tell a dead branch from a live one; and, when the snow fell off, they who had their evergreen outside, had an advantage over many of the trees by which they were surrounded.

It was a time of silence too, and quiet, for the leafless trees were in a half-asleep state, and had no humour to talk. The evergreens were the only ones who, now and then, had spirit enough to keep up a little conversation.

At last, one day, the Spruce-firs decided to consult with a distant relation of their own, the Scotch-fir, on the subject. He formed one of a large grove of his own kind, that grew on an eminence in the wood. But they could only get at him through a messenger; and, when the Squirrel who was sent to enquire whether he ever gave way in his growth to accommodate others, came back with the answer that, "Needs must when there is no help!" the Spruce-firs voted their cousin a degraded being even in his own eyes, and scorned to follow an example so base.

Then they talked to each other of the ill-nature of the world, and tried to persuade themselves that the Birch had put the worst interpretation on their condition, merely to vex them; and told themselves, in conclusion, that they had nothing to fear. But their anxiety was great, and when another spring and summer succeeded to the winter, and all the other trees regained their leaves, and a general waking up of life took place, a serious alarm crept over the Spruce-fir grove; for, alas! the brownness and dryness had spread still further, and less and less of green was to be seen on the thickest branches.

Had they but listened to advice, even then, all might have been well. Even the little birds told them how troublesome it was to hop about among them. Even the Squirrel said he felt stifled if he ran under them for a cone.

But they had got into their heads that it was a fine thing to have an independent spirit, and not mind what anybody said; and they had got a notion that it was a right and justifiable thing to go your own way resolutely, provided you allowed other people to do the same. But, with all their philosophy, they forgot that abstract theories are only fit for solitary life, and can seldom be carried out strictly in a wood.

So they grew on, as before, and the Birch-tree ceased to talk, for either his silver peel had all come off, and he was hardened; or else, he had taught himself to submit unmurmuringly to an evil he could not prevent. Certain it is, that no further argument took place, and the condition of the Spruce-firs attracted no further notice; till, one spring morning, several seasons later, the whole wood was startled by the arrival of its owner, a new master, who was come to pay his first visit among its glades.

The occasional sound of an axe-stroke, and a good deal of talking, were heard from time to time, for the owner was attended by his woodman; and at last he reached the Spruce-fir grove.

Alas! and what an exclamation he gave at the sight, as well he might; for nearly every one of the trees had fallen a victim to his selfish mistake, and had gradually died away. Erect they stood, it is true, as before, but dried, withered, perished monuments of an obstinate delusion.

The owner and the woodman talked together for a time, and remarked to each other that half those trees ought to have been taken away years ago: that they were never fit to live in a cluster together; for, from their awkward way of growing, they were half of them sure to die.

But of all the Grove there was but one who had life enough to hear these words; and to him the experience came too late. All his old friends were in due time cut down before his eyes; and he, who by an accident stood slightly apart, and had not perished with the rest, was only reserved in the hope that he might partially recover for the convenience of a Christmas-tree.

It was a sad, solitary summer he passed, though the fresh air blew freely round him now, and he rallied and grew, as well as felt invigorated by its sweet refreshing breath; and though the little birds sung on his branches and chattered of happiness and love: for those who had thought with him and lived with him, were gone, and their places knew them no more.

Ah, certainly there had been a mistake somewhere, but it did not perhaps signify much now, to ascertain where; and no reproaches or ridicule were cast upon him by his neighbours; no, not even by the freed and happy silver-barked Birch; for a gentler spirit than that of rejoicing in other people's misfortunes, prevailed in the pretty wood.

So that it was not till Christmas came, and his doom was for ever sealed, that the Spruce-fir thoroughly understood the moral of his fate.

But then, when the crowds of children were collected in the brightly-lighted hall, where he stood covered with treasures and beauty, and when they all rushed forward, tumbling one over another, in their struggles to reach his branches; each one going his own way, regardless of his neighbours' wishes or comfort; and when the parents held back the quarrelsome rogues, bidding them one give place to another,—"in honour preferring one another," considering public comfort, rather than individual gratification: then, indeed, a light seemed to be thrown on the puzzling subject of the object and rules of social life; and he repeated to himself the words of the silver-barked Birch, exclaiming—

"Mutual accommodation is certainly the law of the wood, or its inhabitants would all be wretched together."

It was his last idea.

Active and Passive

"They also serve who only stand and wait."
—MILTON.

"Restless life! restless life!" moaned the Weathercock on the church-tower by the sea, as he felt himself swayed suddenly round by the wind, and creaked with dismay: "restless, toiling life, and everybody complaining of one all the time. There's that tiresome weathercock pointing east, cried the old woman, as she hobbled up the churchyard path to the porch last Sunday; now I know why I have got all my rheumatic pains back again. Then, in a day or two, came the farmer by on his pony, and drew up outside the wall to have a word with the grave-digger. A bad look out, Tomkins, said he, if that rascally old weathercock is to be trusted, the wind's got into the wrong quarter again, and we shall have more rain. Was it my fault if he did find out through me that the wind was in, what he called, the wrong quarter? Besides, the wind always is in somebody's wrong quarter, I verily believe! But am I to blame? Did I choose my lot? No, no! Nobody need suppose I should go swinging backwards and forwards, and round and round, all my life, if I had my choice about the matter. Ah! how much rather would I lead the quiet, peaceful existence of my old friend, the Dial, down below yonder on his pedestal. That is a life, indeed!"

"How he is chattering away up above there," remarked the Dial from below; "he almost makes me smile, though not a ray of sunshine has fallen on me through the livelong day, alas! I often wonder what he finds to talk about. But his active life gives him subjects enough, no doubt. Ah! what would I not give to be like him! But all is so different with me, alas! I thought I heard my own name too, just now. I will ask. Halloo! up above there. Did you call, my sprightly friend? Is there anything fresh astir? Tell me, if there is. I get so weary of the dark and useless hours; so common now, alas! What have you been talking about?"

"Nothing profitable this time, good neighbour," replied the Weathercock; "for, in truth, you have caught me grumbling."

"Grumbling . . . ? Grumbling, you?"

"Yes, grumbling, I! Why not?"

"But grumbling in the midst of an existence so gay, so active, so bright," pursued the Dial; "it seems impossible."

"Gay, active, bright! a pretty description enough; but what a mockery of the truth it covers! Look at me, swinging loosely to every peevish blast that flits across the sky. Turned here, turned there, turned everywhere. The sport of every passing gust. Never a moment's rest, but when the uncertain breezes choose to seek it for themselves. Gay, active, bright existence, indeed! Restless, toiling life I call it, and all to serve a thankless world, by whom my very usefulness is abused. But you, my ancient friend, you, in the calm enjoyment of undisturbed repose, steady and unmoved amidst the utmost violence of storms, how little can you appreciate the sense of weariness I feel! A poor judge of my troubled lot are you in your paradise of rest!"

"My paradise of rest, do you call it?" exclaimed the Dial; "an ingenious title, truly, to express what those who know it practically, feel to be little short of a stagnation of existence. Dull, purposeless, unprofitable, at the mercy of the clouds and shades of night; I can never fulfil my end but by their sufferance, and in the seasons, rare enough at best, when their meddling interference is withdrawn. And even when the sun and hour do smile upon me, and I carry out my vocation, how seldom does any one come near me to learn the lessons I could teach. I weary of the night; I weary of the clouds; I weary of the footsteps that pass me by. Would that I could rise, even for a few brief hours, to the energy and meaning of a life like yours!"

"This is a strange fatality, indeed!" creaked the Weathercock in reply, "that you, in your untroubled calm, should yearn after the restlessness I sicken of. That I, in what you call my gay and active existence, should long for the quiet you detest!"

"You long for it because you are ignorant of its nature and practical reality," groaned the Dial.

"Nay, but those are the very words I would apply to you, my ancient friend. The blindest ignorance of its workings can alone account for your coveting a position such as mine."

"If that be so, then every position is wrong," was the murmured remark in answer; but it never reached the sky, for at that moment the mournful tolling of a bell in the old church-tower announced that a funeral was approaching, and in its vibrations the lesser sound was lost.

And as those vibrations gathered in the air, they grouped themselves into a solemn dirge, which seemed as if it rose in contradiction to what had just been said.

For it gave out to the mourners who were following the corpse to its last earthly resting-place, that every lot was good, and blessed to some particular end.

For the lots of all, (it said,) were appointed, and all that was appointed was good.

Little, little did it matter, therefore (it said,) whether the lot of him who came to his last resting-place had been a busy or a quiet one; a high or a low one; one of labour or of endurance. If that which was appointed to be done, had been well done, all was well.

It gave out, too, that every time and season was good, and blessed to some particular purpose; that the time to die was as good as the time to be born, whether it came to the child who had done but little, or to the man who had done much.

For the times and seasons, (it said,) were appointed, and all that was appointed was good.

Little, little did it matter, therefore, (it said,) whether the time of life had been a long one or a short one, if that which was appointed to be used, had been rightly used, all was right.

Echoing and re-echoing in the air, came these sounds out of the bell-tower, bidding the mourners not to mourn, for both the lots and the times of all things were appointed, and all that was appointed was good.

The mourners wept on, however, in spite of the dirge of the bell; and perhaps it was best that they did so, for where are the outpourings of penitence so likely to be sincere, or the resolutions of amendment so likely to be earnest, as over the graves of those we love?

So the mourners wept; the corpse was interred; the clergyman departed, and the crowd dispersed; and then there was quiet in the churchyard again for a time.

Uninterrupted quiet, except when the wandering gusts drove the Weathercock hither and thither, causing him to give out a dismal squeak as he turned.

But at last there was a footstep in the old churchyard again, a step that paced up and down along the paved path; now westward towards the sea, now eastward towards the Lych-gate at the entrance.

It was a weather-beaten old fisherman, once a sailor, who occasionally made of that place a forecastle walk for exercise and pondering thoughts, since the time when age and growing infirmities had disabled him from following regularly the more toilsome parts of a fisherman's business, which were now carried on by his two grown-up sons.

He could do a stroke of work now and then, it is true, but, the nows and thens came but seldom, and he had many leisure hours on his hands in which to think of the past, and look forward to the future.

And what a place was that churchyard for awakening such thoughts! There, as he walked up and down, his own wife's grave was not many yards distant from his feet; and yet, from amidst these relics and bitter evidence of finite mortality, he could look out upon that everlasting sea, which seems always to stretch away into the infinity we all believe in.

Perhaps, in his own way, the sailor had often felt this, although he might not have been able to give any account of his sensations.

Up and down the path he paced, lingering always a little at the western point ere he turned; and with his telescope tucked under his arm ready for use, he stood for a second or two looking seaward, in case a strange sail should have come in sight.

The sexton, who had come up to the churchyard again to finish the shaping of the new grave, nodded to him as he passed, and the sailor nodded in return; but neither of them spoke, for the sailor's habits were too well known to excite attention, and the sexton had his work to complete.

But presently, when half-way to the Lych-gate, the sailor stopped suddenly short, turned around hastily, and faced the sea, steadying the cap on his head against the gale which was now blowing directly on his face—looked up into the sky—looked all around—looked at the Weathercock, and then stood, as if irresolute, for several seconds.

At last, stepping over the grave-stones, he went up to the stone pedestal, on the top of which the Dial lay, waiting for the gleams of sunshine which had on that day fallen rarely and irregularly upon it.

"If the clouds would but break away for a minute," mused the old man to himself.

And soon after they did so, for they had begun to drive very swiftly over the heavens, and the sunlight, streaming for a few seconds on the dial-plate, revealed the shadow of the gnomon cast upon the place of three o'clock.

The sailor lingered by the Dial for several minutes after he had ascertained the hour, examining the figures, inscriptions, and dates. A motto on a little brass plate was let into the pedestal below: "Watch, for ye know not the hour." There was some difficulty in reading it, it was so blotched and tarnished with age and long neglect. Indeed, few people knew there was an inscription there at all; but the old sailor had been looking very closely, and so found it out, and then he spelt it all through, word for word.

It was to be hoped that the engraver (one Thomas Trueman), who claimed to have had this warning put up for the benefit of others, had attended to it himself, for he had long ago—aye! nearly a hundred years ago—gone to his last account. The appointed hour had come for him, whether he had watched for it or not.

Perhaps some such thoughts crossed the sailor's mind, for certainly after reading the sentence, he fell into a reverie. Not a long one, however, for it was interrupted by the voice of the sexton, who, with his mattock over his shoulder, was passing back on his way home, and called out to the sailor to bid him good evening.

"Good-night, Mr. Bowman," said he; "we've rather a sudden change in the wind, haven't we?"

"Aye, aye," answered Bowman, by no means displeased at this deference to his opinion, and he stepped back again to the path, and joined his village friend.

"It is a sudden change, as you say, and an awkward one too, for the wind came round at three o'clock, just at the turn of the tide; and it's a chance but what it will keep this way for hours to come; and a gale all night's an ugly thing, Tomkins, when it blows ashore."

"I hope you may be mistaken, Mr. Bowman," rejoined the sexton; "but I suppose that's not likely. However, they say it's an ill wind that blows nobody good, so I suppose I shall come in for something at last," and here the sexton laughed.

"At your age, strong and hearty," observed the sailor, eyeing the sexton somewhat contemptuously, "you can't have much to wish for, I should think."

"Strong and hearty's a very good thing in its way, Mr. Bowman, I'll not deny; but rest's a very good thing, too, and I wouldn't object to one of your idle afternoons now and then, walking up and down the pavement, looking which way the wind blows. That's a bit of real comfort, to my thinking."

"We don't know much of each other's real comforts, I suspect," observed the sailor abstractedly, and then he added—

"You'll soon be cured of wishing for idle afternoons when they're forced upon you, Tomkins. But you don't know what you're talking about. Wait till you're old, and then you'll find it's I that might be excused for envying you, and not you me."

"That's amazing, Mr. Bowman, and I can't see it," persisted Tomkins, turning round to depart. "In my opinion you've the best of it; but anyhow, we're both of us oddly fixed, for we're neither of us pleased."

With a friendly good-night, but no further remark, the two men parted, and the churchyard was emptied of its living guests.

When the sailor sat down with his sons an hour or two afterwards to their evening meal, said he, "We must keep a sharp look-out, lads, to-night; the wind came round at three with the turn of the tide, and it blows dead ashore. I've been up to the Captain's at the Hall, and borrowed the use of his big boat in case it's wanted, for unless the gale goes down with the next tide,—which it won't, I think,—we might have some awkward work. Anyhow, boys, we'll watch."

"Just what I said," muttered the Dial, as the sound of the last footsteps died on the churchyard path. "Just what I said! Everything's wrong, because everybody's dissatisfied. I knew it was so. We're right in grumbling; that's the only thing we're right in. At least, I'm sure I'm right in grumbling. I'm not so certain about my neighbour on the tower above. Halloo! my sprightly friend, do you hear? Did you notice? Isn't it just as I said? Everything wrong to everybody."

The strong west wind continued to sweep through the churchyard, and bore these observations away; but the Weathercock meanwhile was making his own remarks to himself.

"There, now! There's the old story over again, only now it's the west wind that's wrong instead of the east! I wish anybody would tell me which is the right wind! But this, of course, is an ill wind, and an ugly gale, and they're afraid it will blow all night, (I wonder why it shouldn't, it blows very steadily and well, as I think,) and then they shake their heads at each other, and look up at me and frown. What's the use of frowning? They never saw me go better in their lives. It's a fine firm wind as ever blew, though it does take one's breath rather fast, I own. If it did not make quite so much howling noise, I should have had a word or two about it with my old comrade below, who sits as steady as a rock through it all, I've no doubt. There is one thing I am not quite easy about myself. . . . In case this west wind should blow a little, nay, in short, a great deal harder, even than now, I wonder whether there would be any danger of my being blown down? I'm not very fond of my present quarters, it's true, but a change is sometimes a doubtful kind of thing, unless you can choose what it shall be. I wonder, too, whether people would be glad if I was gone; or whether, after all, I mightn't be rather missed? And I wonder, too—"

But it began to blow too hard for wondering, or talking, or doing anything, but silently holding fast, for the gale was rising rapidly; so rapidly, that before midnight a hurricane was driving over land and ocean, and in its continued roaring, mingled as it was with the raging of a tempest-tossed sea, every other voice and sound was lost.

Tracts of white foam, lying like snow-fields on the water, followed the breakers as they fell down upon the shore with a crash of thunder, and were visible even through the gloom of night.

Hour after hour the uproar continued, and hour after hour the church clock struck, and no one heard. Due west pointed the Weathercock, varying scarcely a point. Firm and composed lay the Dial on his pedestal, and the old church on her foundations, mocking the tumult of the elements by their dead, immovable calm.

In the village on the top of the cliff many were awakened by the noise; and one or two, as they lay listening in their beds, forgot for a time their own petty troubles and trifling cares, and uttered wishes and prayers that no vessels might be driven near that rock-bound shore, on that night of storm!

Vain wishes! vain prayers! As they turned again to their pillows to sleep, with their children around them, housed in security and peace, the blue lights of distress were sent up by trembling hands into the vault of heaven, and agonised hearts wondered whether human eye would see them, or human hand could aid.

And it might easily have happened, that, in that terrible night, no eye had caught sight of the signals, or caught sight of them too late to be of use, or that those who had seen had been indifferent, or unable to help.

But it was not so, or the Weathercock would have pointed, and the Dial have shown the hour, and the sailor looked at both in vain.

And this was not the case!

People were roused from their pillowed slumbers the next morning to hear that a vessel, with a passenger crew on board of her, was driving on the rocks. From cottage casements, and from the drawing-room windows of houses on the top of the cliff, the fatal sight was seen, for the dismasted ship, rolling helplessly on the waters, drifted gradually in front of the village, looking black as with the shadow of death.

Delicate women saw it, who, all unaccustomed to such sights, and shuddering at their own helplessness, could only sink on their knees, and ask if there was no mercy with the Most High.

Men saw it whom age or sickness had made weak as children, but who had once been brave and strong; and their heart burned within them as they turned away and sickened at the spectacle of misery they could not even try to avert.

Children saw it, who, mixing in the village crowd that by degrees gathered on the cliff, never ceased the vain prattling enquiry of why some good people did not go to help the poor people who were drowning in the ship?

"Young 'un, you talk," growled one old fellow who was eyeing the spectacle somewhat coolly through a telescope; "and it's for such as you to talk; but who's to get off a boat over such a surf as yon? Little use there'd be in flinging away more lives to save those that's as good as gone already."

"How you go on, Jonas!" cried a woman from the crowd. "Here's a lady has fainted through your saying that; and what do you know about it? While there's life there's hope. My husband went down to the shore hours and hours ago, before it was light."

"With coffins, I suppose," shouted some one, and the jest went round, for the woman who had spoken was the sexton's wife. But many a voice cried "shame," as Mrs. Tomkins turned away to lend her aid in carrying the fainting lady to her home.

It was strange how time wore on, and no change for better or worse seemed to take place in the condition of the unhappy vessel, as far as those on land could judge of her. But she was at least a mile from shore; and even with a glass it was impossible to detect clearly the movements and state of her crew.

It was evident at one time that she had ceased to drift, and had become stationary, and all sorts of conjectures were afloat as to the cause; the most popular and dreadful of which being, that she was gradually filling with water, and must go down.

This was the reason (old Jonas said) why part of the crew had got into the boat that was being towed along behind by means of a rope, so that, when every other hope was over, the rest of the men might join them, and make a last desperate effort to escape the fate of the sinking vessel.

But still time wore on, and no change took place, nor did the vessel appear to get lower in the water, although at times the breakers rolled over her broken decks, and cries of "It's all over! There she goes!" broke from the crowd. The man at the wheel seemed still to maintain his post; those in the boat behind still kept their places, and the few visible about the ship were busied, but no one could say how.

At last somebody shouted that they were raising a jury-mast, though whether as a signal to some vessel within sight of them, or for their own use, remained doubtful for a time; but by and by a small sail became visible, and soon after, it was observed that the vessel had resumed her course, and that she was no longer drifting, but steering! It was clear, therefore, that she had been anchored previously, that the crew had not given up hope, and that they were now trying to weather the rocky bay, and get into the nearest harbour.

Old Jonas turned away, and lent his glass to others. The vessel was not filling with water, it was true, but could such a battered hulk, rolling as it did, ever live through the "race" at the extremity of the bay? He doubted it, for his part—but he was disposed to doubt!

Others were more hopeful, and many a "Thank God for His goodness" relieved the anxious breasts of those who had hitherto looked on in trembling suspense.

The villagers were gradually dispersing to their different occupations, when a couple of boys, who had gone down by the cliffs to the shore, came running back with the news that the old sailor's (Mr. Bowman's) cottage, the only one near the shore, was shut up, the key gone, and nobody there.

This new surprise was heartily welcome, coming as it did to enliven the natural reaction of dulness that follows the cessation of great excitement; and the good wives of the village, with their aprons over their heads, huddled together, more full of wonder and conjecture over the disappearance of the Bowmans, than over the fate of the still peril-surrounded ship. It was then discovered, but quite by an accident, that some one else had disappeared—no other than Tomkins, the sexton.

A neighbour, on her road home, accidentally dropping in at Mr. Tomkins's door to ask after the lady that had fainted, found the good woman sitting over the fire, rocking to and fro, and crying her heart out.

"Go away, woman!" cried she to her neighbour, as the door opened. "Get away wi' ye! I want none of ye! I want none of your talking! I'll not listen to any of ye till I know whether the ship's gone down or not!"

"The woman's beside herself!" cried the neighbour. "Why, you don't know what you are saying, surely. The ship isn't likely to go down now! There's a mast and a sail up, woman!"

"Aye, aye, but the 'race'!" cried Mrs. Tomkins, rocking to and fro in despair.

"The 'race' will not hurt it, there's a many says. It was only old Jonas that shook his head over that. Eh, woman, but you've lost your head with watching them. Where's your good man?"

Mrs. Tomkins almost shrieked, "There! he's there—with them! I saw him through Jonas's glass."

The neighbour was thunderstruck. Here was news indeed. But she pressed the matter no further, thinking in truth that Mrs. Tomkins's head was unsettled, and so, after soothing her a bit in the best fashion she could, she left her to talk the matter over in the village.

Mrs. Tomkins was not unsettled in her head at all. She had been one of those who had had a peep through Jonas's glass, and, to her horror, had detected, by some peculiarity of dress, the form of her husband sitting in the boat behind the vessel. The terror and astonishment that seized her rendered her mute, and she had retired to her own cottage to think it out by herself—what it could mean, and how it could have happened—but she had caught Jonas's remark about the "race," and on reaching her own fireside all thoughts merged in the one terrible idea that her husband might go down with the devoted ship.

The report of Mrs. Tomkins's hallucination soon spread, and there is no saying to what a pitch of mysterious belief in some supernatural visitation it might not have led, had not the arrival of Bowman's daughter in the village, and the account she gave, explained the whole affair.

Bowman and his sons had not gone regularly to bed at all on the night previous, but, true to their intention, had kept watch in turn, walking up and down along the front of their cottage, which stood upon ground slightly raised above the shore. It was the old man himself who happened to be watching when the first blue lights went up, and it was then considerably past midnight.

"What a mercy!" was his first exclamation, after hurrying to the cottage, and bidding his sons follow him to the Hall; "what a mercy!" and he threw up his right arm with a clenched fist into the air, his whole frame knit up by strong emotion. The boys, not knowing what he meant, had only stared at him in surprise for a moment, for there was no time for talking.

But the mind of the old man had, with the first sight of the lights, gone back to his churchyard lounge, to his observations on the weather, to the startling inscription, and to his determination to watch and provide. It had gone, forward, too, as well as backward. Forward, with the elastic determination and hope, which comes like inspiration to a good cause; and for him, by anticipation, the daring deed had been done, and the perishing crew rescued. "—What a mercy!"—the exclamation comprehended past, present, and future.

As by the position of the signals of distress, Bowman judged it would be best to put off the boat from the place where it usually lay, he locked up his cottage, (for the girl refused to be left there alone,) taking the key with him, and proceeded at once to the Hall; but recollecting that his friend, the sexton, had made an urgent request to be called up, should any disaster occur, one of the lads ran up the cliff to the village, to give notice of what they were about.

But before he was halfway there, he met poor Tomkins himself, who, rendered restless and uneasy by Bowman's fears and the terrible weather, had come out to enquire how matters were going on. Thus, therefore, he joined their expedition at once, while his wife remained as ignorant of his movements as the rest of the village.

The Captain, a fine old sailor, round the evening of whose days the glories of Trafalgar shed an undying halo, had made it clearly understood, when applied to, that, in case of the boat being wanted, his own assistance, also, might be depended upon; and he was true to his word; so that as soon as the dawn had broken, five men were to be seen on the beach under the Hall, up to their waists almost in water, struggling with the foaming breakers, and pushing off, with an energy which nothing but the most desperate resolution could have given them, a boat from the shore.

Few words were spoken; the one gave orders, and the rest obeyed—promptly, implicitly, and willingly, as if they had worked for years in company; and thus, life and death at stake, they rowed over the waste of waters with mute courage, and a hope which never for an instant blinded them to the knowledge of the peril they incurred.

And thus it was that ere the full daylight had revealed to the villagers the disaster at sea, and even while they were shuddering for the fate of the supposed doomed vessel, help and comfort had reached the despairing hearts of the bewildered men on board.

There were plenty of people afterwards to say that anybody might have known—if they had only thought about it—that that man who was lashed to the wheel, and who had never changed his position for an instant, could have been nobody but the grand old Captain who had been so long in the wars!

There were plenty also to say that Bowman, old as he was, was constantly on the look-out, and was sure to be the first to foresee a disaster, and suggest what ought to be done, even when he could not do it himself; and didn't everybody know too, that Tomkins was always foremost to have a hand in a job, whatever it might be?

The vessel cleared the "race," and got safe to the harbour, and half the village went with Bowman's daughter and Mrs. Tomkins (now weeping as hard for joy as she had before done for terror), to meet them as they landed.

What a talking there was! and what bowing to the Captain, who, dripping wet and cold, had nevertheless a joke for everybody, and even made Mrs. Tomkins smile by saying her husband had come with them on the look-out for a job, but happily his professional services had not been required, though he had done his duty otherwise like a man.

But the wet fellow-labourers had to be dried and taken care of, and the half-exhausted crew had to be attended to and comforted; and the time for chatting comfortably over the events of that night did not come till people's minds and spirits had cooled down from the first excitement.

The weather cleared up wonderfully after that terrible storm had passed over, and the following Sunday shone out over village and sea, with all the brilliancy of spring.

It was just as they were issuing from church after morning service, that the Captain observed Bowman standing by the porch, as if waiting till the crowd had passed. He looked far more upright than usual, and had more of a smile upon his face than was commonly seen there. The Captain beckoned to him to come and speak, and Bowman obeyed.

"This has made a young man of you, Bowman," was the Captain's observation, and he smiled.

"It has comforted me, Sir, I'll not deny," was Bowman's answer.

"I hope it will teach as well as comfort you," continued the Captain, with a half good-natured, half stern manner. "You've been very fond of talking of age and infirmity, and 'cumbering the ground,' and all that sort of thing. But what it means, is, quarrelling with your lot. We may not always know what we're wanted for, nor is it for us to enquire, but nobody is useless as long as he is permitted to live. You can't have a shipwreck every day to prove it, Bowman, but this shipwreck ought to teach you the lesson for the rest of your life."

"I hope it will, Sir," cried Bowman.

"Not that you've so much credit in that matter, after all, as I thought," observed the Captain with a sly smile. "By your own account, if it hadn't been for these comrades of yours in the churchyard here," and as he spoke the Captain pointed with his stick to the Dial and Weathercock, "you might have gone to bed and snored composedly all the night through, without thinking of whether the storm would last, or what it would do."

Bowman touched his hat in compliment to the joke, recollecting with a sort of confusion that, as they were bringing the vessel into port, he had told the Captain the whole story of his noticing the change of wind at the particular hour of three, harping nervously and minutely on the importance of each link in the little chain of events, and dwelling much on the half-effaced inscription, the words of which had never left his mind from the moment when he got into the Captain's boat, to that when they reached the shore in safety.

Scarcely knowing how to reply, Bowman began again—

"Well, your honour, it's really true, for if it hadn't been that—"

"I know, I know," interrupted the Captain, laughing. "And now let us see your friends. I must have a peep at the inscription myself."

The old sailor led the way over the grassy graves to the Dial, and pointed out to his companion the almost illegible words.

There was a silence of several minutes, after the Captain had bent his head to read; and when he raised it again, his look was very grave. Except for the mercy that had spared their lives in so great a risk, the hour might have been over for them.

"Bowman," cried the Captain at length, in his old good-natured way, "these comrades of yours shall not go unrewarded any more than yourself. Before another week is over, you must see that this plate is cleaned and burnished, so that all the parish may read the inscription; and as to the Weathercock, I must have him as bright as gilding can make him before another Sunday. Come, here's work for you for the week, and the seeing that this is done will leave you no time for grumbling, eh, old fellow?"

Bowman bowed his lowest bow. It fell in with all his feelings to superintend such an improvement as this.

"And while you're looking after them, don't forget the lesson they teach," continued the Captain.

Bowman bowed again, and was attentive.

"I mean that everything, as well as everybody, is useful in its appointed place, at the appointed time. But neither we nor they can choose or foresee the time."

On the following Sunday, the sun himself scarcely exceeded in brilliancy the flashing Weathercock, which hovered gently between point and point on the old church-tower by the sea, as if to exhibit his splendour to the world. Not a creak did he make as he moved, for all grumbling was over, and he was suspended to a nicety on his well-oiled pole.

Below, and freshly brightened up and cleaned, the Dial basked in the sunlight, telling one by one the fleeting hours, while the motto underneath it spoke its warning, in letters illuminated as if with fire. Many a villager hung about the once-neglected plate, and took to heart those words of divine wisdom,

"Watch, for ye know not the hour,"

and many an eye glanced up to the monitor of storms and weather, and echoed the "What a mercy!" of old Bowman the sailor.

"Are you silent, my sprightly comrade?" enquired the old Dial from below, of his shining friend above.

"Only a little confused and overpowered at first," was the answer of the Weathercock. "My responsibility is great, you know. I have a great deal to do, and all the world is observing me just now."

"That's true, certainly," continued the Dial. "Things are coming round in a singular manner. Everything's right, after all; but under such a cloud as we were a short time ago, it was not very easy to find it out."

"Undoubtedly not, and a more excusable mistake than ours could not well be imagined. People, with fifty times our advantages, are constantly falling into the same errors."

"Which is such a comfort," pursued the Dial, smiling as he glowed in the sunbeams. "However," added he, "that's a good idea of the old gentleman that was here just now, and I shall try and remember it for future occasions, for it really appears to be true. 'Everything is useful in its place at the appointed time.' That was it, wasn't it?"

"Exactly. And, conscious as I feel just now of my own responsibility, I could almost add, (in confidence to you, of course, my ancient friend,) that I have a kind of sensation that everything is useful in its place, always, and at all times, though people mayn't always find it out."

"Just my own impression," was the Dial's last remark.

Daily Bread

"Your heavenly Father knoweth that ye have need of all these things."
—MATTHEW vi. 32.

"I wish your cheerfulness were a little better timed, my friend," remarked a Tortoise, who for many years had inhabited the garden of a suburban villa, to a Robin Redbreast, who was trilling a merry note from a thorn-tree in the shrubbery. "What in the world are you singing about at this time of year, when I, and everybody else of any sense, are trying to go to sleep, and forget ourselves?"

"I beg your pardon, I am sure," replied the Robin; "I did not know it would have disturbed you."

"You must be gifted with very small powers of observation then, my friend," rejoined the Tortoise. "Here have I been grubbing my head under the leaves and sticks half the morning, to make myself a comfortable hole to take a nap in; and always, just as I am dropping off, you set up one of your senseless pipes."

"You are not over-troubled with politeness, good sir, I think," observed the Robin; "to call my performance by such an offensive name, and to find fault with me for want of observation, is the most unreasonable thing in the world. This is the first season I have lived in the garden, and all through the spring and summer you have never objected to my singing at all. How was I to know you would dislike it now?"

"Your own sense might have told you as much, without my giving myself the trouble of explanation," persisted the Tortoise. "Of course, it's natural enough, and not disagreeable, to hear you little birds singing round the place, when there is something to sing about. It rather raises one's spirits than otherwise. For instance, when the weather becomes mild in the early year, and the plants begin to grow and get juicy, and it is about time for me to get up from my winter's sleep, I have no objection to be awakened by your voices. But now, in this miserable season, when the fruits and flowers are gone, and when even the leaves that are left are tough and dry, and there is not a dandelion that I care to eat; and when it gets colder and colder, and damper and damper every day, this affectation of merriment on your part is both ridiculous and hypocritical. It is impossible that you can feel happy yourself, and you have no business to pretend to it."

"But, begging your pardon once more, good sir, I do feel happy, whatever you may think to the contrary," answered the Robin.

"What, do you mean to say that you like cold, and damp, and bare trees, with scarcely a berry upon them?"

"I like warm sunny days the best, perhaps," replied the Robin, "if I am obliged to think about it and make comparisons. But why should I do so? I am quite comfortable as it is. If there is not so much variety of food as there has been, there is, at any rate, enough for every day, and everybody knows that enough is as good as a feast. For my part, I don't see how I can help being contented."

"Contented! what a dull idea, to be just contented! I am contented myself, after a fashion; but you are trying to seem happy, and that is a very different sort of thing."

"Well, but happy; I am happy, too," insisted the Robin.

"That must be then because you know nothing of what is coming," suggested the Tortoise. "As yet, while the open weather lasts, you can pick up your favourite worms, and satisfy your appetite. But, when the ground has become so hard that the worms cannot come through, or your beak get at them, what will you do?"

"Are you sure that will ever happen?" enquired the Robin.

"Oh! certainly, in the course of the winter, at some time or another; and, indeed, it may happen any day now, which makes me anxious to be asleep and out of the way."

"Oh, well, if it happens now, I shall not mind a bit," cried the Robin; "there are plenty of berries left!"

"But supposing it should happen when all the berries are gone?" said the Tortoise, actually teased at not being able to frighten the Robin out of his singing propensities.

"Nay, but if it comes to supposing," exclaimed the Robin, "I shall suppose it won't, and so I shall be happy still."

"But I say it may happen," shouted the Tortoise.

"And I ask will it?" rejoined the Robin, in quite as determined a manner.

"Which you know I cannot answer," retorted the Tortoise again. "Nobody knows exactly either about the weather or the berries beforehand."

"Then let nobody trouble themselves beforehand," persisted the Robin. "If there was anything to be done to prevent or provide, it would be different. But as it is, we have nothing to do but to be happy in the comfort each day brings."

Here the Robin trilled out a few of his favourite notes, but the Tortoise soon interrupted him.

"Allow other people to be happy, then, as well as yourself, and cease squalling out of that tree. I could have forgiven you, had the branches been full of haws; but, as they are all withered or eaten, you have no particular excuse for singing in that particular bush, rather than elsewhere, so let me request you at once to go."

"Of course I will do so," answered the Robin, politely. "It is the same thing to me exactly, so I wish you a good morning, and, if you desire it, a refreshing sleep."

So saying, the Robin flew from the thorn-tree to another part of the grounds, where he could amuse himself without interruption; and the Tortoise began to hustle under the leaves and rubbish again, with a view to taking his nap.

But, by-and-by, as the morning wore away, the frosty feeling and autumnal mists cleared off; and when the sun came out, which it did for three or four hours in the early afternoon, the day became really fine.

The old Tortoise did not fail to discover the fact; and not having yet scratched himself a hole completely to his mind, he came out of the shrubbery and took a turn in the sunshine.

"This is quite a surprise, indeed," said he to himself. "It is very pleasant, but I am afraid it will not last. The more's the pity; but, however, I shall not go to bed just yet."

With these words, he waddled slowly along to the kitchen garden, where he was in the habit of occasionally basking under the brick wall; and now, tilting himself up sideways against it, he passed an hour, much to his satisfaction, in exposing his horny coat to the rays of the sun; a feat which he never dared to perform during the heats of summer.

Meanwhile, the poor little Robin continued his songs in a retired corner of the grounds, where no one objected to his cheerful notes. A tiny grove it was, with a grassy circle in the middle of it, where a pretty fountain played night and day.

During the pauses of his music, and especially after the sun came out, he wondered much to himself about all the strange uncomfortable things the Tortoise had said. Oh, to think of his having wanted to go to sleep and be out of the way; and now here was the sunshine making all the grove as warm as spring itself. If he had not been afraid the Tortoise might consider him intrusive, he would have gone back and told him how warm and pleasant it was, but absolutely he durst not.

Still, he could not, on reflection, shut his eyes to the fact, that there were no other songsters in the grove just now beside himself, and he wondered what was the reason. Time was, when the nightingale was to be heard every night in this very spot; but, now he came to think of it, that beautiful pipe of his had ceased for months, and where the bird himself was, nobody seemed to know.

The Robin became thoughtful, and perhaps a little uneasy.

There was the Blackbird, too;—what was he about that he also was silent? Was it possible that all the world was really as the Tortoise said, thinking it wise to go to sleep and be out of the way?

The Robin got almost alarmed. So much so, that he flew about, until he met with a Blackbird, whom he might question on the subject, and of him he made the enquiry, why he had left off singing?

The Blackbird glanced at him with astonishment.

"Who does sing in the dismal autumn and winter?" said he. "Really, I know of scarcely any who are bold and thoughtless enough to do so except yourself. The Larks may, to be sure, but they lead such strange lives in the sky, or in seclusion, that they are no rule for any one else. Your own persevering chirruping is (in my humble judgment) so out of character with a season, in which every wise creature must be apprehensive for the future, that I can only excuse it on the ground of an ignorance and levity, which you have had no opportunity of correcting."

"It would be kinder to attribute it to a cheerful contentment with whatever comes to pass," cried the Robin, ruffling his feathers as he spoke. "I rejoice in each day's blessing as it comes, and never wish for more than does come. You, who are wishing the present to be better than it is, and fearing that the future may be worse, are meanwhile losing all enjoyment of the hour that now is. You think this wise. To me it seems as foolish as it is ungrateful!"

With these words the Robin flew away as fast as he could, for, to say the truth, he felt conscious of having been a little impertinent in his last remark. He was rather a young bird to be setting other people right; but a Robin is always a bold fellow, and has moreover rather a hot temper of his own, though he is a kind creature at the bottom. He had been insulted, too, there was no doubt; but when people feel themselves in the right, what need is there of ruffling feathers and being saucy?

And the Robin did honestly feel himself in the right; but, oh! how hard it is to resist the influence of evil suggestions, even when one knows them to be such, and turns aside from them. They are so apt to steal back into the heart unawares, and undermine the principle that seemed so steady before.

To a certain extent, this was the case with our poor little friend; and those who are disposed to judge harshly of his weakness, must remember that he was very young and could not be expected to go on right always without a mistake.

Certain it is, that he drooped awhile in spirits, as the winter advanced. He sang every day, it is true, and would still have maintained his own opinions against any one who should have opposed them; but he was decidedly disturbed in mind, and thought sadly too much, for his own peace and comfort, of what both the Tortoise and Blackbird had said.

The colder the days became, the more he became depressed; not that there was any cold then that he really cared about, but he was fidgeting about the much greater cold which he had been told was coming; and, as he hopped about on the grass round the fountain, picking up worms and food, he was ready to drop a tear out of his bright black eye at the thought of the days when the ground was to be so hard that the worms could not come out, or his beak reach them.

Had this state of things gone on long, the Robin would have begun to wish to go to sleep, like the Tortoise; and no more singing would have been heard in the plantation of the suburban villa that year.

But Robins are brave-hearted little fellows, as well as bold and saucy; and one bright day our friend bethought himself that he would go and talk the matter over with an old Woodlark, whom he had heard frequented a thicket at a considerable distance off.

On his way thither, he heard several larks singing high up in the sky over the fields; and by the time he reached the thicket he was in excellent spirits himself, and seemed to have left all his megrims behind.

It was fortunate such was the case, for when, as he approached the thicket, he heard the Woodlark's note, it was so plaintive and low, that it would have made anybody cry to listen to it. And when the Robin congratulated him on his singing, the Woodlark did not seem to care much for the compliment, but confided to his new acquaintance, that although he thought it right to sing and be thankful, as long as there was a bit of comfort left, he was not so happy as he seemed to be, since in reality he was always expecting to die some day of having nothing at all to eat.

"For," said he, "when the snow is on the ground, it is a perfect chance if one finds a morsel of food all day long."

"But I thought you had lived here several seasons," suggested the Robin, who in his braced condition of mind was getting quite reasonable again.

"So I have," murmured the Woodlark, heaving his breast with a touching sigh.

"Yet you did not die of having nothing to eat, last winter?" observed the Robin.

"It appears not," ejaculated the Woodlark, as gravely as possible, and with another sigh; whereat the Robin's eye actually twinkled with mirth, for he had a good deal of fun in his composition, and could not but smile to himself at the Woodlark's solemn way of admitting that he was alive.

"Nor the winter before?" asked he.

"No," murmured the Woodlark again.

"Nor the winter before that?" persisted the saucy Robin.

"Well, no; of course not," answered the Woodlark, somewhat impatiently, "because I am here, as you see."

"Then how did you manage when the snow came, and there was no food?" enquired the Robin.

"I never told you there was actually no food in those other winters," answered the Woodlark somewhat peevishly, for he did not want to be disturbed in his views. "Little bits of things did accidentally turn up always. But there is no proof that it will ever happen again. It was merely chance!"

"Ah, my venerable friend," cried the Robin; "have you no confidence in the kind chance that has befriended you so often before?"

"I can never be sure it will do so again," murmured the Woodlark despondingly.

"But when that kind chance brings you one comfortable day after another, why should you sadden them all by these fears for by and by?"

"It is a weakness, I believe," responded the Woodlark. "I will see what I can do towards enjoying myself more. You are very wise, little Robin; and it is a wisdom that will keep you happy all the year round."

Here the Woodlark rose into the air, and performed several circling flights, singing vigorously all the time. The old melancholy pervaded the tone, but that might be mere habit. The song was, at any rate, more earnest and strong.

"That is better already," cried the Robin gaily; "and for my part, if I am ever disposed to be dull myself, I shall think of what you told me just now of all the past winters; namely, that little bits of things did always accidentally turn up. What a comforting fact!"

"To think of my ever having been able to comfort anybody!" ejaculated the Woodlark. "I must try to take comfort myself."

"Aye, indeed," cried the Robin earnestly; "it is faithless work to give advice which you will not follow yourself."

So saying, the Robin trilled out a pleasant farewell, and returned to the shrubbery grounds, where, in an ivy-covered wall, he had found for himself a snug little winter's home.

It was during the ensuing week, and while the Robin was in his blithest mood, and singing away undisturbed by megrims of any kind, but rejoicing in the comforts of each day as it came, that the Tortoise once more accosted him.

When Robin first heard his voice he was startled, and feared another scolding, but he was quite mistaken. The old Tortoise was sitting by the side of an opening in the ground, which he had scratched out very cleverly with his claws. It was in a corner among some stones which had lain there for years; and there was one large one in particular overhung the entrance of the hole. The wind had drifted a vast quantity of leaves in that direction, and some of them had been blown into the hole, so that it looked like a warm underground bed.

"Hop down to me, little bird!" was the Tortoise's address, in a quite friendly voice; an order with which the Robin at once complied. "Ah, you need not be afraid," continued he, as the Robin alighted by his side. "I am quite happy now. See what a comfortable place I have made myself here in the earth. There, there, put your head in and peep. Did you ever see anything so snug in your life?"

The Robin peered in with his sharp little eye, and really admired the Tortoise's ingenious labour very much.

"Hop in," cried the Tortoise gaily; "there's room enough and to spare, is there not?"

Robin hopped in, and looked round. He was surprised at the size and convenience of the place, and admitted that a more roomy and comfortable winter's bed could not be wished for.

"Who wouldn't go to sleep?" cried the Tortoise; "what say you, my little friend? But you need not say; I see it in your eye. You are not for sleep yourself. Well, well, we have all our different ways of life, and yours is a pleasant folly, after all, when it doesn't disturb other people. And you won't disturb me any more this year, for I have made my arrangements at last, and shall soon be so sound asleep, that I shall hear no more of your singing for the present. It's a nice bed, isn't it? Not so nice, perhaps, as the warm sands of my native land;

but the ground, even here, is much warmer inside it than people think, who know nothing of it but the cold damp surface. Ah, if it wasn't, how would the snowdrop and crocus live through the winter? Well, I called you here to say good-bye, and show you where I am, and to ask you to remember me in the spring; if—that is, of course,—you survive the terrible weather that is coming. You don't mind my having been somewhat cross the other day, do you? I am apt to get testy now and then, and you disturbed me in my nap, which nobody can bear. But you will forgive and forget, won't you, little bird?"

The kind-hearted Robin protested his affectionate feeling in a thousand pretty ways.

"Then you won't forget me in the Spring," added the Tortoise; "but come here and sit on the laurel bush, and sing me awake. Not till the days are mild, and the plants get juicy, of course, but as soon as you please then. And now, good-bye. There's a strange feeling in the air to-day, and before many hours are over there will be snow and frost. Yours is a pleasant folly. I wish it may not cost you dear. Good-bye."

Hereupon the old Tortoise huddled away into the interior of his hole, where he actually disappeared from sight; and as soon afterwards the drifting leaves completely choked up the entrance of the place, no one could have suspected what was there, but those who knew the secret beforehand.

He had been right in his prognostication of the weather. A thick, gloomy, raw evening was succeeded by a bitterly cold night, and towards the morning the over-weighted clouds began to discharge themselves of some of their snow; and as the day wore on, the flakes got heavier and heavier; and as no sunshine came out to melt them, and a biting frost set in, the country was soon covered with a winding-sheet of white. And now, indeed, began a severe trial of the Robin's patience and hope. It is easy to boast while the sun still shines, if ever so little; but it is not till the storm comes, that the mettle of principle is known.

"There are berries left yet," said he, with cheerful composure, as he went out to seek for food, and found a holly-tree by the little gate of the plantation, red with its beautiful fruit. And, after he had eaten, he poured out a song of joy and thankfulness into the cold wintry sky, and finally retreated under his ivy bush at night, happy and contented as before.

But that terrible storm lasted for weeks without intermission; or, if it did intermit, it was but to a partial thaw, which the night of frost soon bound up again, as firmly, or more firmly, than ever.

Many other birds besides himself came to the holly-tree for berries, and it was wonderful how they disappeared, first from one branch, and then from another: but still the Robin sang on. He poured out his little song of thanks after every meal. That was his rule.

Other birds would jeer at him sometimes, but he could not be much moved by jeers. He had brought his bravery, and his patience, and his hope into the field against whatever troubles might arise, and a few foolish jests would not trouble a spirit so strung up to cheerful endurance.

"I will sing the old Tortoise awake yet," said he, many and many a time, when, after chanting his little thanksgiving in the holly-tree, he would hover about the spot where his friend lay asleep in the ground, and think of the spring that would one day come, bringing its mild days and its juicy plants, and its thousand pleasant delights.

I do not say, but what it was a great trial to our friend, when, after dreaming all these things in his day-dreams, he was roused up at last by feeling himself unusually cold and stiff; and was forced to hurry to his ivy home to recover himself at all.

The alternations, too, of winter, are very trying. The long storm of many weeks ceased at last, and a fortnight of open weather ensued, which, although wet and cold, gave much more liberty to the birds, and allowed of greater plenty of food. The Robin could now hop once more on the grass round the fountain, and get at a few worms, and pick up a few seeds. And he was so delighted with the change, that he half hoped the winter was over; and he sat in the laurel tree by the Tortoise's cave, and poured out long ditties of anticipative delight. But the bitterest storm of all was yet in store,—the storm of disappointed hope.

Oh, heavy clouds, why did you hang so darkly over the earth just before the Christmas season? Oh, why did the fields become so white again, and the trees so laden with snow wreaths, and the waters so frozen and immovable, just when all human beings wanted to rejoice and be glad?

Did you come—perhaps you did!—to rouse to tender pity and compassionate love, the hearts of all who wished to welcome their Saviour with hosannas of joy? but who cannot forget, if they read the gospel of love, that whosoever does a kindness to one of the least of His disciples, does it unto Him. Surely, thus may the bitter cold, and the trying weather of a biting, snowy Christmas, be read. Surely, it calls aloud to every one, that now is the moment for clothing the naked, for feeding the hungry, and for comforting the afflicted.

Heavily, heavily, heavily, it came down. There were two days in which the Robin never left his ivy-covered hole, but hunger took him at last to the holly-tree by the little gate. Its prickly leaves were loaded with snow, and on one side the stem could not be seen at all.

Was it his fancy, or was the tree really much less than before? He hopped from one white branch to another, and fancied that large pieces were gone. He peered under and over, picked at the leaves, and shook down little morsels of snow; but nowhere, nowhere, nowhere, could a single berry be found!

The Robin flew about in distress, and in so doing caught sight of a heap of holly, laurel, and bay branches that were laid aside together to be carried up to the house to decorate its walls. He picked two or three of the berries from them as they lay there,—ripe, red berries, such as he had gathered but lately from the tree; and then came the gardener by, who carried the whole away. He flew after the man as he walked, and never left him until he disappeared with his load into the house. Its unfriendly doors closed against the little wanderer, and no one within knew of the wistful eyes which had watched the coveted food out of sight.

"I have eaten; let me be thankful," was the Robin's resolute remark, as he flew away from the house and returned to the holly-tree, which had so lately been his storehouse of hope, and from its now stripped and barren branches, poured out, as before, his lay of glad thanksgiving for what he had had.

Not a breath of wind was blowing, not a leaf stirred; not a movement of any kind took place, save when some overloaded branch dropped part of its weight of snow on the ground below; as the sweet carol of the still hungry little bird rose through the air on that dark, still winter's afternoon.

What did it tell of? Oh, surely, that clear bell-like melody, that musical tone, that exquisite harmonious trill, told of something—of something, I mean, besides the tale of a poor little desolate bird, whose food had been snatched away before his eyes, and who might be thought to have eaten his last meal.

Surely, those solitary notes of joy, poured into the midst of a gloom so profound, were as an angel's message, coming with a promise of peace and hope, at a moment when both seemed dead and departed.

Homeward from his day's work of business, there passed by, at that moment, the owner and inhabitant of the little suburban villa. It had been a melancholy day to him, for it was saddened by painful recollections. It was the anniversary of the day on which his wife had been laid in her churchyard grave, and since that event two sons had sailed for the far-off land of promise, which puts a hemisphere between the loved and loving on earth. So that far-distant land held them, whilst one—not so distant, perhaps, but more unattainable for the present—held the other.

No wonder, therefore, that on that owner's face, as he approached his home, there hung a cloud of suffering and care, which not even the thought of the Christmas-day at hand, and the children yet spared to his hearth, could prevent or dispel.

Verily the autumn of man's life comes down upon him as the autumn season descends upon the earth. Clouds and tears mixed with whatever brightness may remain.

All at once, however, the abstracted look of sorrow is startled. What is it that he hears? He is passing outside the little plantation which skirts the grounds. He is close to the little gate near which the holly-tree grows. He pauses,—he stops—he lifts up those troubled eyes. Surely, a wholesome tear is stealing over the cheek. Beautiful, tender, affecting, as the voice of the cuckoo in spring, there swept over the listener's heart, the autumnal song of the Robin.

Sing on, sing on, from the top of your desolate tree, oh, little bird of cheerfulness and hope! Pour out again that heaven-taught music of contentment with the hour that now is. Shalt thou be confident of protection, and man destitute of hope! Shalt thou, in the depth of thy winter's trial, have joy and peace, and man never look beyond the cloud?

Poor little innocent bird, he sang his pretty song to an end, and then he flew away. Quarrel not with him, if in painful recollection of the holly-berries that had been carried into the house, he hovered round its windows and doors, with anxious and curious stealth. Whether across the middle of one window he observed a tempting red cluster hanging down inside, no one can say. But the tantalising pain of such a sight, if he felt it, was soon over, for just then the window was opened, and along its outside ledge something was strewn by a careful hand. The window was closed again immediately, and, whoever it was within, retreated backwards into the room.

From a standard rose-bush, whither he had flown, when the window was opened, our little friend watched the affair.

Presently a fragrant odour seemed to steal towards him,—something unknown yet pleasant, something tempting and very nice. Was there any risk to be feared? All seemed quiet and still. Should he venture? Ah, that odour again! it was irresistible.

In another minute he was on the ledge, and boldly, as if a dozen invitations had bidden him welcome to the feast, he was devouring crumb after crumb of the scattered bread.

A burst of delighted laughter from within broke upon his elysium of joy for a moment, and sent him back with sudden flight to the rose-bush. But no disaster ensued, and he was tempted again and again.

The children within might well laugh at the saucy bird, whom their father had, by his gift of bread-crumbs, tempted to the place. They laughed at the bold hop,—the eager pecking,—the brilliant bead-like eye of their new guest,—and at the bright red of his breast; but it was a laugh that told of nothing but kind delight.

"Little bits of things do accidentally turn up always, indeed!" said the Robin to himself, as he crept into his ivy hole that evening to sleep; and he dreamt half the night of the wonderful place and the princely fare. And next morning, long before anybody was awake and up, he was off to the magical window-ledge again, but neither children nor bread-crumbs were there. (How was he to know about breakfast hours, and the customs of social life?) So it almost seemed to him as if his evening meal had been a dream, too good a thing to be true, or if it had ever been true, too good to return. Yet a sweeter song was never heard on a summer eve, than that with which the Robin greeted that early day, the Christmas morning of the year.

Perched in the laurel bush near the Tortoise's retreat, he told his sleeping friend a long, marvellous tale of his yesterday's adventures, and promised him more news against the time when he should return to wake him up in the spring.

Nor did he promise in vain; for whether the Tortoise would be patient enough to listen or not, there was no doubt the Robin had plenty to tell. He had to tell of the daily meal that was spread for him, by those suddenly raised up friends—that daily meal that had never failed; of the curious tiny house that was erected for him at the end of the ledge, which, carpeted as it was with cotton-wool and hay, formed almost too warm a roosting-place for his hardy little frame.

But even to the Tortoise he could never tell all he had felt during that wonderful winter; for he could never explain to any one the mysterious friendship which grew up between himself and his protectors. He could never describe properly the friendly faces that sat round the breakfast-table on which at last he was allowed to hop about at will.

He told, however, how he used to sing on the rose-tree outside, every morning of every day, to welcome the waking of his friends, and how, in the late afternoons, the father would sometimes open the window, and sit there alone by himself, listening to his song.

"Come, come, my little friend," remarked the Tortoise, when he did awake at last, and had come out of his cavern-bed, and heard the account; "I have been asleep for a long time, and I dare say have been dreaming all manner of fine things myself, if I could but think of them. Now, I suspect you have had a nap, as well. However, I am very glad to see you alive, and not so half-starved looking as I expected. But as to your having sung every day, and had plenty to eat every day, and been so happy all the time,—take my advice, don't try to cram older heads than your own with travellers' tales!"

Daily Bread

"Your heavenly Father knoweth that ye have need of all these things."
—MATTHEW vi. 32.

"I wish your cheerfulness were a little better timed, my friend," remarked a Tortoise, who for many years had inhabited the garden of a suburban villa, to a Robin Redbreast, who was trilling a merry note from a thorn-tree in the shrubbery. "What in the world are you singing about at this time of year, when I, and everybody else of any sense, are trying to go to sleep, and forget ourselves?"

"I beg your pardon, I am sure," replied the Robin; "I did not know it would have disturbed you."

"You must be gifted with very small powers of observation then, my friend," rejoined the Tortoise. "Here have I been grubbing my head under the leaves and sticks half the morning, to make myself a comfortable hole to take a nap in; and always, just as I am dropping off, you set up one of your senseless pipes."

"You are not over-troubled with politeness, good sir, I think," observed the Robin; "to call my performance by such an offensive name, and to find fault with me for want of observation, is the most unreasonable thing in the world. This is the first season I have lived in the garden, and all through the spring and summer you have never objected to my singing at all. How was I to know you would dislike it now?"

"Your own sense might have told you as much, without my giving myself the trouble of explanation," persisted the Tortoise. "Of course, it's natural enough, and not disagreeable, to hear you little birds singing round the place, when there is something to sing about. It rather raises one's spirits than otherwise. For instance, when the weather becomes mild in the early year, and the plants begin to grow and get juicy, and it is about time for me to get up from my winter's sleep, I have no objection to be awakened by your voices. But now, in this miserable season, when the fruits and flowers are gone, and when even the leaves that are left are tough and dry, and there is not a dandelion that I care to eat; and when it gets colder and colder, and damper and damper every day, this affectation of merriment on your part is both ridiculous and hypocritical. It is impossible that you can feel happy yourself, and you have no business to pretend to it."

"But, begging your pardon once more, good sir, I do feel happy, whatever you may think to the contrary," answered the Robin.

"What, do you mean to say that you like cold, and damp, and bare trees, with scarcely a berry upon them?"

"I like warm sunny days the best, perhaps," replied the Robin, "if I am obliged to think about it and make comparisons. But why should I do so? I am quite comfortable as it is. If there is not so much variety of food as there has been, there is, at any rate, enough for every day, and everybody knows that enough is as good as a feast. For my part, I don't see how I can help being contented."

"Contented! what a dull idea, to be just contented! I am contented myself, after a fashion; but you are trying to seem happy, and that is a very different sort of thing."

"Well, but happy; I am happy, too," insisted the Robin.

"That must be then because you know nothing of what is coming," suggested the Tortoise. "As yet, while the open weather lasts, you can pick up your favourite worms, and satisfy your appetite. But, when the ground has become so hard that the worms cannot come through, or your beak get at them, what will you do?"

"Are you sure that will ever happen?" enquired the Robin.

"Oh! certainly, in the course of the winter, at some time or another; and, indeed, it may happen any day now, which makes me anxious to be asleep and out of the way."

"Oh, well, if it happens now, I shall not mind a bit," cried the Robin; "there are plenty of berries left!"

"But supposing it should happen when all the berries are gone?" said the Tortoise, actually teased at not being able to frighten the Robin out of his singing propensities.

"Nay, but if it comes to supposing," exclaimed the Robin, "I shall suppose it won't, and so I shall be happy still."

"But I say it may happen," shouted the Tortoise.

"And I ask will it?" rejoined the Robin, in quite as determined a manner.

"Which you know I cannot answer," retorted the Tortoise again. "Nobody knows exactly either about the weather or the berries beforehand."

"Then let nobody trouble themselves beforehand," persisted the Robin. "If there was anything to be done to prevent or provide, it would be different. But as it is, we have nothing to do but to be happy in the comfort each day brings."

Here the Robin trilled out a few of his favourite notes, but the Tortoise soon interrupted him.

"Allow other people to be happy, then, as well as yourself, and cease squalling out of that tree. I could have forgiven you, had the branches been full of haws; but, as they are all withered or eaten, you have no particular excuse for singing in that particular bush, rather than elsewhere, so let me request you at once to go."

"Of course I will do so," answered the Robin, politely. "It is the same thing to me exactly, so I wish you a good morning, and, if you desire it, a refreshing sleep."

So saying, the Robin flew from the thorn-tree to another part of the grounds, where he could amuse himself without interruption; and the Tortoise began to hustle under the leaves and rubbish again, with a view to taking his nap.

But, by-and-by, as the morning wore away, the frosty feeling and autumnal mists cleared off; and when the sun came out, which it did for three or four hours in the early afternoon, the day became really fine.

The old Tortoise did not fail to discover the fact; and not having yet scratched himself a hole completely to his mind, he came out of the shrubbery and took a turn in the sunshine.

"This is quite a surprise, indeed," said he to himself. "It is very pleasant, but I am afraid it will not last. The more's the pity; but, however, I shall not go to bed just yet."

With these words, he waddled slowly along to the kitchen garden, where he was in the habit of occasionally basking under the brick wall; and now, tilting himself up sideways against it, he passed an hour, much to his satisfaction, in exposing his horny coat to the rays of the sun; a feat which he never dared to perform during the heats of summer.

Meanwhile, the poor little Robin continued his songs in a retired corner of the grounds, where no one objected to his cheerful notes. A tiny grove it was, with a grassy circle in the middle of it, where a pretty fountain played night and day.

During the pauses of his music, and especially after the sun came out, he wondered much to himself about all the strange uncomfortable things the Tortoise had said. Oh, to think of his having wanted to go to sleep and be out of the way; and now here was the sunshine making all the grove as warm as spring itself. If he had not been afraid the Tortoise might consider him intrusive, he would have gone back and told him how warm and pleasant it was, but absolutely he durst not.

Still, he could not, on reflection, shut his eyes to the fact, that there were no other songsters in the grove just now beside himself, and he wondered what was the reason. Time was, when the nightingale was to be heard every night in this very spot; but, now he came to think of it, that beautiful pipe of his had ceased for months, and where the bird himself was, nobody seemed to know.

The Robin became thoughtful, and perhaps a little uneasy.

There was the Blackbird, too;—what was he about that he also was silent? Was it possible that all the world was really as the Tortoise said, thinking it wise to go to sleep and be out of the way?

The Robin got almost alarmed. So much so, that he flew about, until he met with a Blackbird, whom he might question on the subject, and of him he made the enquiry, why he had left off singing?

The Blackbird glanced at him with astonishment.

"Who does sing in the dismal autumn and winter?" said he. "Really, I know of scarcely any who are bold and thoughtless enough to do so except yourself. The Larks may, to be sure, but they lead such strange lives in the sky, or in seclusion, that they are no rule for any one else. Your own persevering chirruping is (in my humble judgment) so out of character with a season, in which every wise creature must be apprehensive for the future, that I can only excuse it on the ground of an ignorance and levity, which you have had no opportunity of correcting."

"It would be kinder to attribute it to a cheerful contentment with whatever comes to pass," cried the Robin, ruffling his feathers as he spoke. "I rejoice in each day's blessing as it comes, and never wish for more than does come. You, who are wishing the present to be better than it is, and fearing that the future may be worse, are meanwhile losing all enjoyment of the hour that now is. You think this wise. To me it seems as foolish as it is ungrateful!"

With these words the Robin flew away as fast as he could, for, to say the truth, he felt conscious of having been a little impertinent in his last remark. He was rather a young bird to be setting other people right; but a Robin is always a bold fellow, and has moreover rather a hot temper of his own, though he is a kind creature at the bottom. He had been insulted, too, there was no doubt; but when people feel themselves in the right, what need is there of ruffling feathers and being saucy?

And the Robin did honestly feel himself in the right; but, oh! how hard it is to resist the influence of evil suggestions, even when one knows them to be such, and turns aside from them. They are so apt to steal back into the heart unawares, and undermine the principle that seemed so steady before.

To a certain extent, this was the case with our poor little friend; and those who are disposed to judge harshly of his weakness, must remember that he was very young and could not be expected to go on right always without a mistake.

Certain it is, that he drooped awhile in spirits, as the winter advanced. He sang every day, it is true, and would still have maintained his own opinions against any one who should have opposed them; but he was decidedly disturbed in mind, and thought sadly too much, for his own peace and comfort, of what both the Tortoise and Blackbird had said.

The colder the days became, the more he became depressed; not that there was any cold then that he really cared about, but he was fidgeting about the much greater cold which he had been told was coming; and, as he hopped about on the grass round the fountain, picking up worms and food, he was ready to drop a tear out of his bright black eye at the thought of the days when the ground was to be so hard that the worms could not come out, or his beak reach them.

Had this state of things gone on long, the Robin would have begun to wish to go to sleep, like the Tortoise; and no more singing would have been heard in the plantation of the suburban villa that year.

But Robins are brave-hearted little fellows, as well as bold and saucy; and one bright day our friend bethought himself that he would go and talk the matter over with an old Woodlark, whom he had heard frequented a thicket at a considerable distance off.

On his way thither, he heard several larks singing high up in the sky over the fields; and by the time he reached the thicket he was in excellent spirits himself, and seemed to have left all his megrims behind.

It was fortunate such was the case, for when, as he approached the thicket, he heard the Woodlark's note, it was so plaintive and low, that it would have made anybody cry to listen to it. And when the Robin congratulated him on his singing, the Woodlark did not seem to care much for the compliment, but confided to his new acquaintance, that although he thought it right to sing and be thankful, as long as there was a bit of comfort left, he was not so happy as he seemed to be, since in reality he was always expecting to die some day of having nothing at all to eat.

"For," said he, "when the snow is on the ground, it is a perfect chance if one finds a morsel of food all day long."

"But I thought you had lived here several seasons," suggested the Robin, who in his braced condition of mind was getting quite reasonable again.

"So I have," murmured the Woodlark, heaving his breast with a touching sigh.

"Yet you did not die of having nothing to eat, last winter?" observed the Robin.

"It appears not," ejaculated the Woodlark, as gravely as possible, and with another sigh; whereat the Robin's eye actually twinkled with mirth, for he had a good deal of fun in his composition, and could not but smile to himself at the Woodlark's solemn way of admitting that he was alive.

"Nor the winter before?" asked he.

"No," murmured the Woodlark again.

"Nor the winter before that?" persisted the saucy Robin.

"Well, no; of course not," answered the Woodlark, somewhat impatiently, "because I am here, as you see."

"Then how did you manage when the snow came, and there was no food?" enquired the Robin.

"I never told you there was actually no food in those other winters," answered the Woodlark somewhat peevishly, for he did not want to be disturbed in his views. "Little bits of things did accidentally turn up always. But there is no proof that it will ever happen again. It was merely chance!"

"Ah, my venerable friend," cried the Robin; "have you no confidence in the kind chance that has befriended you so often before?"

"I can never be sure it will do so again," murmured the Woodlark despondingly.

"But when that kind chance brings you one comfortable day after another, why should you sadden them all by these fears for by and by?"

"It is a weakness, I believe," responded the Woodlark. "I will see what I can do towards enjoying myself more. You are very wise, little Robin; and it is a wisdom that will keep you happy all the year round."

Here the Woodlark rose into the air, and performed several circling flights, singing vigorously all the time. The old melancholy pervaded the tone, but that might be mere habit. The song was, at any rate, more earnest and strong.

"That is better already," cried the Robin gaily; "and for my part, if I am ever disposed to be dull myself, I shall think of what you told me just now of all the past winters; namely, that little bits of things did always accidentally turn up. What a comforting fact!"

"To think of my ever having been able to comfort anybody!" ejaculated the Woodlark. "I must try to take comfort myself."

"Aye, indeed," cried the Robin earnestly; "it is faithless work to give advice which you will not follow yourself."

So saying, the Robin trilled out a pleasant farewell, and returned to the shrubbery grounds, where, in an ivy-covered wall, he had found for himself a snug little winter's home.

It was during the ensuing week, and while the Robin was in his blithest mood, and singing away undisturbed by megrims of any kind, but rejoicing in the comforts of each day as it came, that the Tortoise once more accosted him.

When Robin first heard his voice he was startled, and feared another scolding, but he was quite mistaken. The old Tortoise was sitting by the side of an opening in the ground, which he had scratched out very cleverly with his claws. It was in a corner among some stones which had lain there for years; and there was one large one in particular overhung the entrance of the hole. The wind had drifted a vast quantity of leaves in that direction, and some of them had been blown into the hole, so that it looked like a warm underground bed.

"Hop down to me, little bird!" was the Tortoise's address, in a quite friendly voice; an order with which the Robin at once complied. "Ah, you need not be afraid," continued he, as the Robin alighted by his side. "I am quite happy now. See what a comfortable place I have made myself here in the earth. There, there, put your head in and peep. Did you ever see anything so snug in your life?"

The Robin peered in with his sharp little eye, and really admired the Tortoise's ingenious labour very much.

"Hop in," cried the Tortoise gaily; "there's room enough and to spare, is there not?"

Robin hopped in, and looked round. He was surprised at the size and convenience of the place, and admitted that a more roomy and comfortable winter's bed could not be wished for.

"Who wouldn't go to sleep?" cried the Tortoise; "what say you, my little friend? But you need not say; I see it in your eye. You are not for sleep yourself. Well, well, we have all our different ways of life, and yours is a pleasant folly, after all, when it doesn't disturb other people. And you won't disturb me any more this year, for I have made my arrangements at last, and shall soon be so sound asleep, that I shall hear no more of your singing for the present. It's a nice bed, isn't it? Not so nice, perhaps, as the warm sands of my native land;

but the ground, even here, is much warmer inside it than people think, who know nothing of it but the cold damp surface. Ah, if it wasn't, how would the snowdrop and crocus live through the winter? Well, I called you here to say good-bye, and show you where I am, and to ask you to remember me in the spring; if—that is, of course,—you survive the terrible weather that is coming. You don't mind my having been somewhat cross the other day, do you? I am apt to get testy now and then, and you disturbed me in my nap, which nobody can bear. But you will forgive and forget, won't you, little bird?"

The kind-hearted Robin protested his affectionate feeling in a thousand pretty ways.

"Then you won't forget me in the Spring," added the Tortoise; "but come here and sit on the laurel bush, and sing me awake. Not till the days are mild, and the plants get juicy, of course, but as soon as you please then. And now, good-bye. There's a strange feeling in the air to-day, and before many hours are over there will be snow and frost. Yours is a pleasant folly. I wish it may not cost you dear. Good-bye."

Hereupon the old Tortoise huddled away into the interior of his hole, where he actually disappeared from sight; and as soon afterwards the drifting leaves completely choked up the entrance of the place, no one could have suspected what was there, but those who knew the secret beforehand.

He had been right in his prognostication of the weather. A thick, gloomy, raw evening was succeeded by a bitterly cold night, and towards the morning the over-weighted clouds began to discharge themselves of some of their snow; and as the day wore on, the flakes got heavier and heavier; and as no sunshine came out to melt them, and a biting frost set in, the country was soon covered with a winding-sheet of white. And now, indeed, began a severe trial of the Robin's patience and hope. It is easy to boast while the sun still shines, if ever so little; but it is not till the storm comes, that the mettle of principle is known.

"There are berries left yet," said he, with cheerful composure, as he went out to seek for food, and found a holly-tree by the little gate of the plantation, red with its beautiful fruit. And, after he had eaten, he poured out a song of joy and thankfulness into the cold wintry sky, and finally retreated under his ivy bush at night, happy and contented as before.

But that terrible storm lasted for weeks without intermission; or, if it did intermit, it was but to a partial thaw, which the night of frost soon bound up again, as firmly, or more firmly, than ever.

Many other birds besides himself came to the holly-tree for berries, and it was wonderful how they disappeared, first from one branch, and then from another: but still the Robin sang on. He poured out his little song of thanks after every meal. That was his rule.

Other birds would jeer at him sometimes, but he could not be much moved by jeers. He had brought his bravery, and his patience, and his hope into the field against whatever troubles might arise, and a few foolish jests would not trouble a spirit so strung up to cheerful endurance.

"I will sing the old Tortoise awake yet," said he, many and many a time, when, after chanting his little thanksgiving in the holly-tree, he would hover about the spot where his friend lay asleep in the ground, and think of the spring that would one day come, bringing its mild days and its juicy plants, and its thousand pleasant delights.

I do not say, but what it was a great trial to our friend, when, after dreaming all these things in his day-dreams, he was roused up at last by feeling himself unusually cold and stiff; and was forced to hurry to his ivy home to recover himself at all.

The alternations, too, of winter, are very trying. The long storm of many weeks ceased at last, and a fortnight of open weather ensued, which, although wet and cold, gave much more liberty to the birds, and allowed of greater plenty of food. The Robin could now hop once more on the grass round the fountain, and get at a few worms, and pick up a few seeds. And he was so delighted with the change, that he half hoped the winter was over; and he sat in the laurel tree by the Tortoise's cave, and poured out long ditties of anticipative delight. But the bitterest storm of all was yet in store,—the storm of disappointed hope.

Oh, heavy clouds, why did you hang so darkly over the earth just before the Christmas season? Oh, why did the fields become so white again, and the trees so laden with snow wreaths, and the waters so frozen and immovable, just when all human beings wanted to rejoice and be glad?

Did you come—perhaps you did!—to rouse to tender pity and compassionate love, the hearts of all who wished to welcome their Saviour with hosannas of joy? but who cannot forget, if they read the gospel of love, that whosoever does a kindness to one of the least of His disciples, does it unto Him. Surely, thus may the bitter cold, and the trying weather of a biting, snowy Christmas, be read. Surely, it calls aloud to every one, that now is the moment for clothing the naked, for feeding the hungry, and for comforting the afflicted.

Heavily, heavily, heavily, it came down. There were two days in which the Robin never left his ivy-covered hole, but hunger took him at last to the holly-tree by the little gate. Its prickly leaves were loaded with snow, and on one side the stem could not be seen at all.

Was it his fancy, or was the tree really much less than before? He hopped from one white branch to another, and fancied that large pieces were gone. He peered under and over, picked at the leaves, and shook down little morsels of snow; but nowhere, nowhere, nowhere, could a single berry be found!

The Robin flew about in distress, and in so doing caught sight of a heap of holly, laurel, and bay branches that were laid aside together to be carried up to the house to decorate its walls. He picked two or three of the berries from them as they lay there,—ripe, red berries, such as he had gathered but lately from the tree; and then came the gardener by, who carried the whole away. He flew after the man as he walked, and never left him until he disappeared with his load into the house. Its unfriendly doors closed against the little wanderer, and no one within knew of the wistful eyes which had watched the coveted food out of sight.

"I have eaten; let me be thankful," was the Robin's resolute remark, as he flew away from the house and returned to the holly-tree, which had so lately been his storehouse of hope, and from its now stripped and barren branches, poured out, as before, his lay of glad thanksgiving for what he had had.

Not a breath of wind was blowing, not a leaf stirred; not a movement of any kind took place, save when some overloaded branch dropped part of its weight of snow on the ground below; as the sweet carol of the still hungry little bird rose through the air on that dark, still winter's afternoon.

What did it tell of? Oh, surely, that clear bell-like melody, that musical tone, that exquisite harmonious trill, told of something—of something, I mean, besides the tale of a poor little desolate bird, whose food had been snatched away before his eyes, and who might be thought to have eaten his last meal.

Surely, those solitary notes of joy, poured into the midst of a gloom so profound, were as an angel's message, coming with a promise of peace and hope, at a moment when both seemed dead and departed.

Homeward from his day's work of business, there passed by, at that moment, the owner and inhabitant of the little suburban villa. It had been a melancholy day to him, for it was saddened by painful recollections. It was the anniversary of the day on which his wife had been laid in her churchyard grave, and since that event two sons had sailed for the far-off land of promise, which puts a hemisphere between the loved and loving on earth. So that far-distant land held them, whilst one—not so distant, perhaps, but more unattainable for the present—held the other.

No wonder, therefore, that on that owner's face, as he approached his home, there hung a cloud of suffering and care, which not even the thought of the Christmas-day at hand, and the children yet spared to his hearth, could prevent or dispel.

Verily the autumn of man's life comes down upon him as the autumn season descends upon the earth. Clouds and tears mixed with whatever brightness may remain.

All at once, however, the abstracted look of sorrow is startled. What is it that he hears? He is passing outside the little plantation which skirts the grounds. He is close to the little gate near which the holly-tree grows. He pauses,—he stops—he lifts up those troubled eyes. Surely, a wholesome tear is stealing over the cheek. Beautiful, tender, affecting, as the voice of the cuckoo in spring, there swept over the listener's heart, the autumnal song of the Robin.

Sing on, sing on, from the top of your desolate tree, oh, little bird of cheerfulness and hope! Pour out again that heaven-taught music of contentment with the hour that now is. Shalt thou be confident of protection, and man destitute of hope! Shalt thou, in the depth of thy winter's trial, have joy and peace, and man never look beyond the cloud?

Poor little innocent bird, he sang his pretty song to an end, and then he flew away. Quarrel not with him, if in painful recollection of the holly-berries that had been carried into the house, he hovered round its windows and doors, with anxious and curious stealth. Whether across the middle of one window he observed a tempting red cluster hanging down inside, no one can say. But the tantalising pain of such a sight, if he felt it, was soon over, for just then the window was opened, and along its outside ledge something was strewn by a careful hand. The window was closed again immediately, and, whoever it was within, retreated backwards into the room.

From a standard rose-bush, whither he had flown, when the window was opened, our little friend watched the affair.

Presently a fragrant odour seemed to steal towards him,—something unknown yet pleasant, something tempting and very nice. Was there any risk to be feared? All seemed quiet and still. Should he venture? Ah, that odour again! it was irresistible.

In another minute he was on the ledge, and boldly, as if a dozen invitations had bidden him welcome to the feast, he was devouring crumb after crumb of the scattered bread.

A burst of delighted laughter from within broke upon his elysium of joy for a moment, and sent him back with sudden flight to the rose-bush. But no disaster ensued, and he was tempted again and again.

The children within might well laugh at the saucy bird, whom their father had, by his gift of bread-crumbs, tempted to the place. They laughed at the bold hop,—the eager pecking,—the brilliant bead-like eye of their new guest,—and at the bright red of his breast; but it was a laugh that told of nothing but kind delight.

"Little bits of things do accidentally turn up always, indeed!" said the Robin to himself, as he crept into his ivy hole that evening to sleep; and he dreamt half the night of the wonderful place and the princely fare. And next morning, long before anybody was awake and up, he was off to the magical window-ledge again, but neither children nor bread-crumbs were there. (How was he to know about breakfast hours, and the customs of social life?) So it almost seemed to him as if his evening meal had been a dream, too good a thing to be true, or if it had ever been true, too good to return. Yet a sweeter song was never heard on a summer eve, than that with which the Robin greeted that early day, the Christmas morning of the year.

Perched in the laurel bush near the Tortoise's retreat, he told his sleeping friend a long, marvellous tale of his yesterday's adventures, and promised him more news against the time when he should return to wake him up in the spring.

Nor did he promise in vain; for whether the Tortoise would be patient enough to listen or not, there was no doubt the Robin had plenty to tell. He had to tell of the daily meal that was spread for him, by those suddenly raised up friends—that daily meal that had never failed; of the curious tiny house that was erected for him at the end of the ledge, which, carpeted as it was with cotton-wool and hay, formed almost too warm a roosting-place for his hardy little frame.

But even to the Tortoise he could never tell all he had felt during that wonderful winter; for he could never explain to any one the mysterious friendship which grew up between himself and his protectors. He could never describe properly the friendly faces that sat round the breakfast-table on which at last he was allowed to hop about at will.

He told, however, how he used to sing on the rose-tree outside, every morning of every day, to welcome the waking of his friends, and how, in the late afternoons, the father would sometimes open the window, and sit there alone by himself, listening to his song.

"Come, come, my little friend," remarked the Tortoise, when he did awake at last, and had come out of his cavern-bed, and heard the account; "I have been asleep for a long time, and I dare say have been dreaming all manner of fine things myself, if I could but think of them. Now, I suspect you have had a nap, as well. However, I am very glad to see you alive, and not so half-starved looking as I expected. But as to your having sung every day, and had plenty to eat every day, and been so happy all the time,—take my advice, don't try to cram older heads than your own with travellers' tales!"

Motes in the Sunbeam

It was a bright, sunshiny day at Christmas-tide, when, once upon a time, two little girls were sitting on their mamma's sick-bed. One was a very little thing, who could only just talk, and she was leaning her curly head against the bed-post. The other, some two or three years older, was sitting on a pillow near her mother.

The children were not talking much, for there was a new baby in the house, and everybody was very quiet, though very happy; and these two little sisters of the new-comer had only been admitted to see poor mamma, on condition that they would be very good and make no noise.

But the active spirits of young animals cannot be long kept under; and so it happened that a strong gleam of winter sunshine, entering into the room through a half-opened shutter, shot right across the middle of the bed, and attracted the eyes and attention of both the children; for up and down in this narrow strip of light danced innumerable sparkling motes.

The elder child, the Kate of our story, had a little open box in her hand, and she stretched it out, up and down, into the beam, and whispered in a half-giggle of delight, "I'll catch the stars." Her mamma looked on and smiled, for the merry Kate made the play very amusing to herself. She pretended to catch the shining motes in the empty box; and then put on a face of mock surprise and disappointment at finding nothing inside when she peeped to see. Moreover, she kept up a little talk all the time: "There's one:—oh, he's such a beauty!—I must have him!" and then she dashed the box once more into the streak of light.

But this sport and the smiles on mamma's face soon became irresistible to the little Undine child by the bed-post, and she said, very gently, "Give me some, too."

"Some 'what?', my little Undine?" asked mamma: "what are they?"

Undine glanced at her mother, and then at the motes, and then she said, "Stars;"—but there was a misgiving look on her face as she spoke.

"No, they're not stars,—are they, Mamma?" observed the wiser Kate: "they're nothing but dust;"—and the box danced about quicker than ever.

"They're not dust," pouted the offended little one: "they're stars!"

"Well then, here, you shall have a boxful," cried Kate, thrusting the box on to Undine's lap, and covering it over with her pinafore: "Take care of them—take care of them—or they'll all go out."

Very carefully and slowly did Undine uncover the box, and with a very grave and enquiring face did she examine it both inside and out, in search of the stars; and then, in one of those freaks of change so common to children, she burst into a gay laugh, tossed the box up like a ball, and cried out, "They're nothing but dust—nothing but nasty, dirty dust! There they go!"

And, "There they go!" echoed Kate; and forthwith the children commenced a jumping and noise, which quickly brought the nurse to the room, and an order for the removal of the riotous little damsels.

"But, Mamma," enquired Kate, in a grave whisper, before she went away, "why does the dust look so like stars?"

"Because the sun sent his light upon it," answered mamma. "Sunshine is like love, Kate,—it makes everything shine with its own beauty. You and Undine," added she, kissing her little girl's fat cheek, "are stars in my eyes, because I see you in the sunshine of love."

"But we're not 'nothing but nasty, dirty dust,' in reality," observed Kate, shaking her head very knowingly, as she led her little sister from the room.

Those of my young readers who have lived in the North of England, will remember the fine old Christmas hymn that is sung in that part of the country. They will remember the many happy snowy Christmas-eves on which they went to bed, delighted at the thought of hearing it in the night; and how a curious thrill of pleasure came over them when they really were roused from sleep by the solemn and beautiful sounds of—

"Christians awake! salute the happy morn
Whereon the Saviour of mankind was born;"

—sung by the village waits, usually the church singers of the place. As I think of these things myself, I almost hear the grand old melody; and can just fancy some little urchin, more hardy than the rest of his companions, creeping out of his snug bed to peep behind the blind at the well-known old men and girls, all wrapped up in great coats and cloaks, to protect them from the stormy December night.

I can fancy, too, how, after feeling very chilly as he stood at the window, he would go back to the warm bed, and say how cold the poor waits must be! and how, between whispering about the waits and listening to the music, those children would while away one of the happiest hours of merry Christmas; and then, after hearing the sounds revive and die away in other more distant parts of the village, would drop asleep as easily as tired labourers at night.

Well! you wonder what this Christmas hymn has to do with my story of Kate and Undine? Merely this,—that one of the verses begins thus:—

"Oh may we keep and ponder in our mind,
God's wondrous love in saving lost mankind."

And this is taken from a passage in Scripture, to which I want to call your attention—namely, that wherein it is said of the Virgin Mary, that she "kept and pondered in her heart" the wonderful things the shepherds had told her of our Saviour.

Other people talked about them, and made a fuss about them, and then very likely forgot them; but Mary "pondered them in her heart;" a practice which has, alas! gone sadly too much out of fashion; for everybody nowadays is so busy either learning or talking, that for "pondering things in the heart" there seems to be neither time nor inclination.

Nevertheless, mothers are still more apt to do it than anybody else. Indeed, they are constantly pondering in their minds the things that their children say, or the things that people say of them. Sometimes they may ponder foolishly, but I hope not often, especially if they ponder in their hearts, and not in their heads only.

Now the mother of Kate and Undine was a great ponderer; and as she had, especially just then, nothing else to do, you may be sure how she pondered over the pretty scene of her two little ones and the motes in the sunbeam. And the dust did look very like stars, she confessed to herself, as she lay looking up at the light.

"But how wise," thought she, "the sober Kate felt at her own superior knowledge! how proud to recognise dust for dust, even under its most sunny aspect! And yet how often, before life is ended, may she not make Undine's mistake herself, and take even dust for stars, merely because the sun shines upon it!"

And here the poor mamma uttered a short prayer that she might be enabled to instil good principles into her children's minds, that so Kate, and Undine too, might know dust for dust whenever they saw it, let the outward world shine upon it never so brightly.

And then she looked up at the sunbeam, as it streamed across her sick-bed, till she thought it was like so many things, she felt her head becoming quite confused.

It was like love, as she had said—yes; but it was like cheerfulness—like good-temper—like the Gospel charity: for do not the commonest things of life, and the dullest duties of life, shine, star-like, under their rays? Yes; but it was most of all like "the peace of God, which passeth all understanding;" for that lightens up the dark career of earthly existence, and leads the soul upward along the bright path of its rays, till it reaches the everlasting home of light itself.

"Ay, ay," thought the mother, as she looked once more: "Motes in the sunbeam as we are—miserable dust and ashes in ourselves—the light streams down upon us and transfigures us: we follow the light upwards, and become the children of light ourselves."

Her head had indeed become confused amidst similes, and fancies, and half-waking dreams; but before she could think the matter over, clearly and distinctly, she had fallen fast asleep.

Red Snow

"Or tu chi se', che vuoi sedere a scranna,
Per giudicar da lungi mille miglia
Con la veduta corta d'una spanna?"
    DANTE.

"And who art thou, that on the stool wouldst sit
To judge at distance of a thousand miles,
With the short-sighted vision of a span?"
    CARY'S Translation.

    Little Siegfried, the widow's son, climbed day by day up the hill which overlooked his mother's cottage, and rambled about on the top, running after birds and insects, and gathering the beautiful wild-flowers that grow on the Swiss Alps.
    There the dark blue gentians and the Alpine rose, as it is called, and campanulas and salvias, are almost as common as the cowslips and daisies of English fields, and, from the brightness of their colours, make the hillsides look like gardens, instead of uncultivated ground.
    Little Siegfried's father had been killed in battle, some months before his child's birth, and so, when he came into the world, he was cradled in tears instead of smiles; and what wonder if he grew up less thoughtless and gay than other boys of his age?
    It was his mother who had first shown Siegfried where to climb the hill, and where to find the finest flowers; and had made him look at the hills still higher than their own, by which their valley was enclosed, and had pointed out to him Mont Blanc in the distance, looming like a shadowy giant in the sky.
    For thus and thus had her husband shown her all these things, during the few happy months of their marriage, before he was called away to the wars; and on the same heights where the child now roamed after flowers, his parents had sat together among them, in quiet summer evenings, sometimes talking, sometimes reading, always praising God for the happiness He was permitting them to enjoy.
    But having thus led her child to the spot so fondly endeared to herself, and bidden him rejoice in the sights and scenes of Nature, and told him of the

protecting God of goodness who ruled over all, the widowed mother went back alone to her cottage, to weep out in secret her re-awakened grief.

Siegfried, meanwhile, amused himself on the flowery heights, his new playground; and after he had gathered for his mother the nosegay she had asked him to bring, he lay down on the soft turf, and looked round at the hills, and up to the snowy sides of the huge Mont Blanc, (of which he could see so much more here than down in the valley below,) till it took possession of his fancy as something wonderful and grand; something far beyond the flowers, bright and lovely as they were.

And ever afterwards, day by day, when he had had enough of chasing and rambling, he used to lie down in the same place, and look at the hills in the same way, that he might feel again what he had felt at first.

Yet he found no sameness in the sight. The clouds that sometimes lifted themselves up from, and at other times came down over, the mountain, were never quite alike. The shadows that flitted across it varied from day to day in their shape and size and course; and the sunshine that broke over it was of many different tints, and lit it up in a thousand different ways. At one time it was wrapt in a silvery haze; at another the air became so clear, that the child could see the glittering of the snow atoms, as they seemed to dance in and out, like the stars in the sky.

So Siegfried never wearied of watching the huge mountain, but got to love it more and more, with a love mixed with respectful awe, and a feeling as if it had some sort of life and consciousness.

At last, one day, when his mother was putting his little basket in his hand, that he might go on the hill as usual to play, he asked her if he might go to the top of Mont Blanc instead, and if she would show him the way.

It was no wonder that the good widow smiled, as she told him that neither he nor she were able to climb up such a terrible mountain. But she did smile; and although she noticed how the little face flushed over as she spoke, she thought, naturally enough, that this was because of his disappointment. So, kissing him lovingly, she said:

"You must be a great strong man, Siegfried, before you can scramble up the heights of Mont Blanc: and even for great strong men the way is very dangerous. And even if you were there, you would find nothing but cold and snow and misery; neither life nor flowers; our own hills are as pleasant again."

So Siegfried went away with his basket; but instead of running about and picking flowers, he threw himself at once upon the ground, and looked at the mountain, and cried, for he felt very sorry at what his mother had said.

Presently, however, he wiped his eyes, and looked again; then sprang up and stared before him as if surprised.

All the distance was bathed in bright sunshine, and the air was more transparent than usual, and, lo! a round rosy-coloured patch was visible on the far-off snows. He had never seen it before. What could it be? He thought he knew; and running hastily down to the cottage, threw open the door, and shouted in delight, "Mother! there is a rose on Mont Blanc!"

Siegfried's mother did not laugh now, for she saw the child was excited; and she was grieved for him. Ah! he had only half the love that should have been his; she must console him as best she could; he was not like other boys, she knew—and thinking this, she took him on her knee, and tried to explain to him that it must be only some accidental light from the sky that caused the rosy patch, for that no vegetation of any kind grew on the sides of the snowy mountain; there could be no roses there; and she knew that it often looked pink in the evening sun—only now it was not evening.

Siegfried was silent for a few seconds, and hung down his head; but presently he murmured out, "Why?"

"Ah, Siegfried!" cried his mother, "is it not enough that God chooses it to be so? It is He who sends the everlasting snows there, and the flowery herbage here."

"I am very sorry for the mountain," persisted little Siegfried, sadly; so sadly that his mother grieved for the fanciful child, and asked should she go up with him again to the hill, and see the rosy patch on the snow herself? On which the smiles came back to Siegfried's face, and they went away together very happily, and with the basket as usual; for, said the mother, "You came back empty-handed to-day, Siegfried, and brought me no flowers."

But, by the time they reached the spot, heavy mists had come down over the landscape, and neither Mont Blanc nor its rosy patch could be seen. Even Siegfried laughed at the journey they had had for nothing, and, after filling his basket, was contented to return home; but in doing so, he began to talk again.

"If we had fewer flowers, Mother, we should be quite as happy, and then the great mountain could have some too. I wish God would make things equal."

"Hush, little Siegfried, hush!" cried his mother, in a half whisper; "God has a right to do what He pleases, and we must not dispute about it, nor wish it otherwise. He chooses that there shall be desolate places as well as pretty ones in the world; outcast ends of the earth, as it were, which nobody seems to care for, as well as happy valleys. I am afraid it is the same with human beings—men and women, I mean—which is much worse. I am afraid there are many outcast,

God-deserted men, as well as desolate mountains. But you are too young to understand such things."

The mother sighed as she spoke. Verily, she did not understand such things herself.

And so they walked on a few steps farther, and then the boy began again,—

"At any rate, the top of the mountain is nearer Heaven than our hill, Mother. It goes right into the blue."

"No, no," cried the widow, passionately; "it only looks to be so. It is no nearer the real Heaven than we are. If it were, oh! would I not have gone there long ago, at the risk of life itself!"

The child looked very surprised at his mother; for she spoke in tones very unusual to her; and seeing how sad her face, he wondered to himself if she, also, were fretting that Mont Blanc was so miserable and forlorn.

And, snatching the nosegay from the basket, he flung the flowers as far into the air as he could, exclaiming, "There! I wish you had wings, and would fly away to the mountain, and make it look beautiful, too!"

Nothing more was spoken between them, but after little Siegfried had said his evening prayers, and gone to bed, and while the mother was sitting alone in the chamber below, she heard a sound of crying; and, going upstairs, found the boy in tears, the only account he could give of which was, that he could not help thinking about the poor outcast, God-deserted mountain.

Now, she had not called the mountain God-deserted. That was his own disturbed idea; a confusion he had got into from what his mother had said. But how hard this was to explain! How painful to touch the chords of a subject which jarred so cruelly against the natural hopes and faith of a gentle heart!

How difficult also for one who had known the stern realities of sorrow, to "feel along" the more delicate "line" of an infant's dreamy griefs!

He was soothed by degrees, however, and after she left him, her thoughts soon wandered away from what she felt to be his fanciful troubles about the desolate mountain, to her own struggles with her desolate heart.

The next day was Sunday, and Siegfried was able to walk to the somewhat distant church, and even to repeat a few of the prayers, and listen, now and then, to bits of the sermon, when his mother thought there was something he could understand, and drew his attention to it.

But on this particular day there was no need for her to call his attention to the preacher; nay, had she been able, she would have been very glad to have prevented his hearing him at all. But how could he help hearing, when the pastor, addressing his flock, asked if there was a single one, young or old, among them, who had not gazed hundreds and hundreds of times at the giant mountain of their land—the snow-covered, inaccessible heights of Mont Blanc?

Siegfried and his mother looked at each other, and his heart leapt within him, to think that now, at last, he should hear something about his mysterious friend; and, clasping his mother's hand tightly in his own, he listened for every word.

But alas! for what he heard. The pastor, after describing the mountain in all the magnificence of its size and form, painted it as being, nevertheless, the region of hopeless desolation; the abode of everlasting lifelessness and despair. Cold, hard, insensible, what could rouse it from its death-like torpor? The life-giving sun shone upon it from day to day, from age to age; but no influence from its rays ever penetrated that frozen bosom. The dews fell upon it, the storms burst over it, equally in vain. Unmoved, it lifted up its gloomy crest to Heaven, as if defying its very Maker to touch the stony depths and bid the waters flow, or warm and soften them into life and gladness!

Siegfried was already in tears, but what followed was still worse, for the pastor now called upon his congregation to consider whether there was not something in the moral world of which the insensible mountain was but the too faithful type? And then he answered himself. Yes!—the hardened human heart, the wicked natural heart, the Pharaoh-heart of the multitude, on which the sunshine of Divine Grace and the storms of Divine wrath were equally poured out in vain.

Yet, that "offences must needs come," he was well aware; that such God-deserted beings as he had spoken of, must come up and be cut down, he knew: "vessels of wrath appointed to destruction." But, oh! might none of the congregation now before him be of the number of those lost ones! Might all there present take warning henceforth, as they turned their eyes to the stiff-necked hill of their native country, and flee from the wrath of the Lamb!

Siegfried's sobs had by this time become so uncontrollable, that the neighbours were disturbed; and the widow thought the best thing she could do, was to rise up and leave the church with her child.

There was no use arguing with him; he was both too young and too much distressed; added to which, his mother was scarcely less pained by the stern words than he was.

She, too, could have wept to think of "vessels of wrath appointed to destruction," and longed to hope against hope for the world of her fellow-creatures. In the material world she had but little interest, for she knew but little about it, and had not sufficiently considered the text which says that "God's mercy is over all His works;" not limited to one class of creatures, or even to one sort of life.

Feeling as she did, therefore, she entered into no discussion with her boy, but through the home evening contrived to divert his mind, by reading him pleasant stories of good people who had lived in favour with God, and had died full of hope and peace.

Nevertheless, Siegfried's last thought, as he fell asleep, was not of comfort and joy in the righteous, but of pity and almost love for all the wretched things for whom there seemed no hope.

The next day, his mother would fain have persuaded him to remain below in the valley, and seek some new amusement, but finding she could not reconcile him to the idea of forsaking his favourite haunt, she gave way, though with a sigh; and so, after his little daily tasks and helps to her were ended, he climbed up the heights as usual.

It was well that he had promised his mother to tease her no more about the matter. Otherwise, on that day, he would have made more fuss than ever, for, when the sun was at the highest, the rosy flush re-appeared on the distant snow, only not now confined to one small patch, but spread in broad tracts of delicate colour, which threatened to cover the whole mountain with its Aurora-like tint.

Once or twice Siegfried's resolution to keep his promise nearly gave way, but he held out manfully even to the last, contenting himself, on his return into the valley, with enquiring of a neighbour's son, whom he met driving home his father's cattle, why some of the snow on the hills looked pink?

At first the boy said he didn't know, but presently he recollected that he had heard it said, that red snow fell sometimes out of the sky. Very likely that was it; but what it was, or what became of it, he had no notion. Only it went away as it came. Nothing ever stopped on the hill but the snow that was always there.

Hearing this, Siegfried had no longer even a wish to speak to his mother about it. She would say it was because the mountain was so cold and hard, no good thing, even from Heaven, could stay upon it!

And thus a day or two passed, and the tracts of rosy colour grew fainter, and finally disappeared, as the farmer's son had said was always the case; and Siegfried never spoke about it again, but sat on the hill-side daily, wondering and dreaming to himself.

But he was interrupted at last. One morning, when the snow looked colder and whiter than ever against the blue sky, and he had been sitting for a while, with his face hidden by his hands, a voice he did not know called to him, asking what he was doing. And when he lifted up his eyes, a stranger stood between him and Mont Blanc.

A child always answers "Nothing" to such a question, for children never feel thinking to be doing anything.

But the stranger would not be so easily satisfied, and smiling, persisted in his enquiries.

"What are you thinking of, then, little boy? One must be either doing or thinking while one is awake. And I want you to talk to me. I have come from such a long way off, and am so weary."

Here the stranger seated himself by Siegfried's side on the grass.

"First," continued he, "I want you to tell me, if you can, whether I can get to the town of ——, through the pretty valley here at the bottom of this hill? Then, I want you to tell me for whom you have picked this basket of flowers? Then, why you are on this wild hill-side alone? Then, what you think about when you cover up your face with your hands? Now, then, can I get to the town through the valley?"

The voice that asked was so good-natured, and the smile on the stranger's face so kind, that Siegfried was won at once, and looking full at his new friend, and smiling himself, nodded ascent to this first question.

"Does your nod always mean 'yes,' little boy?" asked the stranger, amused.

Siegfried nodded again.

"Very good. Now we understand each other. Will you answer my other questions?"

Siegfried gave another nod, and then they both laughed, and the stranger went on.

"For whom have you gathered the flowers?"

"For my mother."

"And why are you here alone?"

"To play."

"What, alone? Why?"

"I have nobody else to play with."

"And what is it you think of when you sit with your face covered up?"

Siegfried's heart melted within him, and, pointing by a sorrowful nod to the giant mountain, he answered, "I think of it."

"Of it?" What can you find in it to think about?"

"I am so sorry for it!" cried little Siegfried, passionately; "so sorry it is so miserable and outcast, and that God will let nothing grow there, while we have all these flowers!"

And once more he tossed the flowers contemptuously out of the basket.

"Ah, little boy," said the stranger, putting his arm kindly around the child, and drawing himself nearer to him. "You must answer another question now. Who put such strange fancies into your heard? Who told you this about the poor mountain?"

"They all say so," murmured Siegfried. "The pastor preached about it on Sunday, and mother says so, too, and the farmer's son, and everybody; and I am so sorry, so very sorry!"

The young voice died away, as it were, in regret.

"And why do you care so much about the mountain, little boy?"

Siegfried looked up, puzzled, for a moment, but very soon out came the simple, child-like answer, "I look at it so much when I come up here to play."

It was the stranger's turn now to feel his eyes moisten, as he thought of the solitary child sending out his heart into the inanimate creation around him.

Extremely interested, therefore, he made a few more enquiries, and, by degrees, brought out a part, at any rate, of what Siegfried's mother and the pastor between them had told and taught of outcast countries and God-deserted men. All was confusion in the child's account, but the drift of it could easily be discovered.

Without making a single remark, however, the stranger smiled again, and said, quite cheerfully, "I will tell you a secret, little boy. Neither the pastor, nor your mother, nor the farmer's son were ever up the mountain, I suspect, so they cannot know very much about it."

"I wanted to go, but they would not let me," interposed Siegfried. "They said I was not able to get up."

"They said right," replied the stranger. "But I, you see, am older and stronger, and could go; and I have been."

Quietly as he purposely spoke, the effect of what he said was, as he expected, very great. Siegfried jumped up; then sat down; then once more started from his seat, and was far more anxious to run down the hill and tell his mother the news, than to remain quietly where he was, and hear what more the stranger had to tell. He allowed himself to be controlled, however, and his friend went on talking as if he had not been interrupted.

"And the place is neither lifeless nor deserted. God sends it the beautiful red snow plant instead of flowers. I have been gathering it for days."

As he spoke, he unfastened from the leathern strap that went across his shoulders a small tin box, and, opening it for a moment, let Siegfried peep at a bright carmine-coloured mass of something within.

The child was speechless at first, overpowered by admiration and delight, but presently exclaimed, "Then that was what I saw!" adding gently, "And it really came down from Heaven, then?" He was thinking of what the farmer's son had said.

"All good things come from Heaven, that is, from the God of Heaven," answered the stranger. "But this is as much a plant as the Alpine rose by your side. It did not drop down from the sky, but grows in the very snow itself, and covers over miles and miles of the hill you thought so desolate. God sends good things everywhere, though not everywhere alike."

Oh, the joy of such a doctrine! The simplest child could understand it, and be glad! All was explained now, too; the rosy patch and the broad tracts of colour were both accounted for, and Siegfried was as happy as he now believed the mountain to be. And, embracing his new friend, he forthwith began such a blundering account of what he, and his mother, and the farmer's boy, had thought about the rosy patch, that the stranger could do nothing but laugh, and at last stopped him by exclaiming:

"Then you see you were all wrong; but never mind. Take me to your mother's cottage, and we will tell her all about it, too, and I will show it to you both, for even you have not really seen it yet."

Siegfried's mother welcomed the friendly stranger whom her son brought to her door with all the heartiness of a Swiss welcome; and not the less when she found he was an English traveller, on his way to a neighbouring town to visit a well-known officer there, who had been deprived of a limb in the same action in which Siegfried's father had lost his life.

And as the town was but a few miles off, and the summer evenings so long, the stranger was easily persuaded to rest for a few hours in the Swiss cottage, and tell the widow and her son the history of his adventures on Mont Blanc, and of the red snow plant he had brought from it. Not that telling its history only would have been enough; nor was there anything either beautiful or wonderful-looking in the red, jelly-like mass in the tin box, when looked at only with the naked eye. The stranger had far more in store for them than that.

"I am going to show you," he began, at last, and after busying himself in unpacking that revealer of secrets, a microscope,—"that God has sent many more gracious things into the world than our natural eyes are able to see. Do you like to know this, little Siegfried?" he added, turning purposely to the child.

Siegfried nodded his heartiest nod of assent, and the widow said, with a smile, "You should have asked that question, Sir, of me. It is I who have not believed, because I did not see. He has had the instinct of the truth all along."

"Well, then, good Mother," replied the stranger, "you shall see and believe what will, I think, comfort you for life—namely, that God makes the very wilderness to burst forth and blossom like a rose: that there are no outcast ends of the earth, uncared for by Him; no desolate corners where His goodness is not shown forth."

As he spoke he finished the last adjustment of the microscope, and touching the red jelly in the tin box with the fine point of a porcupine's quill, he placed the tiny morsel so obtained in a glass, to be looked at, and called to Siegfried to have the first peep.

The widow, struck as she had been with the stranger's words, had her own doubts as to what there could be to be seen, for she had not been able to detect anything on the porcupine's quill, but she said nothing, and very soon Siegfried's shouts of delight announced that something, at any rate, was there.

And, truly, what there was, was a very pretty sight. Four or five bright little red balls, and two or three colourless ones among them, were lying like gems in the few drops of water which had been put in to keep them separate.

The child believed at once, but at the first moment the mother could scarcely credit what she saw. That this should be a bit of the shapeless stuff she had looked at in the tin box—it was marvellous indeed.

The stranger now proceeded to explain. He told them that each of the red balls was a perfect plant in itself. That it was a little colourless bag, finer than gold-beater's skin, filled with a red substance, which shone through. That, as soon as it was full grown, the red substance within divided into four, eight, and sometimes sixteen separate red balls, of course of the tiniest size possible, all which immediately began to grow very fast, and grew, and grew, and grew, till the little bag in which they lived could hold them no longer, but burst, and dropt them out.

"These," said he, "are the young plants; and when each of them is full grown, the same thing happens again. The red substance in each divides into other tiny balls, and, as these grow, they burst out from the parent bag, (called a cell, properly,) and begin life for themselves. And thus comes another generation of the ball-like plants, and so another and another; and all this so quickly, that, in a few hours, millions of them have sprung from a few single cells. So now, little Siegfried, you know why, when you looked the second time at the rosy patch, it had spread into those great broad tracts of colour which, in fact, covered over miles of the poor snow with its beauty. It was no wonder, was it?"

No, that was no wonder; but that such things were, of which so many people did not know, was a wonder from which the good widow could not easily recover. Besides, she was thinking of the pastor having made such a mistake.

As for Siegfried, he had not lived long enough to know why he should be so much surprised about the red snow plant; was it a bit more really strange than the growth of the Alpine rose, which astonished nobody? So his chief feeling was extreme delight at there being something on the mountain to make amends for its want of flowers.

"And now," said the stranger, "is there anything more you would like to ask?"

The mother was about to speak at once, but hesitated and drew back. She knew so little; she feared to seem so ignorant and foolish.

Reassured, however, she begged to be told how the marvellous plant could live amidst nothing but snow; could come up, and bring forth a thousand fold, with nothing to nourish and support it?

The stranger repeated the word "nothing" with a smile.

"Nothing, because we see nothing!"

"Ah, see what a bad habit is!" cried the mother. "I had forgotten already. Then you think there may be things I do not know of, in what we call the cold, barren snow?"

"Ay, ay," was the answer; "germs of life, hidden and buried, perhaps, for years; seeds scattered no one can tell how or when; and salts and chemical properties, needing only some accident of a sunbeam, or dew, or state of the very air, to make all work together, and the frozen surface to become moist, and the red snow plant to spring up by millions."

Here he paused, and seeing little Siegfried looking wistfully at him, as if trying to understand, he took him on his knee caressingly, and said, "That microscope is a very curious thing, is it not?"

The child nodded his "yes" as heartily as ever, and then laid his head, contentedly, on his friend's shoulder, while he went on talking.

"Yes; it is very curious, for it shows us quantities of things we could not see without it; but the best lesson it teaches is, how much more there may be of which, even with its help, we can see and know nothing; for, although there is a limit to our power of seeing God's works, no naturalist dares to think he has reached the limits of the works themselves. In this life we cannot hope to know a hundredth part of the creations which surround us. You can believe this now, good Mother?"

"With all my heart," was her answer.

"And, further," he added, "You can judge now for yourself, that even of the things we do what we call see with the naked eye, there are a great many of which we can never know anything like the real truth, without such aid as this (pointing to the microscope). What was the red snow plant to you at first? A piece of shapeless jelly. What did it become to your more enlightened eye? A living organism, unmistakably from Almighty hands, endowed with a system of life, if not of life-enjoyment, peculiarly its own. This is something to have discovered, certainly, but is it all? Ah! as I tell it, I feel how imperfect the account is—how much remains behind. All we have done is but to have made a step or two out of complete ignorance.

"'The rest remaineth unrevealed.'"

Yet a glory comes into our hearts from the thought of the worlds beyond reach of our present senses, like the reflection from lightning below our own horizon, and both faith and hope ought to be strengthened."

The widow did not speak.

"I have one more word to say," continued the stranger guest, "If you will allow me to say it, and can forgive the old traveller for preaching as well as teaching. I have taught you something of God's doings in the natural world, which has given you comfort and hope. What, then, you believe of His works, believe also of His mercies. If you cannot find a limit to the one, suspect and hope that the other, too, may be infinite—far beyond our comprehension. Will you try and take this last lesson to heart?"

The poor mother's eyes filled with tears. She had passed tremblingly through life, and sadly needed the good counsel.

After a short pause, her counsellor went on, firmly, but very kindly—

"You have seen how weak and short-sighted the natural eye is; can you for a moment suppose that the spiritual eye is more far-seeing and better able to acquaint you with God's purposes and doings? Are His works to be infinite, and His mercies bounded, so that a man can point to the limit, and say, Here God's mercy ceases; here there is no hope—but only everlasting lifelessness and despair? Oh, good Mother, to whom is entrusted the rearing of a very tender plant, take heed what you teach, and foster in it, above all other virtues, the charity which 'hopeth all things,' and then can both believe and endure."

The lesson was not spoken in vain even then, and it was never forgotten. And Siegfried grew on, and the stranger revisited the cottage many times, and by and by aided in the education of the child whose acquaintance he had made in so singular a manner. And, after many years, the young man, Siegfried, became a teacher himself—a pastor—though not in his own country.

But never, through a long life, did he forget his early hopes, and fears, and fancies, about the desolate mountain, nor the lesson he learnt from the stranger traveller. And into whatever scenes of darkness and ignorance he forced his way; whatever he met of sin and sorrow; however often baffled, thrown back, and disappointed, he never despaired; for he used to recall the past, and take comfort to himself by thinking, "It may be God's will yet, that the red snow plant may one day burst into life on the cold hillside."

Whereunto?

"I see in part
That all, as in some piece of art,
Is toil cöoperant to an end."
       TENNYSON.

"This is dreadful! What can I do?"

"Why, follow me, to be sure! Here! quick! sideways! to the left! into this crevice of the rock! there! all's right!"

"Oh, it's easy to talk, when people can trip away as lightly as you do. But look at me with the ground slipping away wherever I try to lay hold."

"Come along; all's right," repeated the Crab (for such was the speaker) from his crevice in the rock.

And all was right certainly, as far as he was concerned; but as for the poor Star-fish, who was left on the sand, all was as wrong as possible, for he was much too hot; and no wonder.

It was a low tide—a spring tide—and even for a spring tide, a particularly low one; for there was very little wind astir, and what there was, blew off the shore.

So the rocks were uncovered now, which seldom tasted the air, and the stems of the great oarweed, or tangle, which grew from them, were bent into a half-circle by the weight of their broad leathery fronds, as, no longer buoyed up by the sea, they lay trailing on the sands.

What a day it was, to be sure! one of those rare, serene ones, when there is not a cloud in the delicate blue sky, and when the sea lies so calm and peaceful under it, that one might almost be persuaded to believe nothing would ever again ruffle its surface. The white-sailed vessels in the distance, too, looked as if they had nothing in the world to do for ever, but to float from one beautiful end of the world to the other, in security and joy.

Yet delicious—unspeakably delicious—as the day was, it brought discomfort to some who lived under it. The numberless star-fishes, for instance, who had been unexpectedly left stranded on the shore by the all-too-gently-retreating waves, how could they rejoice in the beautiful sunshine, when it was streaming so pitilessly on their helpless limbs, and scorching them by its dry cruel heat? And as for the jelly-fishes, who had shared a similar fate, they had died almost at once from the shock, as the wave cast them ashore; so of the merits of the delicious day they knew nothing at all.

All creatures did not suffer, of course. The Crab, for instance, who had given such good advice to his friend (if he could but have followed it), did very well. In the first place, he liked the air nearly as well as the water, so that being left high and dry on the shore now and then was quite to his taste.

Moreover, he could scuttle off and hide in a crevice of the rocks whenever he chose. Or he could shelter under the large sea-weeds, and because of his hard coat was even able to take a short walk from time to time, to see how matters went on, and observe how far the tide had gone down; and if the sun did happen to bake him a little too much, he had only to run off to a pool and take a bath, and then was as fresh as ever in a minute.

And now, just as the tide was at the lowest, where it was likely to beat about for some time without much change, two other creatures appeared on the sands, and approached the very spot where the Star-fish lay in his distress, and near which the Crab was hid. Now there was a ledge of rocks here, which would have furnished seats for dozens of human beings, and from the front of it grew almost a forest of oarweed plants.

What the creatures were who came up to this place and stopped to observe it, I shall not say; but one of them remarked to the other, "Here again, you see; the same old story as before. Wasted life and wasted death, and all within a few inches of each other! Useless, lumbering plants, not seen half a dozen times in the year; and helpless, miserable sea-creatures, dying in health and strength, one doesn't know why."

As the creature who spoke said this, it lifted up two or three tangle fronds with a stick it carried in its hand, and then let them flop suddenly down on the sand; after which it used the end of the same stick to chuck the unhappy Star-fish into the air, who, tumbling by a lucky accident under the shelter of the tangle, was hid for a time from sight.

"And so we go up, and so we go down, ourselves," continued the creature; "a good many of us, with no more end in life, and of no more use, that one can see, than these vile, useless seaweeds; coming into the world, in fact, for no earthly purpose but to go out of it, in some such wretched manner as this!"

And here the creature kicked three or four more stranded star-fishes across the narrow sands, till he had fairly kicked them into the sea; muttering as he did so, "What did you come into the world for, I wonder, and you, and you, and you? Purposeless life and purposeless death—the fate of thousands. And I for one as useless as any of them, but at any rate having the grace to acknowledge that the world would get on quite as cleverly without me as with! Whereunto, whereunto, whereunto? Answer it if you can!"

As the creature finished speaking, the two moved on together; but what the companion answered was never exactly known; for though the voice sounded as if in dispute, what was said was not heard by those who were left behind, for they began at once to chatter among themselves.

And first out popped the head of the Crab from the crevice he had taken shelter in; and he cocked his eyes knowingly, first to one side, and then to the other, and began to talk; for he had always plenty to say for himself, and was remarkably bold when there was no danger.

"Miserable sea-creatures!" was his first exclamation, repeating what the land-creature had said. "I suppose I am included in that elegant compliment. I say! where are you, old Lilac-legs? Have you contrived to crawl away after all? Come out of your corner, or wherever you are, for a bit. Who was the creature that was talking such nonsense just now? Only let me come across him, that's all! Helpless sea-creatures, indeed! I should like to have seen him hiding in a crevice as nimbly as I can do! He'd better not come within reach of me any more, I can tell him!"

It was all very well for the Crab to sit outside the rock looking so fierce, and brushing his mouth so boldly with his whisker-like feelers, now that there was nobody to fight with. How he would have scuttled away sideways into his hole, if the creature had re-appeared, everybody can guess.

"You happy fellow!" answered the meek voice of the Star-fish, Lilac-legs; "you can afford to joke about everything, and can do whatever you please. You have so many things in your favour—your stiff coat, and your jointed legs, and your claws with pincers at their ends; and your large eyes. Dear me, what advantages! and yet I have an advantage too, and that a very great one, over you all, so I shall not grumble, especially not now that I am in the shade. That sun was very unpleasant, certainly; I felt something between scalded and baked. Horrible! but I am sheltered now. And how did that come to pass, do you think?"

The Star-fish paused for an answer; but the Crab declared he couldn't think—had no time for thinking; it was too slow work to suit him. So Lilac-legs told him how she had been chucked into the air by the stick, and how she had come down in the midst of the tangle, and fallen under shelter.

"So you see," added she in conclusion, "that you were quite right in saying what nonsense the creature talked. Why, he said he was as useless as these vile useless seaweeds, and had come into the world, like them, for nothing; whereas, don't you see, he was born to save me, which was something to be born for, at any rate, that's quite clear; and so was the vile useless seaweed, as he called it, too. I, with my advantages, can tell them both that!"

"You go in and out, and in and out, over people's remarks, till you make me quite giddy, I get so puzzled," replied the Crab; "and then you are always talking of your advantages," he continued, whisking his feelers backwards and forwards conceitedly as he spoke, "and I can't make out what they are. I wish you would say at once what you mean."

"Oh, my advantages, you want to know about?" answered Lilac-legs. "Well, I certainly have one in each leg, near the end, with which I—but I don't think I can describe it exactly. You have several advantages yourself, as I told you just now, and we have one or two in common; for instance, the loss of a leg or two is nothing to either of us; they grow again so quickly; but still I am very helpless now and then, I must admit! on the sand, for instance—it is so soft—and the more I try to lay hold, the more it slips away.

"Still these advantages in my legs make amends for a good deal, for at any rate I know my own superiority, and there's a great comfort in that; I can't explain, but you may safely take it for granted, that with my advantages, I know a good deal more than you give me credit for. I know, for instance, that the poor ignorant creature need not consider himself useless, since he was the means of chucking me here, and that this fine old tangle hasn't lived for nothing, since it is sheltering me."

"How conceited some people are with their advantages!" murmured a silver voice from one of the tangle fronds. "If the tangle had come into the world for nothing but to shelter you, there would have been a fuss to very little purpose indeed! Can't your advantages tell you there are other creatures in the world quite as important as yourself, if not more so, you poor helpless Lilac-legs? Do you know who is speaking? It is the blue-eyed limpet, I beg to say—the Patella pellucida, if you please.

"I have an advantage or two myself! My coat is harder even than the crab's, and it is studded with a row of azure spots, as bright as the turquoise itself. That is something to reflect upon in one's solitude, I can assure you! and the tangle plants are the natural home and food of our lovely race. The creature was ignorant enough in calling them useless, therefore, of course; but you were not much wiser in thinking they were put into the world to shelter you.

"I flatter myself I have said enough! To be the home and the food of beings like us, is cause sufficient—almost more than sufficient, I venture to think—for the existence of any vegetable that fringes these shores. And while they live for us, our turquoise-gemmed backs are, in return, their highest ornament and pride. The whole thing is perfect and complete. Anybody with half an eye, and a grain of understanding, may see that!"

"Oh, the narrow-mindedness of people who live under a shell!" murmured a score of whispers, in unison, from another tangle frond close by. "Oh, the assurance of you poor moveable limpets in talking about your home, when you do but stick to first one part of these vast leaves and then another, moving from place to place, and never fairly settling anywhere! Home, indeed, you call it? What sort of a home is it, when an unlucky chance can force you off at any moment, or some passing creature pick you from your hold? The pretension would be disgusting, if it were not so absurd. Think of mere travellers, as one may say, talking of their lodging-house as if it were their own, and belonged to them by a natural right!—how ridiculous, if not wrong! We can afford to speak—we, of whose dwelling-places it is the foundation and support. Talk of the useless tangle, indeed! Yes, the creature was ignorant indeed who said so. Little he knew that it was the basis of the lives of millions. Little he knew of the silver net-work we spread over it from year to year, or of the countless inhabitants of the beautiful web—a fairyland of beings, so small, that the crab can scarcely see us, yet spreading so far and wide, and accomplishing so much; but that is because we work in unison, of course. We never quarrel among ourselves, as some folks do—not altogether unlike the crab in the crevice yonder. We work to one end, so that we are sure to continue strong. Useless tangles, forsooth! when they have been the foundations of colonies like ours from the beginning of the world! Of course the thing is clear enough to those who choose to look into it; any one who knows us, can tell people what the tangle is in the world for, I should think!"

"Hear how they talk," murmured another shell-fish, no distant relation of the blue-eyed limpet who had spoken before, and who lay hidden in the midst of the twisted roots by which the tangle stem held fast to the rock; "hear how the poor scurfy creatures talk, to be sure, as if there was nobody in the world but themselves. But anything can talk, which has so many mouths to talk with. I could say a good deal myself, if I chose to try, with only one; but I don't care to let out my secrets into everybody's foolish ears. Much better hold my tongue, than let certain people, not a hundred miles off, know I am here. I don't fancy being sucked at by star-fishes, or picked out of my place by crab's claws. Of course I know what the tangle is in the world for, as well as anybody else. For while they are fighting merely about his flapping leathery ends, here I sit in the very heart of the matter; safe in the roots themselves, knowing what's what with the cleverest of them. Useless tangle, the creature said—useless enough, perhaps, as far as he could tell, who only looked at the long, loose, rubbishy leaves; but those who want to know the truth of the matter, must use their eyes to a little more purpose, and find out what's going on at the roots. Ah, they'd soon see then what the tangle is for! I don't speak of myself alone, though of course I know one very sufficient reason why the tangle is in the world, if I chose to say. Am I right, little Silver-tuft, in the corner there, with the elegant doors to your house?"

Now, little Silver-tuft, the coralline, piqued herself particularly on the carving of the curious doors which guarded the front of every one of the numberless cells in which her family lived; so she was flattered by the compliment, and owned that the limpet was right in the main. She was, nevertheless, rather cool in her manner, for, thought she to herself:

"The rough fellow forgets that he is but a lodger here, as the sea-mat said of his blue-eyed cousin; whereas everybody knows that I am a bona fide inhabitant, though with a little more freedom of movement than people who stick to their friends so closely as to cover them up! No offence to the sea-mat, or anybody who can't help himself. Nevertheless, my fibres being firmly interlaced with the roots, I am here by right for ever. These limpets may talk as they please, but nobody in their senses can suppose the tangle came into the world merely to accommodate chance travellers like them, even though they may now and then spend their lives in the place. But vanity blinds the judgment, that's very clear. Roots and plants have to grow for such as myself and my silver-tuft cousins, however; but that's quite another affair. There's a reason in that—a necessity, I may say; we want them, and of course, therefore, they are here. The thing is as straightforward and plain to anybody of sense, as—"

But, unfortunately, the simile was lost; for a wave of the now-returning tide interrupted Silver-tuft's speech, by breaking suddenly over the tangle with a noisy splash. It drew back again for a bit immediately after; but, meantime, both plants and animals were revelling in the delicious moisture, and for a few moments thought of nothing else. And just then, hurrying along the narrow strip of sand that yet remained exposed, as fast as their legs could carry them, came the land-creature and its companion.

Before, however, they had passed the spot where they had stopped to talk when the tide was low, another wave was seen coming; to avoid which, the friends sprang together on the ledge of rock, and from thence watched the gathering water, as it fell tumbling over the forest of tangle plants. And again and again this happened, and they remained to observe it, and see how the huge fronds surged up like struggling giants, as the waves rushed in below; and how by degrees, as the tide rose higher and higher, their curved stems unbent, so that they resumed their natural position, till at last they were bending and bowing in graceful undulations to the swell of the water, as was their wont.

And, "Look at them!" cried the creature's companion. "For the existence of even these poor plants in the world, I could give you a hundred reasons, and believe that as many more might be found. Of their use, I could tell you a hundred instances in proof; there is not one of them but what gives shelter to the helpless, food to the hungry, a happy home to as many as desire it, and vigour and health to the element in which it lives. Purposeless life you talk of! Such a thing exists nowhere. Come, I will explain. To begin—but see, we must move on, for the wind as well as the tide is rising, and we might chance to be caught. Follow me quick, for even we might be missed; and, besides, it is cowardly to shirk one's appointed share of work and welldoing before one's time. For if the vile seaweeds are able to do good in the world, how much more—"

But here, too, the discourse was cut short by the roar of a breaking wave, which carried the conclusion out of hearing.

People talk of the angry sea; was he angry now at what he had heard? No, he was only loud and in earnest, after all. But undoubtedly he and the risen wind between them contrived to make a great noise over the tangle beds. And he gave his opinion pretty strongly on the subject in hand. For, cried he:

"You foolish creatures, one and all! what is all this nonsense about? Who dares to talk of useless seaweeds while I am here to throw their folly in their face? And you, poor little worms and wretches, who have been talking your small talk together, as if it was in your power to form the least idea of anything an inch beyond your own noses—well, well, well, I won't undeceive you! There, there! believe what you like about yourselves and your trumpery little comforts and lives; but if any really philosophical enquirer wants to know what seaweeds are in the world for, and what good they do, I will roar them the true answer all day long, if they please—to keep me, the great sea, pure, and sweet, and healthy! There, now, that's the reply! They suck in my foul vapours as food, and give me back life-supporting vapours in return. Vile and useless! What fool has called anything so? Only let me catch him—thus—"

Bang!—with what a roar that wave came down! and yet it did no harm—didn't even dislodge the Crab from the new crevice he had squeezed himself into for the present. And as to Star-fish Lilac-legs, she was spreading herself out in the rocking water, rejoicing in her regained freedom, and telling all her friends of her wonderful escape, and of the creature who had been born into the world on purpose to save her from an untimely death.

It was a very fine story indeed; and the longer she told it, the more pathetic she made it, till at last there was not a creature in the sea who could listen to it with dry eyes.

Purring When You're Pleased

"Out of the abundance of the heart the mouth speaketh."
—MATT. xii. 34.

They had been licked over hundreds of times by the same mother, had been brought up on the same food, lived in the same house, learnt the same lessons, heard the same advice, and yet how different they were! Never were there two kittens more thoroughly unlike than those two! The one, with an open, loving heart, which never could contain itself in its joy, but purred it out at once to all the world; the other, who scarcely ever purred at all, and that never above its breath, let him be as happy or as fond as he would.

It was partly his mother's fault, perhaps, for she always set the children the example of reserve; rarely purring herself, and then only in a low tone. But, poor thing, there were excuses to be made for her; she had had so many troubles. Cats generally have. Their kittens are taken away from them so often, and they get so hissed about the house when people are busy, and the children pull them about so heedlessly, and make the dogs run after them—which is so irritating—that really the wonder is they ever purr at all.

Nevertheless, her not feeling inclined to purr much herself was no good reason for her thinking it silly or wrong in other people to purr when they were pleased; but she did, and she and her purring daughter were always having small tiffs on the subject.

Every morning, for instance, when the nice curly-headed little boy brought the kittens a saucer of milk from his breakfast, there was sure to be a disturbance over the purring question; for, even before the saucer had reached the floor, Puss Missy was sure to be there, tail and head erect and eager, singing her loudest and best, her whole throat vibrating visibly; while Puss Master, on the contrary, took his food, but said very little about it, or, if ever tempted to express his natural delight, did it in so low a tone that nobody could hear without putting their ears close down to him to listen.

Now this was what the mother cat called keeping up one's dignity and self-respect, so it can easily be imagined how angry she used to get with the other child. "Wretched little creature!" she would say to poor Puss Missy, who, even after the meal was over, would lie purring with pleasure in front of the fire; "what in the world are you making all that noise and fuss about? Why are you to be always letting yourself down by thanking people for what they do for you, as if you did not deserve it, and had not a right to expect it? Isn't it quite right of them to feed you and keep you warm? What a shame it would be if they left you without food or fire! I am ashamed to see you make yourself so cheap, by showing gratitude for every trifle. For goodness' sake have a little proper pride, and leave off such fawning ways! Look at your brother, and see how differently he behaves!—takes everything as a matter of course; and has the sense to keep his feelings to himself; and people are sure to respect him all the more. It keeps up one's friends' interest when they are not too sure that one is pleased. But you, with your everlasting acknowledgments, will be seen through, and despised very soon. Have a little more esteem for your own character, I do beg! What is to become of self-respect if people are to purr whenever they are pleased?"

Puss Missy had not the least notion what would become of it in such a case, but she supposed something dreadful; so she felt quite horrified at herself for having done anything to bring it about, and made a thousand resolutions to keep up her dignity, save self-respect from the terrible unknown fate in store, and purr no more.

But it was all in vain. As soon as ever anything happened to make her feel happy and comfortable, throb went the little throat, as naturally as flowers come out in spring, and there she was in a fresh scrape again! And the temptations were endless. The little boy's cousin, pale, and quiet, and silent as she was, would often take Puss Missy on her knee, and nurse her for half an hour at a time, stroking her so gently and kindly—how could any one help purring?

Or the boy would tie a string, with a cork at the end of it, to the drawer-handle of a table, so that the kittens could paw it, and pat it, and spring at it, as they pleased—how was it possible not to give vent to one's delight in the intervals of such a game, when the thing was swinging from side to side before their very eyes, inviting the next bound?

And when there was nothing else to be pleased about, there were always their own tails to run after, and the fun was surely irresistible, and well deserved a song.

Yet the brother very seldom committed himself in that way—that was the great puzzle, and Puss Missy grew more perplexed as time went on. Nay, once, when they were alone together, and her spirits had quite got the better of her judgment, she boldly asked him, in as many words:

"Why do you not purr when you are pleased?" as if it was quite the natural and proper thing to do. Whereat he seemed quite taken by surprise, but answered at last:

"It's so weak-minded, mother says; I should be ashamed. Besides," added he, after a short pause, "to tell you the truth—but don't say anything about it—when I begin there's something that chokes a little in my throat. Mind you don't tell—it would let me down so in mother's eyes. She likes one to keep up one's dignity, you know."

Had Mother Puss overheard these words, she might have been a little startled by such a result of her teaching: but, as it was, she remained in happy ignorance that her son was influenced by anything but her advice . . . Yet, strange to say, she had that choking in the throat sometimes herself! . . .

But, at last, a change came in their lives. One day their friend, the curly-headed boy, came bounding into the kitchen where Puss and her kittens were asleep, in raptures of delight, followed by the pale, quiet, silent cousin, as quiet and silent as ever. The boy rushed to the kittens at once, took up both together in his hands, laid one over the other for fun, and then said to the girl:

"Cousin, now they're going to give us the kittens for our very own, just tell me which you like best, really? I'm so afraid you won't choose for yourself when they ask you, and then, if I have to choose instead, I sha'n't know which you would rather have! And I want you to have the one you like most—so do tell me beforehand!"

"Oh, I like them both!" answered the girl, in the same unmoved, indifferent tone, in which she generally spoke.

"So do I," replied her cousin; "but I know which I like best for all that; and so must you, only you won't say. I wonder whether you like to have the kittens at all?" added he, looking at the pale child a little doubtfully; then whispering, as he put them both to her face to be kissed, "Cousin, dear, I wish I could see when you were pleased by your face! See! give a smile when the one you like best goes by. Do—won't you—this once—just for once?" . . .

It was in vain! He passed the kittens before her in succession, that she might see the markings of their fur, but she still only said she liked both, and, of course, was glad to have a kitten, and so on; till, at last, he was disheartened, and asked no more.

It is a great distress to some people when their friends will not purr when they are pleased; and as the children went back together to the drawing-room, the little boy was the sadder of the two, though he could not have explained why.

And then, just what he expected happened—the choice between the two kittens was offered first to the girl; but, instead of accepting it as a favour, and saying "Thank you" for it, and being pleased as she ought to have been, she would say nothing but that she liked both, and it could not matter which she had; nay, to look at her as she spoke, nobody would have thought she cared for having either at all!

How was it that she did not observe how sorrowfully her aunt was gazing at her as she spoke; aye, and with a sorrow far beyond anything the kittens could occasion?

But she did not; and presently her aunt said: "Well, then, as she did not care, the boy should choose." On which the poor boy coloured with vexation; but when he had sought his cousin's eyes again and again in vain for some token of her feelings, he laid sudden hold on Puss Missy, and cuddled her against his cheek, exclaiming—

"Then I will have this one! I like her much the best, mother, because she purrs when she is pleased!"

And then the little girl took up Puss Master, and kissed him very kindly, but went away without saying another word.

And so a week passed; and though the children nursed their kittens, they never discussed the question of which was liked best again, for a shyness had sprung up about it ever since the day the choice had been made.

But at the end of the week, one sunshiny morning, when the boy was riding his father's pony, and only the little girl was in the house, her aunt, coming suddenly into the school-room, discovered her kneeling by the sofa, weeping a silent rain of tears over the fur-coat of Puss Missy, who was purring loudly all the time; while her own kitten, Puss Master, was lying asleep unnoticed by the fire.

Now, the pale, silent little girl had been an orphan nearly two years—father and mother having died within a few weeks of each other; and she had been ever since, till quite lately, under the care of a guardian, who, though married, had no children, and was more strict and well-intentioned than kind and comprehending; so that, between sorrow at first and fear afterwards, joined to a timid, shrinking nature, she had, without knowing anything about it, shut herself up in a sort of defensive armour of self-restraint, which, till now, neither aunt, nor uncle, nor even loving cousin, had been able to break through.

But they had gently bided their time, and the time had come at last, and Puss Missy pointed the moral; for, with her aunt's arms folded round her, and a sense of her comforting tenderness creeping into the long-lonely heart, she owned that she had fretted all the week in secret because—actually because—it was so miserable to nurse a kitten who would not purr when he was pleased!

Anybody may guess how nice it was, ten minutes afterwards, to see the little girl, with the roused colour of warm feeling on her cheeks, smiling through her tears at the thought of how like the unpurring kitten she had been herself! Anybody may guess, too, with what riotous joy the loving boy-cousin insisted on her changing kittens at once, and having Puss Missy for her very own.

And now, on the other hand, he set to work himself, with a resolute heart, to make Puss Master so fond of him that purr he must, whether he would or no; and how that, now and then, by dint of delicate attentions, such as choice morsels of food and judicious rubbing under the ears, he worked the creature up to such a pitch of complacency, that the vibrations of his throat became, at any rate, visible to sight, and perceptible to touch.

Truly, they were a very happy party; for after Puss Master took Puss Missy for friend, confidante, and adviser, he grew so loving and fond, that he could not help showing his feelings in a thousand pretty pleasant ways: and the mother-cat herself relaxed by degrees; perhaps because she found her kittens were not taken away—partly, perhaps, because Puss Missy's openheartedness stole into her heart at last, with a sense of comfort—who knows?

Certainly she left off scolding and lecturing, and would not only watch their gambols, but join in them at times herself. And if neither she nor her son ever purred quite so much, or so loudly as their neighbours, the reason, no doubt, was only that tiresome choking in the throat!

Why, the pale little girl herself complained of having felt something very like it, during the sad two years before her kind aunt made her happy again! It always used to come on when she wanted to say what she felt.

And, perhaps, there is always something that chokes in the throat when people do not purr when they are pleased.

Let us hope so!

The Voices of the Earth

"Let everything that hath breath, praise the Lord."
—PS. cl. 6.

"Would that I could pass away, and cease to be!" murmured the Wind, as it performed its circuits round the earth, long ages ago. "Would that I could cease to be! Since the creation of man, existence has become insupportable."

"Thou art mad!" cried the Mountains and Valleys, over whom the wind was passing, with its outcry of lamentation. "Is not man the glory of the world, the favourite of Heaven? Surely thou art mad, or else jealous of the greatness of others—jealous of the masterpiece of creation. Oh thou, ungrateful and unwise, to whom is committed the privilege of refreshing the earth and its inhabitants, why turn aside to hold judgment and condemn? Enough that thou fulfil thine own appointed work, and, in so doing, exist to the glory of the Creator."

"Yet, hear me in patience," wailed the Wind. "It is for the honour of man, and the glory of his Creator, that I am so troubled. Hence comes all my misery. I, who know no rest but in His will, and once went on my way rejoicing—I now am, of all creatures, the most miserable.

Oh Earth, with thy mountains and valleys, and forests, and fast-flowing rivers and seas, do me justice! Thou knowest it was not so with me of old, when I was first called into being. Thou knowest with what joy I roamed over thy confines, and beheld the universal beauty that then was spread around; how tenderly I whispered through thy flowers, how joyfully I carried up their fragrant odours as a thank-offering to heaven; how merrily I sported on the hills, or taught the branches of thy lofty trees to bow, as in obeisance to Him who made them!

"Thou knowest that I even failed not in due obedient love, when storms were needed; whether to drive the sluggish vapours through the sky, or rouse the sea itself to healthy action. When have I ever failed? Have I not always fulfilled His word? For even now, in these my days of misery, I carry out unweariingly the great decree. Still I bear aloft from tropical seas, in ceaseless revolution round the world, those vapours which must descend in northern latitudes as dew, or rain, or snow. Still I labour—still I love to labour in the way ordained.

"But woe for me! another burden than labour is upon me now! Woe for the pollution I have suffered, since the earth was overspread by the wretched race of men! Woe for their civilised lands, which I must needs pass through! Woe for the cities, and towns, and villages, their haunts and habitations, which I cannot avoid! Woe! for I bear thence in my bosom the blasphemies of the multitudes, and am laden with the burden of ingratitude, denial, and doubt. Woe that I must spread these black results of misguided reason from pole to pole! Woe that I must carry up the jests of the scorner and the oaths of the intemperate, as incense from man to his Maker: from man formed in His image, and boasting in his faculties of sense!

Oh that I could pass away, and cease from being! and that with me might perish these fruits of an evil heart of unbelief!"

"Thou hast numbered curses," breathed the Mountains and Valleys in reply; "and alas! that such should ever defile thee, thou messenger of blessing. But this is not all thou bearest upon thy wings. Other outpourings stream into thy bosom; other voices are wafted upon thee to the skies; other sounds are spread by thee from pole to pole. Hast thou weighed in the balance, against the utterances of the rebellious, the prayers of the faithful, the childlike, and the pure; the steadfast avowal of martyrs; the daily thanksgiving of saints; the songs of holy praise and joy?"

"Yet what are these but what are due, and more than due, ten hundred thousand fold?" exclaimed the angry Wind. "What merit can you find in these? How strike a balance between them and the unnatural sin which says, 'There is no God'? All His works everywhere have praised Him from the beginning: only among men is there silence and doubt. And shall the remnant take credit for not joining in their sin? Inanimate creation and the beasts have never swerved from their allegiance. What room is there for boasting in man? Has he done more than these, from the foundation of the world?"

"But he alone of all creation, with a free, intelligent will."—The words came up in soft response from the Earth, and spread like harmony upon the air.—"He alone of all creation, with a free, intelligent will. Merit there can be none, indeed; but acceptability—where can it ever be found, but in the free-will worship of a spirit which has choice? And if choice, then, of necessity, liberty to err. And with liberty to err, comes, alas! the everlasting contest between right and wrong. Yet why do I say, 'alas'? Obedience to a law which cannot be resisted is not the service of the heart—not the highest tribute to the Creator's glory. Far dearer to Him may be the struggle by which the human will is subdued to unison with the will Divine, in anticipation of that day when all its wisdom shall be made known. Have patience, then, with the contest between good and evil, so long as the good is accepted of Heaven; and while this is so, be contented to labour and to be!"

"Yet listen once again," sighed the Wind. "I have been jealous for the glory of the Maker, it is true, and troubled for the honour of man. But I am also wretched for myself. Oh Earth, Earth, Earth! The Creator has made His human favourite mortal! The mountains stand fast for ever, the hills cannot be moved, the very trees survive from generation to generation; but man—the chosen—passes away like a shadow; he cometh up and is cut down as the grass; I go over him, and his place knows him no more. Alas for the misery I am doomed to share! The breath of the dying has passed into my soul for ages; it is borne upon every breeze; it has tainted every air. I am filled with those bitter agonies, and loathe my very being. Would that I could pass away into nothing, and be as though I had never been, that so I might taste no more the vile dishonour of death."

"Thou judgest with the judgment of those who see and know but in part," came up the soothing answer from the Hills. "What, if the dying breath, which falls so sadly on thy breast, releases from its prison-house of clay some spirit more ethereal than thine own, some essence subtler far than thine, which thou must bear before the mercy-seat? Shall not the Judge of all the earth do right? Canst thou not trust the Almighty with His own? Why grieve for the last sigh of perishing flesh, if it be also the first breathing of a freed immortal soul? How rail at death, if it is He who strikes the chord of everlasting life?"

"Yet once more hear me, and be just," persisted the Wind. "Not the breath of the dying only overwhelms me with this wild desire to be at rest. The breath of the living who suffer on is even worse. The sigh of natural grief, which none can blame; the moanings of the afflicted in mind, body, or estate; the outcries of the oppressed and desperate; the shrieks of madness and of pain, the groanings of despair; all, all are outpoured on me! Those dreadful voices haunt me from all sides. This mass of human woe corrodes my soul. I meet it in the cottage, and pass through to find it in the palace; I rush from the battle-field to the cloister, but in vain! for no seclusion can shut out man from sorrow. Wherever the chosen creature is found, there must I gather up the voices of grief; for lo! as the sparks fly upwards, so man is born to trouble. Oh that I might pass away for ever, and cease to know the wretchedness I have no power to avert!"

"Yet wait, wait, wait," implored another whisperer from the Earth. "What, if in human sorrow may be found an answer to the riddle of human guilt?

What, if amidst its saddest cries, thou carriest up the voice of heartfelt penitence on high? Wilt thou not weigh against the transient earthly grief the joy in heaven for one repenting sinner? Or, if amidst the mortal agony of the righteous, the triumph-songs of faith grow loud as those the angels sing round the throne,—'Thy will, Thy will, Thy will—doing or suffering—Thy will be done;'—wouldst thou not fear to take away the one, lest the other perchance should fail from off the earth? Watch well the balance between suffering and its fruits; but while these rise acceptable on thee to Heaven, well mayst thou rest contented in thy work, and rejoice both to labour and to be."

"Yet is man—the favourite—of all creatures the most wretched," moaned the Wind, "since he alone must purchase happiness with pain."

"Unjust! unjust!" expostulated the Earth. "Thou keepest record of men's sighs, hast thou no consciousness of the unceasing breathings of simple, natural joys? Yet, number the one by thousands, and by tens of thousands of the other will I answer and refute thy words. The peaceful respirations of health, unnoticed and, alas! how often unthankfully enjoyed through years, count them if thou canst! Count them as they float to thee, while the night hours pass over the sleeper's head: count them when he wakes with the young daylight to a fresh existence. Count the laughs of frolic childhood. Count the murmurs of happy love. Count the stars if thou wilt, but thou canst never count the daily outpourings of common earthly joys. Alas for those who judge of life only by startling periods, and are deaf to the still small voices, which tell of hourly mercies, hour by hour!"

"Yet once more listen," cried the Wind, "for more and worse remains behind. The utterances of vice—oh innocent Earth, in whom the glory of the Creator is yet left visible to all!—I sicken at the thought of what I know; of what I bear unwillingly about. The loathsome words of sin—the lies of the deceiver—the prating of the fool—the seductions of the dissolute—the shouts of drunken revelry—the songs of the profane—the gifts of speech and thought misused to evil:—those voices horrible to God and man...."

"Be they as dust before thee, and thou as the angel of the Lord scattering them!" shouted a cry of indignation from the Earth. "Yet wait, wait, wait! For thyself, be thou still contented to labour and to be. Wouldst thou be wiser than the Judge? Wilt thou lose patience, while He yet forbears? No! watch the balance as before, and weigh the evil and the good. And so long as the prayers which the faithful pour on thy bosom outvalue the words of the scorner; so long as the blessings of the righteous float above the curses of the blasphemer; so long as the voice of penitence follows close upon the utterances of sin; so long as pious submission makes harmony of the cries of grief; so long as thou carriest up daily thanksgiving for unnumbered daily mercies; so long as souls of saints are breathed up to Heaven by death:—so long be thou contented to have patience, and labour and be."

"But should the day ever come," shouted the Wind in return, "when the balance is reversed; when vice, only tolerated now, becomes triumphant; when sin reigns on the altars, and no man pulls it down; when the voice of the good man's worship is drowned in the bad man's scorn, and I cannot lift it to the skies; when the wretched curse God and die, and men have forgotten to be thankful;—then, then at last wilt thou acknowledge the justice of my complaints, and help me to pass away in peace? Promise this, and till then I will watch the struggle, and be contented to labour and to be."

And the Earth paused and consented, and the Wind fled satisfied away.

L'envoi to the Reader.

And he is still careering round the world; still gathering "the Voices of the Earth;" still watching the struggle between good and evil. In our public walks he meets us face to face. In our private chambers he is with us still. There is no secret corner where he cannot come; no whisper which is not breathed into his ear. It behoves us well, then, to be careful, lest, by thoughtlessness or sin, we add weight to the wrong side of the scales. For if the balance should ever incline to evil, and the wind cease to blow—what would become of the world?

The Master of the Harvest

"That which thou dost not understand when thou readest, thou shalt understand in the day of thy visitation; for there are many secrets of religion which are not perceived till they be felt, and are not felt but in the day of a great calamity."
—JEREMY TAYLOR.

The Master of the Harvest walked by the side of his corn-fields in the early year, and a cloud was over his face, for there had been no rain for several weeks, and the earth was hard from the parching of the cold east winds, and the young wheat had not been able to spring up.

So, as he looked over the long ridges that lay stretched in rows before him, he was vexed, and began to grumble, and say, the harvest would be backward, and all things would go wrong. At the mere thought of which he frowned more and more, and uttered words of complaint against the heavens, because there was no rain; against the earth, because it was so dry and unyielding; against the corn, because it had not sprung up.

And the man's discontent was whispered all over the field, and all along the long ridges where the corn-seeds lay; and when it reached them they murmured out:

"How cruel to complain! Are we not doing our best? Have we let one drop of moisture pass by unused, one moment of warmth come to us in vain? Have we not seized on every chance, and striven every day to be ready for the hour of breaking forth? Are we idle? Are we obstinate? Are we indifferent? Shall we not be found waiting and watching? How cruel to complain!"

Of all this, however, the Master of the Harvest heard nothing, so the gloom did not pass away from his face. On the contrary, he took it with him into his comfortable home, and repeated to his wife the dark words, that all things were going wrong; that the drought would ruin the harvest, for the corn was not yet sprung.

And still thinking thus, he laid his head on his pillow, and presently fell asleep.

But his wife sat up for a while by the bedside and opened her Bible, and read, "The harvest is the end of the world, and the reapers are the angels."

Then she wrote this text in pencil, on the fly-leaf at the end of the book, and after it the date of the day, and after the date the words, "Oh, Lord, the husbandman, Thou waitest for the precious fruit Thou hast sown, and hast long patience for it! Amen, O Lord, Amen!"

After which the good woman knelt down to pray, and as she prayed she wept, for she knew that she was very ill.

But what she prayed that night was heard only in heaven.

And so a few days passed on as before, and the house was gloomy with the discontent of its master, but at last, one evening, the wind changed, the sky became heavy with clouds, and before midnight there was rain all over the land; and when the Master of the Harvest came in next morning, wet from his early walk by the corn-fields, he said it was well it had come up at last, and that, at last, the corn had sprung up.

On which his wife looked at him with a smile, and said, "How often things came right, about which one had been anxious and disturbed." To which her husband made no answer, but turned away and spoke of something else.

Meantime, the corn-seeds had been found ready and waiting when the hour came, and the young sprouts burst out at once; and very soon all along the ridges were to be seen rows of tender blades, tinting the whole field with a delicate green. And day by day the Master of the Harvest saw them and was satisfied; but because he was satisfied, and his anxiety was gone, he spoke of other things, and forgot to rejoice.

And a murmur arose among them,—"Should not the Master have welcomed us to life? He was angry but lately, because the seed he had sown had not yet brought forth; now that it has brought forth, why is he not glad? What more does he want? Have we not done our best? Are we not doing it minute by minute, hour by hour, day by day? From the morning and evening dews, from the glow of the midday sun, from the juices of the earth, from the breezes which freshen the air, even from clouds and rain, are we not taking in food and strength, warmth and life, refreshment and joy; so that one day the valleys may laugh and sing, because the good seed hath brought forth abundantly? Why does he not rejoice?"

As before, however, of all they said the Master of the Harvest heard nothing; and it never struck him to think of the young corn-blades' struggling life. Nay, once, when his wife asked him if the wheat was doing well, he answered, "Very fairly," and nothing more. But she then, because the evening was fine, and the fairer weather had revived her failing powers, said she would walk out by the corn-fields herself.

And so it came to pass that they went out together.

And together they looked all along the long green ridges of wheat, and watched the blades as they quivered and glistened in the breeze, which sprang up with the setting sun. Together they walked, together they looked; looking at the same things, and with the same human eyes; even as they had walked, and looked, and lived together for years, but with a world dividing their hearts; and what was ever to unite them?

Even then, as they moved along, she murmured half-aloud, half to herself, thinking of the anxiety that had passed away,—"Thou visitest the earth, and blessest it; Thou makest it very plenteous."

To which he answered, if answer it may be called,—"Why are you always so gloomy? Why should Scripture be quoted about such common things?"

And she looked in his face and smiled, but did not speak; and he could not read the smile, for the life of her heart was as hidden to him as the life of the corn-blades in the field.

And so they went home together, no more being said by either; for, as she turned round, the sight of the setting sun, and of the young freshly-growing wheat-blades, brought tears into her eyes.

She might never see the harvest upon earth again—for her that other was at hand, whereof the reapers were to be angels.

And when she opened her Bible that night she wrote on the fly-leaf the text she had quoted to her husband, and after the text the date of the day, and after the date the words, "Bless me, even me also, oh my Father, that I may bring forth fruit with patience!"

Very peaceful were the next few weeks that followed, for all Nature seemed to rejoice in the weather, and the corn-blades shot up till they were nearly two feet high, and about them the Master of the Harvest had no complaints to make.

But at the end of that time, behold, the earth began to be hard and dry again, for once more rain was wanted; and by degrees the growing plants failed for want of moisture and nourishment, and lost power and colour, and became weak and yellow in hue. And once more the husbandmen began to fear and tremble, and once more the brow of the Master of the Harvest was overclouded with angry apprehension.

And as the man got more and more anxious about the fate of his crops, he grew more and more irritable and distrustful, and railed as before, only louder now, against the heavens, because there was no rain; against the earth, because it lacked moisture; against the corn-plants, because they had waxed feeble.

Nay, once, when his sick wife reproved him gently, praying him to remember how his fears had been turned to joy before, he reproached her in his turn for sitting in the house and pretending to judge of what she could know nothing about, and bade her come out and see for herself how all things were working together for ill.

And although he spoke it in bitter jest, and she was very ill, she said she would go, and went.

So once more they walked out together, and once more looked over the corn-fields; but when he stretched out his arm, and pointed to the long ridges of blades, and she saw them shrunken and faded in hue, her heart was grieved within her, and she turned aside and wept over them.

Nevertheless she said she durst not cease from hope, since an hour might renew the face of the earth, if God so willed; neither should she dare to complain, even if the harvest were to fail.

At which words the Master of the Harvest turned round, amazed, to look at his wife, for her soul was growing stronger, as her body grew weaker, and she dared to say now things she would have had no courage to utter before.

But of all this he knew nothing, and what he thought, as he listened, was, that she was as weak in mind as in body; and what he said was, that a man must be an idiot who would not complain when he saw the bread taken from under his very eyes!

And his murmurings and her tears sent a shudder all along the long ridges of sickly corn-blades, and they asked one another, "Why does he murmur? and, Why does she weep? Are we not doing all we can? Do we slumber or sleep, and let opportunities pass by unused? Are we not watching and waiting against the times of refreshing? Shall we not be found ready at last? Why does he murmur? and, Why does she weep? Is she, too, fading and waiting? Has she, too, a master who has lost patience?"

Meantime, when she opened her Bible that night, she wrote on the fly-leaf the text, "Wherefore should a man complain, a man for the punishment of his sins?" and after the text the date of the day, and after the date the words: "Thou dost turn Thy face from us, and we are troubled: but, Lord, how long, how long?"

And by and by came on the long-delayed times of refreshing, but so slowly and imperfectly, that the change in the corn could scarcely be detected for a while. Nevertheless it told at last, and stems struggled up among the blades, and burst forth into flowers, which gradually ripened into ears of grain. But a struggle it had been, and continued to be, for the measure of moisture was scant, and the due amount of warmth in the air was wanting.

Nevertheless, by struggling and effort the young wheat advanced, little by little, in growth; preparing itself, minute by minute—hour by hour—day by day, as best it could, for the great day of the harvest.—As best it could! Would the Master of the Harvest ask more?

Alas! he had still something to find fault with, for when he looked at the ears and saw that they were small and poor, he grumbled, and said the yield would be less than it ought to be, and the harvest would be bad.

And as more weeks went on, and the same weather continued, and the progress was very, very slow, he spoke out his vexation to his wife at home, to his friends at the market, and to the husbandmen who passed by and talked with him about the crops.

And the voice of his discontent was breathed over the corn-field, all along the long ridges where the plants were labouring, and waiting, and watching. And they shuddered and murmured,—"How cruel to complain! Had we been idle, had we been negligent, had we been indifferent, we might have passed away without bearing fruit at all. How cruel to complain!"

But of all this the Master of the Harvest heard nothing, so he did not cease to complain.

Meantime another week or two went on, and people, as they glanced over the land, wished that a few good rainy days would come and do their work decidedly, so that the corn-ears might fill. And behold, while the wish was yet on their lips, the sky became charged with clouds, darkness spread over the country, a wild wind arose, and the growling of thunder announced a storm.

And such a storm! People hid from it in cellars, and closets, and dark corners, as if now, for the first time, they believed in a God, and were trembling at the new-found fact; as if they could never discover Him in His sunshine and blessings, but only thus in His tempests and wrath.

And all along the long ridges of wheat-plants drove the rain-laden blast, and they bent down before it and rose up again, like the waves of a labouring sea. Ears over ears they bowed down; ears above ears they rose up. They bowed down, as if they knew that to resist was destruction: they rose up, as if they had a hope beyond the storm. Only here and there, where the whirlwinds were strongest, they fell down and could not lift themselves again. So the damage done was but little, and the general good was great.

But when the Master of the Harvest saw here and there patches of over-weighted corn yet dripping from the thundershowers, he grew angry for them, and forgot to think of the long ridges that stretched over his fields, where the corn-ears were swelling and rejoicing.

And he came in gloomy to his home, when his wife was hoping that now, at last, all would be well; and when she looked at him the tumult of her soul grew beyond control, and she knelt down before him as he sat moody in his chair, and threw her arms round him, and cried out:

"It is of the Lord's mercies that we are not utterly consumed. Oh, husband! pray for the corn and for me, that it may go well with us at the last! Carry me upstairs!"

And his anger was checked by fear, and he carried her upstairs and laid her on the bed, and said it must be the storm which had shaken her nerves. But whether he prayed for either the corn or her that night, she never knew.

And presently came a new distress; for when the days of rain had accomplished their gracious work, and every one was satisfied, behold, they did not cease. And as hitherto the cry had gone up for water on the furrows, so now men's hearts failed them for fear lest it should continue to overflowing, and lest mildew should set in upon the full, rich ears, and the glorious crops should be lost.

And the Master of the Harvest walked out by his corn-fields, his face darker than ever. And he railed against the rain, because it would not cease; against the sun, because it would not shine; against the wheat, because it might perish before the harvest.

"But why does he always and only complain?" moaned the corn-plants, as the new terror was breathed over the field. "Have we not done our best from the first? And has not mercy been with us, sooner or later, all along? When moisture was scant, and we throve but little, why did he not rejoice over that little, and wait, as we did, for more? Now that abundance has come, and we swell, triumphant in strength and in hope, why does he not share our joy in the present, and wait, in trust, as we do, for the future ripening change? Why does he always complain? Has he himself some master, who would fain reap where he has not sown and gather where he has not strawed, and who has no pity for his servants who strive?"

But all of this the Master of the Harvest heard nothing. And when the days of rain had rolled into weeks, and the weeks into months, and the autumn set in, and the corn still stood up green in the ridges, as if it never meant to ripen at all, the boldest and most hopeful became uneasy, and the Master of the Harvest despaired.

But his wife had risen no more from her bed, where she lay in sickness and suffering, yet in patient trust; watching the sky through the window that faced her pillow; looking for the relief that came at last. For even at the eleventh hour, when hope seemed almost over, and men had half learned to submit to their expected trial, the dark days began to be varied by a few hours of sunshine; and though these passed away, and the gloom and rain returned again, yet they also passed away in their turn, and the sun shone out once more.

And the poor sick wife, as she watched, said to those around her that the weather was gradually changing; and that all would come right at last; and sighing a prayer that it might be so with herself also, she had her Bible brought to the bed, and wrote in the fly-leaf the text, "Some thirty, some sixty, some an hundredfold;" and after the text the date of the day, for on that day the sun had been shining steadily for many hours. And after the date the words: "Unto whom much is given, of him shall much be required; yet if Thou, Lord, be extreme to mark iniquity, O Lord, who may stand?"

And day by day the hours of sunshine were more in number, and the hours of rain and darkness fewer, and by degrees the green corn-ears ripened into yellow, and the yellow turned into gold, and the harvest was ready, and the labourers not wanting. And the bursting corn broke out into songs of rejoicing, and cried, "At least we have not waited and watched in vain! Surely goodness and mercy have followed us all the days of our life, and we are crowned with glory and honour. Where is the Master of the Harvest, that he may claim his own with joy?"

But the Master of the Harvest was bending over the bed of his dying wife.

And she whispered that her Bible should be brought. And he brought it, and she said, "Open it at the fly-leaf at the end, and write, 'It is sown in corruption, it is raised in incorruption: it is sown in dishonour; it is raised in glory: it is sown in weakness; it is raised in power: it is sown a natural body; it is raised a spiritual body.' " And she bade him add the date of the day, and after the date of the day the words, "O Lord, in Thy mercy say of me—She hath done what she could!" And then she laid her hand in his; and so fell asleep in hope.

And the harvest of the earth was gathered into barns, and the gathering-day of rejoicing was over, and the Master of it all sat alone by his fireside, with his wife's Bible on his knee. And he read the texts, and the dates, and the prayers, from the first day when the corn-seeds were held back by drought; and as he read, a new heart seemed to burst out within him from the old one—a heart which the Lord of the other Harvest was making soft, and the springing whereof He would bless.

And henceforth, in his going out and coming in from watching the fruits of the earth, the texts, and the dates, and the prayers were ever present in his mind, often rising to his lips; and he murmured and complained no more, let the seasons be what they would, and his fears however great; for the thought of the late-sprung in his own dry, cold heart, and of the long-suffering of Him who was Lord and Master of all, was with him night and day. And more and more as he prayed for help, that the weary struggle might be blessed, and the new-born watching and waiting not be in vain; so more and more there came over his spirit a yearning for that other harvest, where he, and she who had gone before, might be gathered in together.

And thus,—in one hope of their calling,—the long-divided hearts were united at last.

The Deliverer

"Sages, leave your contemplations,
Brighter visions beam afar."
   CHRISTMAS HYMN.

For years there had been abroad over the earth a whisper that a Deliverer was about to arise: a Deliverer who had been promised from the earliest ages of the world. Some mighty man or king, some sage or conqueror, who would bring back lost justice, goodness, and happiness to the suffering race of men, and begin a reign of everlasting peace.

And the hearts of all whom the whisper reached caught fire at the thought; for who so dull as not to know his own wretchedness, or not see that things around him might be better than they were? Ah! men knew it but too well. Death, sickness, the necessity of labour, labour bestowed in vain, wronged affections, the triumph of might over right, wars and tumults, household divisions, and the thousand other miseries of life, had from year to year in every age unfolded to each man in succession, as he awoke to reason, the strange, sad fact, that some prevailing disorder existed in the world in his own particular day; while at the same time a strong instinct in his soul, told him, that it had not always been so,—would not be so for ever.

So the whisper of a Deliverer stole into all hearts with a promise of better things in store; but, obscure and indefinite, it was interpreted by many minds in as many different ways, according to the bent of different wishes and feelings. Only in one thing all agreed, namely, that at the advent of this Mighty One, sorrow and evil should flee away, and joy and peace be spread over the earth as the waters cover the sea.

A Deliverer!—what should He deliver them from, if not from the death so abhorrent to every instinct of their being; from the grinding sicknesses which made life a burden even to the young; from the toil that kept the strong man back from ease and enjoyment; from the disappointments which racked the tenderest and best emotions of their hearts; from the chains of unjust oppression; from the strife of parties and of tongues; from the weakness of their own souls, which left them a prey to evil imaginations from within and a thousand temptations from without?

Truly such life was but a weariness at the best: and "Oh for a Deliverer!" was the cry that went up from each man's heart as his own particular burden bore him down. Oh that the everlasting doors were lifted up, that the King of Glory might come in, and touch the earth with some magic sceptre, restoring all things to order and joy!

But the name of the Mighty One was to be called "Wonderful, Counsellor, The Mighty God, The Everlasting Father, The Prince of Peace." And the government was to be upon His shoulders, although He was to be a son, and born a child. Where, then, but in palaces could He be expected, or looked for; where but in palaces brought forth and nurtured? Surely, kings must be His nursing fathers and their queens his nursing mothers. Oh happy parents of a happy child!—who great enough, who high enough to be so favoured? Yet the child of these great ones was to be greater and mightier than all, to rule and triumph over all!—A King of kings, a Lord of lords! Well might the longing eyes of hope be fixed on palaces and regal halls! Well might the murmured question arise, "Can this be He?" when the cry of a new-born prince was heard within their walls! What wonder if Sybil and Poet sang, by anticipation of His fame!

But ever as the children of these great ones grew up to manhood, they merged by the common lot of suffering and sin into common men, and hope was darkened: yet though darkened not extinguished—and the Deliverer was still looked for as before.

Some, however, there were who found in the titles "Wonderful, Counsellor," another meaning and another aim. Kingly the Deliverer might be by influence and character, but not necessarily in His human birth. The kingship of man's noblest faculty—Reason—might be at hand, to overthrow all kingships of mere blood; the triumph of mind over material things, the kingship of intellect over brute passion and force.

The poor wise man who saved the city, but had neither thanks nor honour for his pains, was a type of a state of things now at last about to pass away. And the midnight oil had not been wasted, nor the brain racked in vain, if this were so indeed: if the day and hour were at hand when He should be exalted as universal Counsellor, whom wisdom had made fit to rule; He be called Wonderful who was great by the secrets of His mind.

And as Sages and Philosophers meditated on these things, there glowed in their bosoms aspirations which bordered on devotion. And they stretched out supplicating hands to the Unseen Ruler of all, asking that the Wonderful, the Counsellor, might bring them light and truth indeed, and conquer with those arms alone the ignorance and errors of the world.

Oh for the rising of that day, when the real majesty and power of the human mind should be revealed to the ignorant multitude in all its magnificence! Here is the only greatness worth the name! Here the only power fit for universal rule!

But year after year the wise man died as the fool, and his children followed him, and neither among them had the Deliverer arisen, but must be looked for as before.

Again: "Prince of Peace!" mused others. In this, all is comprehended. The conquering spoken of is but the overcoming of all wish for strife; the rule in store, the sovereignty of love, suppressing all desires but that for universal joy.

Ah! surely, when the Deliverer came it would be to make all men happy alike, and pour a healing balsam into every wound! Then would all the old griefs be buried and forgotten, and the soothed minds of contented men trouble themselves no more with struggle and labour.

Oh for the dawning of that morn when each man should be king and kingdom to himself, and the world resound once more to the songs of rejoicing which gladdened the golden age! Had not the Sybils so spoken, and had not the Poet so sung? Then should every man sit under his own vine and his fig-tree, and poor and rich alike cease from the land, for all should be equal and all happy.

But whence should such a Deliverer be looked for—where be expected to arise?—Ah! surely only in some happy spot of Nature, some valley peaceful and beautiful as that of Cashmere, among a race of pastoral simplicity; in some perfect household, where disturbance was never known, and one mind prevailed. Thence alone could come He who would cause the cruel swords of war to be turned into ploughshares, and spears into reapinghooks, and animate and inanimate Nature to join in one general song of joy.

So these looked to the lovely valleys and the quiet nooks of Nature for the magic spot where discord had never entered. But they, too, looked and waited in vain—yet looked and waited on as before, and called upon Nature herself to confirm their hopes.

And the inanimate Earth awoke at last to the consciousness of some great approaching event, and listened to the whisper of deliverance, even as before she had suffered and sunk under the ancient curse. And spring by spring, as she adorned herself in beauty, putting on verdure and flowers, the sense of the Mighty One who was to restore and renovate her lost glories swelled through every pulse. But she could not be troubled with the discordant expectations of men. . . .

"Come as He will," she cried, "as King, as Conqueror, as Sage, as God: thus, thus, thus, in my bloom and beauty, do I make myself meet and ready for His advent; thus, thus, thus am I worthy to receive my Lord and King! When He comes shall not all the hills leap for joy, and the valleys laugh and sing, and the trees of the forest rejoice?

So spring after spring she adorned herself in hope, and, summer after summer, she glowed with longing expectation; but spring and summer fled away and no Deliverer had come. And when the sap must return back again to the roots of trees and plants, and flowers and leaves decay, and a torpor as of death prevail over them for a while, she wept with tears of regret while they took sad leave of each other, but said—

"With a new season there will be hope once more." And Earth echoed the words, but, cold and desolate, she felt no confidence, and showed no signs of hope. Only the Evergreens cheered her up, for said they:

"While better things cannot be had, be contented with us; at any rate, we will remind you of what is to come."

Oh ignorant man and ignorant earth alike! While darkness was over the mind of one, and deadness over the face of the other—when the eyes of the common world were fixed on earthly palaces, and the thoughts of the wise on the fruits of earthly wisdom; yea, when the lovers of pleasure hoped for a Deliverer in scenes of earthly enjoyment—behold, God had chosen "the foolish things of the world to confound the wise; . . . the weak things of the world to confound the things which are mighty; . . . and base things of the world, and things which are despised," had He chosen, "that no flesh should glory in His presence."

Turn aside your eyes from earthly grandeurs, ye prisoners of hope! Put away from your hearts the confidence of human wisdom! Generation after generation had passed away, and the whole world lay yet in wickedness, for "in the wisdom of God, the world by wisdom knew not God;" and not many wise men after the flesh, not many mighty, not many noble, are called by Him.

And then, lo! in the stable of a village inn, where the beasts of the field were wont to take their rest, a weary foot-worn maiden had lain down for shelter and ease, for no other room could be found. And hark to the cry of a new-born babe which rose thence, unnoticed by the busy world without! The first-born of a mother, whose husband earned their bread by daily toil—what mattered this common birth to other men?

Yet—hark to another cry which went up amidst the wailings of the lowly child: a cry of thanksgiving and praise. "Glory be to God in the Highest, and on earth peace, good-will toward men." "Unto you is born this day, in the city of David, a Saviour, which is Christ the Lord!" And they who sang this glad Hosanna were the angels of Heaven!

Oh day of glory and delight! the Deliverer had come at last; the day of redemption was there; but what was the sign whereby the long-expected Mighty One might be known? Had kings at last given birth to Him? Had sages at last found Him?

Nay!—to simple shepherds abiding in the field, keeping watch over their flocks by night, was the news declared, amidst the shining of the glory of the Lord; and the sign whereby He was to be known, was, that He should be found wrapped in swaddling clothes, and lying in a manger.

Oh ignorant man and ignorant earth alike! When the cry of that helpless infant broke forth in the shed of the village inn, who, untaught of Heaven, could have dreamt that at that moment, and thus, the Desire of all nations had come among men?

Yet thus, thus, thus, in the counsels of God it was decreed it should be! Thus at His first coming He should come, an Example to all men.

Aye! thus, thus, thus,—in poverty and lowliness. Thus, thus, thus—while Nature lay torpid and hopeless, and half the world was winter-wrapt in snow. Thus, thus, thus—with healing on His wings, but not the healing they sought for: not a deliverance from death or sorrow, not a freedom from toil or pain, not even a ransom from temptation and sin; but, behold, by the strength and wisdom of God's right hand, and the power of His Holy Spirit, to make men through all these things "more than conquerors."

We strive after signs and wonders, we look for visible manifestations, we long for sensible experiences, and when unanswered we fall back without a hope; but how often, and often, and often, must the lesson of the Advent be repeated. Not always where and how we look for Him does the Divine One make His presence known to ourselves. Not always even when we are hopeful and earnest. Not always when in confidence we cry, "Thus, thus, thus, am I meet to receive my Lord and King," does He come indeed.

Then hang up the holly, the ivy and the yew, over the Christmas snows, as memorials of a hope which human reason could never teach. Not by the glories of summer was the Comforter ushered into the world. In the season of cold and of darkness He came to His own. In the winter and humiliation of our souls, when the robes of earthly righteousness have been laid aside, it may be He will draw near again.

When learning and research cannot find Him, it may be He will reveal Himself to the simple in heart. When the expectations of great men perish, He may come with healing on His wings to the soul of the lowly and meek.

Inferior Animals

"How? when? and I whence? The gods give no reply.
Let so it is suffice, and cease to question why."
    GOETHE.

What do they say?—what do they say?—what do they say?—

What can they have to say, those noisy, cawing rooks, as they sail along the sky over our heads, gathering more and more friends as they go, to the appointed place of meeting?

What have they to say?—What have we to say, they may equally ask. They have life, and labour, and food, and children to say their say about; and if they do not say it in what we are pleased to call language, they say it in a way intelligible to each other, which is all that is wanted.

That they do understand each other's say is clear, for they are collecting from far and near in large numbers for a definite object—viz. that of assembling in some field, or open pasturage, or park, where they will settle down together for upwards of an hour, and walk or hop about, as if they had serious thoughts of giving up flying altogether, and taking to an earthly life; saying a say, all the while, whereof we are altogether as ignorant as they would be of ours round a large dinner-table, if they had the opportunity of hearing it.

We call their say noisy cawing; what they would call ours round the large dinner-table one cannot guess; but if they concluded it had no meaning, because they did not happen to understand it, their judgment would not be worth much.

As to the noises, there is not much to choose between them in the matter of agreeableness. Nay, of the two, perhaps the din produced by human voices is the more discordant and confused.

If you never thought of this before, O reader, think of it now, and take an early opportunity of listening and judging for yourself. Listen, not as listening to the meaning of what is uttered, but to the mass of noise as mere noise.

Listen to it, as you might imagine a rook to do, ignorant of human speech, and judging only of the hubbub of sounds; and then own to yourself—for conscience will force you so to do—that there is neither sweetness nor sublimity, neither melody or majesty, in the shouting, and piping, and whistling, and hissing, and barking, of closely intermixed human voices and laughter.

Alas, for the barriers which lie so mysteriously between us and the other creatures among whom we are born, and pass our short existence upon earth!—Alas!—for a desire for intercommunion is one of the strong instincts of our nature, and yet it is one which, as regards all the rest of creation, but our human fellow-beings, we have to unlearn from babyhood.

See the little child as she babbles to her cat on the rug, and would fain be friends with the soft plaything. Observe in every action how she expects it to understand her, and return her love. Look at the angry disappointment, if a vicious bite or scratch disturb the security of the affectionate dream. It is not pain alone the child feels, let the matter-of-fact observer say what he will; there is the vexation of hurt feelings as well. Puss should not have behaved so to her; puss, with whom she had so gladly shared her breakfast of milk; puss, whom she had nursed on her knee; puss, who must have known how much she loved her! . . . .

And then follows the lesson:—it may have been given before, but it has to be given again; and while mamma tells her little one that poor pussy does not know what she means, cannot hear what she says, cannot talk as she can, has no sense to know how much she loves her, and therefore is not to blame for biting, although she must be slapped when she does it, to make her remember not to do it again;—behold! how the wistful eyes of the listening child haze over with a dull dreaminess as she becomes more and more perplexed.

It is all far too puzzling for her to understand, and when she turns again to puss—as if by looking at her to make it out—lo! the veil between the two natures remains as thick as before; neither the bite, nor anything else, has been explained.

But, practically, the unlearning of the instinct has begun, and so, practically, the lesson goes on, until we get so used to it, we forget it was ever a lesson at all; and only a few of us, here and there in grown-up life, are haunted, as we stand among the lower forms of creation, by a painful wonder at the gulf which lies between.

That the lower should not fully understand the higher; that they should not understand us, is comprehensible enough; nay, is a necessity involved in the very idea of a lower and higher; let the philosophers rave as they will at the chains thereby hung around their own necks. But that the higher should not fully understand them, is a mystery indeed, and one of which no solution has been offered.

What more natural than that the dog should not know much about his master? What more strange than that the master should know so little of his dog? In one sense, of course, he knows all about him, i.e. the uses he can put him to, and what he may expect from him; but of the inner world of the dog's life, his feelings and motives of action, he knows almost nothing.

Nay, even of his physical capabilities he has no complete idea. Who has ever explained by what power a dog will take a short cut across the country to the house where his master is, although he has never been the road before? or why he never, even by any accident or mistake, brings back any but the stone his master threw—thrown, perhaps, with a gloved hand, and into wet meadow grass, and not found for several minutes?

Verily, in more than one sense, we are "strangers and pilgrims upon earth;" for, from the first moment of waking to conscious thought, we find ourselves in a country where all utterances but our own are to us a blank; all the creatures strange; all life unintelligible, both in its beginning and its end: all the present, as well as the past and future, a mystery.

"Only children, or child-like men," says Novalis, "have any chance of breaking through the charm which holds nature thus as it were frozen around us, like a petrified magic city." Oh, if this be true, who would not be a child again? Reader, can you hear this and remain unmoved, or shall you and I become children in heart once more? Come! own with me how hateful were the lessons which undeceived us from our earlier instincts of faith and sweet companionship with all created things: and let us go forth together, and for a while forget such teaching.

Hand in hand, in the dear confiding way in which only children use, let us go forth into the fields, and read the hidden secrets of the world. Clasp mine firmly as I clasp yours. See, there is magic in the action itself! So we placed our hands in those of our parents; so our children love to place theirs in our own. So, then, even so, let us two walk trustingly and lovingly together for a while, and join again the broken threads of old feelings, wishes, friendships, and hopes.

Hush! is it a parliament, or a congregation, or what, that darkens over yonder field? Are rook-politics, or rook-faith, or rook domestic hopes and fears, the subjects of that everlasting cawing, those restless movements, those hoppings and peckings, and changes of position?

Cower down here with me by this hole in the hedge;—let us lean against this old elm-root and look through. See! the honeysuckle is twined in the thorn above our heads, and is giving out its scent around us, as if to bid us welcome.

Oh, dear companion, do you see the dark glossy creatures at their play? Their play? am I not bold to do so? They have come here for some object—with some distinct intention and purpose. Yonder, in the tall oak that overlooks the field in the opposite corner, I see the sentinel guard, who will never stir from his post until the assembly has dispersed, unless he hears or sees symptoms of danger or interruption, and then he will dash out and fly among them, making his warning cry, so different from all others, that any one who has once heard it, will recognise it again. We must whisper our remarks very softly then, or he may give notice of our presence here, and all the flock may forsake the field.

How solemn and grave, yet how keen and attentive he looks! How patient and observant! Contented not to join the fun himself, so that he may but promote it. Unselfish, dark watchman, are you paid for your trouble, and if so, how?

Or do you do it out of love and affection for your brethren, expecting love and affection from them in return, on some future occasion, when one of them will watch, and you be allowed to play? Play, I still say; but can this be only play indeed? Surely something graver and more important than play must have brought these different companies and families from their often distant homes, to this spot?

Alas! how vain are my questionings! nature remains mute around me, and man is ignorant and unable to answer, let him say what he will.

Hear this, oh you philosophers,—you lights of the world, with your books and papers and diagrams, and collected facts, and self-confidence unlimited! You who turn the bull's-eye of your miserable lanthorns upon isolated corners of the universe, and fancy you are sitting in the supreme light of creative knowledge! Hear this; you are ignorant and unable to answer; or disprove it if you can, by showing me that you do know this one simple thing which puzzles me now! Tell me what the rooks are doing and saying; those inferior animals about whom you, in your wisdom, ought to know everything. Tell me that, and I will own that your eyes have been opened indeed, and that you are as gods, knowing good and evil.

Tell me what these grand assemblies are for; tell me how they are called; tell me how they are conducted; tell me by what message the distant colonies are warned of the particular spot and hour of meeting. Tell me by what rules the place is chosen. Tell me how the messenger is instructed. Tell me by what means he delivers his message. Tell me why they meet on level ground and walk like men, and not rather in their own deep woods, where they might fly and roost on branches, and run no danger, and need no guard?

Tell me what do they say, what do they say, what do they say, when they meet at last, and whether they are here for business or for play. Tell me these things, and then I will listen to you when you point out to me the counsels and the workings of the Creator of rooks and of men.

But, miserable guides, miserable comforters are ye all! Better a thousand times to be a child as I am now, lying under this twining honeysuckle, and listening reverently to the unknown murmurs in the field! But oh! twining honeysuckle, why do you breathe out only scent around me? Stoop, stoop, stoop! I know you know! Why not whisper in my ear, then, what they say?

Tell me, what do they say? Childlike, I ask, childlike must I always ask in vain?

But hush for a moment! some one speaks; some stranger interrupts us already!—calls, "gentlemen!" as if gentlemen were here. Oh! go, go, go, whoever you may be. There are no gentlemen here—only children: children for one brief hour of weary grown-up life. Leave us; let us dream our dream in peace.

But how is this? I see no one near, yet the voice is louder than before. Companion, where are you? Look! There is no disturbance in the field; the sentry sits firm at his post; the rest are hopping, pecking, jumping as before; and yet I hear—oh, what do I hear?—a voice—and from among the rooks themselves! Have my senses left me, or have I received another? Anyhow the spell is broken at last, and language, language, language, resounds on every side! Quick, then, my tablets! Let me record what I see and hear.

One among them comes forward—a crowd surrounds him—he is congratulated—he inclines his head—he thanks his friends for a reception so far beyond his merits or his hopes.... Oh, folly! are they aping the mockeries of men? Wait! he is serious once more, and here on my tablets I record,

WHAT THE ROOK SAYS.

"The origin, therefore, of these creatures,—these men,—whom we equally fear and dislike, is decidedly the most useful of all subjects of study. How can it be otherwise? Their treatment of us, and our feelings to them, can never be placed on a proper footing, until we know something of the nature of the people themselves. In fact, my friends, I base my whole enquiry upon these two assumptions; first, that it is desirable to ascertain the exact truth on the subject; secondly, that it is possible to ascertain the exact truth upon any subject, if one chooses to try.

"Whoever goes along with me on these points, will be so good as to rise from the ground by a hop, and give a caw. . . .

. . . "Thank you, thank you, gentlemen, for your applause! My recognition of our common capabilities is acceptable to you I perceive. Unlimited faith in them is indeed the keystone of all knowledge. . . . Thank you, thank you, once more!"

—But I—the transcriber of this arrogant nonsense—am ready, as I listen to their senseless caws, to throw down my tablets in despair. Oh! to think of finding the false glozings of philosophical conceit among the birds of the air, and as welcome as . . . but hush! he speaks again.

"How, when, whence, and why, then, are the questions we must put and learn to answer. How came this creature in the land, and whence? when was he first our foe, and why? Why also is he here at all?

"These are difficult questions indeed, and before we answer them, let us look at the facts of the case. Unhappily they are too well known to need much description. It is, and has been from time immemorial (I have made enquiry of our oldest relations), a system of encroachment on one side, and retreat on the other. He comes near us and we fly; he pursues us again, and again we retire before him. Old solitudes and woodland homes are invaded, and made public; and we seek fresh retreats, only to be driven out afresh. It is a terrible position, and a time will certainly come when we must seek a new world, or cease to exist, unless some remedy for the threatened evil can be found.

"Now, the WHY of our yielding our place to man is fear. We can none of us deny it: a cowardly terror which seems to have possessed our race as far back as our oldest grandsires can recollect.

"But the WHY of this fear? What is that? Well! I am told on all sides that it is our sense of man's superiority to ourselves. Hence we give way, overawed by his presence. And here I will at once confess, that I was for a long time myself as firm a believer in this old tradition as any of you can be at the present moment. When I beheld ancient woods deserted, ancient homes forsaken, how could I fail to tremble before him who, I was told, was the mighty cause of such disturbance? But thanks to the awakened spirit of enquiry, I emerged at last from the labyrinth of what I now believe to be an old wife's tale.

"The why of our giving way, was fear: that was obvious enough; the why of the fear, man's superiority. So it was said, at least; but of this, what proofs? was my next demand; and no one could give me an answer! Here was a position for an intelligent creature! Everything mysterious, unknown, and taken for granted; nothing proved. I shouted for proofs till I was hoarse, but every one turned away silent. Who can wonder, then, that my next enquiry was a doubt.

"Is man superior to ourselves after all? No one can show me the fact by proofs. May not this old tradition then be a mere myth? the delusion of timid minds imposed upon weak ones for truth? My friends! the moment when I asked myself these questions was the turning-point of my life. Henceforth I resolved to enquire and investigate for myself, and the result of my labours I am going to place before you.

"Yet, lest you should accuse me also of mere assertion-making, let me guide you into examining the facts of the matter fairly for yourselves.

"Now all common observation is against the superiority of man. While we fly swiftly through the sky, behold him creeping slowly along the ground. While we soar to the very clouds, a brief jump and come down again is all his utmost efforts can accomplish, though I have seen him practising to get higher and higher, in his leaps, as if at a game. And at all times, if one of his legs is up, the other is obliged to be down, or the superior creature would be apt to tumble on his nose. Yet it is in this miserable lop-sided manner he moves from place to place, unless he can get some other being, more skilful than himself, to carry him along.

"Again, while we are clothed in a natural glossy plumage, available equally for summer or winter, behold man, not possessing in himself the means of protection against any sort of weather whatever! Neither the warmth of summer nor the cold of winter suits his uncomfortable skin. In all seasons he must wear clothes. Clumsy incumbrances, with which he is driven by a sad necessity to supply the place of the feathers or fur with which every other creature on earth but himself is blessed. What sort of superiority is this?

"One more instance out of many, and I shall have said enough for the present. It is one, the force of which every philosophical mind will appreciate. While we are satisfied with ourselves and all around us, man is ever discontented and uneasy, seeking rest in everlasting change, but neither finding it himself, nor allowing it to others, as we know to our bitter cost.

"Ah, my friends, if restless dissatisfaction be a proof of superiority, who would not be glad to be an inferior animal?

"Now then, have I shaken the old faith in the old tradition? If so, you will be better disposed to accept the new. Whoever is satisfied of this, let him soar from the ground and give a caw!"

—What a rising of dark forms in the air; what an outburst of caws! Verily 'tis a beautiful language after all, and beautiful creatures they are themselves! Only I am not sure I do not like them better so, than in the would-be wisdom of men. Yes! if they had but the sense not to sit in judgment upon things beyond their power! . . . But hush! he speaks again.

"One objection remains to be answered. It was suggested by a keen-sighted friend, now, I am proud to say, a warm supporter of my views. In some of the unmannerly invasions of our premises already alluded to, painful events occur. While standing under our roosting trees, these creatures, men, will occasionally level at us sticks, of the most contemptible size, but which, owing to some contrivance which I have not at present had the time to investigate, make suddenly an abominable banging noise and a very unpleasant smoke. And no sooner do our youngsters see and hear all this, than some of them are pretty sure to fall down upon the ground, as if crouching at the very feet of our foe. All fathers of families here present will admit the truth of this description, and know the terrible result. The prostrate young ones are carried away unresisting, and are never heard of more.

"Now this has actually been brought forward as a proof of the superiority of man; though in what way wanton cruelty proves superiority, I confess I am unable to see. But what cannot we flatter ourselves we have proved when our minds are warped by a theory! I, looking at the fact with an unprejudiced eye, see in it nothing but the miserable fruits of a delusion encouraged through so long a succession of ages, that we have transmitted to our very offspring an inheritance of paralysing fear! For, observe, it is rarely—very rarely—the grown-up bird who is the victim of this terror. Only the tender and susceptible young ones, with no experience of life to counteract the insane cowardice which our obstinate adherence to the old wife's tale has bequeathed to their constitutions.

"Enough of this. I pass now to the pleasanter part of my task! The statement of a theory respecting the origin of men, which affords a beautiful and consistent explanation of all the puzzling facts we have been considering, and opens up a vista of triumph to the whole rook race!"

—Mercy! what thunders of applause!—I am deafened, but curiosity is awakened at last.—What folly!—Yet if ingenuity were wisdom. . . . Well, well, if it were, judges would be overruled by barristers, and a thousand unjust verdicts become law. Again he opens his bill. . . .

"My friends, man is not our superior, was never so, for he is neither more nor less than a degenerated brother of our own race! Yes, I venture confidently to look back thousands on thousands of generations, and I see that men were once rooks! Like us they were covered with feathers, like us lived in trees, flew instead of walking, roosted instead of squatting in stone boxes, and were happy and contented as we are now!

"This is a bold proposition, and I do not ask you to assent to it at once. But if on testing it in various ways, you are forced to admit that by it you are able to explain things hitherto inexplicable, and to account for things otherwise unaccountable, though ocular proof cannot be had, then I insist that you cannot reasonably reject my solution, without offering me a better one in exchange. If things are not so, how are they? is the ground I stand upon. For remember we have already laid down the maxim that everything ought to be and can be explained.

"Well! here then I advance another step forward. I give an explanation (supported of course by facts), and I challenge you either to accept it, or to answer the searching enquiry, 'If things are not so, how are they?' Gentlemen who see the justice of this remark, will, perhaps, afford me a congratulatory caw.

"Almost unanimous, I declare! and my venerable friends who hesitate—well, well—it is from the young I look for support. A natural distaste to disturbance of ideas comes on with declining years. Thank you, gentlemen, again; the voices of my young supporters are loud and impressive."

—Oh, birds of the air, the world and the vanities and follies of it are as deep in your hearts as in ours! But again he resumes—

"The test I begin with is this. Supposing that my theory be true, and that men are degenerated rooks, what would be the condition of their minds, what their feeling and conduct towards us, the original race? Would not the painful sense of degradation, in the first place, cause them to be restless and uneasy with their present condition, as in fact we see they are? And would it not, in the second place stimulate them to an incessant craving for re-association—a desire to be with us, among us, of us, and like us, once more? What more natural then than that they should pursue us with almost tiresome pertinacity (a fact inexplicable on the theory of man's superiority), and that when we retreat before them in fear, they should still follow us, not, however, as we have for so long imagined, with evil intent, but with the outstretched arms of love?

"My friends, I feel the moisture tremble in my eyes at the thought of the gross misconceptions we have cherished with respect to this much-maligned human race. How cruel, how cold we must have appeared to them! How heartless—pardon my emotion! . . . Give me encouragement by an approving caw." . . .

Louder than ever, only hoarse with suppressed emotion. The dream of nonsense is becoming real and exciting! He speaks—

"And now, even for the terrible loss of our young ones, an explanation dawns; and their probable fate becomes clear; and happily it is one of which, in the midst of parental regrets, we cannot but be proud. Yes! I boldly picture to myself those lost young ones, carried away to become the friends and instructors of the race we have dreaded as enemies. I do not hesitate to imagine them tenderly nursed and watched in the stone boxes into which we cannot see, but which they inhabit as homes—every movement an object of interest to their captors, every action creating admiration, and made a subject of imitation—and I see no improbability in the picture!

"For if, as I shall presently show by unanswerable proofs, men are imitating not only our appearance, but our very customs and manners, their being able to do so can only be attributed to the instructions imparted to them, whether by example or precept, by our own offspring,—for who else can have taught them? Ages may pass away before the re-union of the two races takes place, but when it does (and I look forward to it in confident faith), it will be our own children who will have been the means of bringing the long-parted brethren together: those children who once fell down in fear at the feet of men, and over whose fate, hitherto, the veil of an impenetrable mystery has been thrown. My friends, it is my proud delight at this moment to lift that veil, and reveal to the affectionate mourners the bright and pleasurable reality!

"And thus the mysteries of man's pursuit, and apparent ill-usage of us, become in the light of my theory natural and intelligible facts. But you have a right to reply. 'Clear as all this would be, if the thing itself could be, that still remains to be shown. By what possible means could birds ever degenerate into men?'

"Nothing can be more reasonable than the enquiry; nothing more conclusive I believe than the explanation I am able to give.

"At this very moment, then, my friends, we are ourselves living examples of a first step in the same direction! Here we are assembled from all quarters of the country, having deserted our trees and woods, to meet in an open field, as men meet; walk lopsided as they walk, with one leg up and the other down; or jump in short hops instead of using our wings. What account can we give of this? To descend to the earth for a few moments for food, sticks, or wool, as they are needed, is one thing; to prolong our stay upon it, as we do now, is a matter of dangerous choice. Alas! indolence and a fatal tendency to yield to the ease of the moment, are the causes of our own conduct; and so they were, I can have no doubt whatever, of the degradation of our ancestors.

"Ages indeed may pass away without any perceptible effect being produced upon the individuals of a race, by the bad habits in which all are indulging. In fact, where a gradual change is creeping over all, it attracts the attention of none. But heap ages upon ages, and other ages upon them, in a succession to which the century-lives of our grandfathers are a tiny fraction of time, and what then? Anything is possible in the course of such a period. Can any one disprove what I say? If so, let him caw it publicly out; if not, let him hold his tongue. You are silent: I perceive that you assent.

"Now, then, let us imagine a race of bygone rooks, less energetic even than ourselves; nay, we will, if you please, imagine them with some temporary weakness in their wings (such deviations from a general standard are quite possible), and indulging gradually more and more in the relief afforded to the evil by this pernicious habit of ground-walking.

"There seems to me to be no great difficulty in believing that a weakness so indulged should gain ground in proportion to the extent of the indulgence, until, in the course of the long ages alluded to, and by many inheritances of increased want of power, the mischief, once trifling, became insurmountable, and a race incapable of using their wings at all, arose.

"Now, it is well known to you all, by observation of our young ones, that wings grow by use. After the young brood make efforts at flying, those necessary appendages increase. Thus much therefore is clear. Practice brings power, and power brings on growth and enlargement. And, in a similar manner, want of practice brings a falling away of strength, and diminution in size.

"Why then should there be any insuperable difficulty in further believing it possible that the never-used and consequently constantly diminishing wings of generation after generation, should disappear at last entirely as wings, leaving only the outer bone remaining, as a sort of claw whereby to lay hold on what was wanted—bared of all its beauty and ornament,—in fact, the long uncouth arm of the present man?

"And I can hardly doubt that in a similar manner, the other unused feathers on back and breast and legs, would also gradually fail. No air blowing through them, no freedom of action, no battling with the breeze. On the contrary, a stuffy life in close stone boxes, inclosed on all sides. Well might wings diminish in size, and feathers decrease in quantity, until at length, in the naked, claw-armed, bare-legged creature, not a trace of them could be found!

"Every probability is in favour of such a result, provided you only allow time enough for the imperceptible action of the change.

"And now reflect upon the miserable creature presented to your imagination! Enlarged, it is true, in length, for his lazy habits encourage that sort of feeble growth; and the power which once produced feathers, must needs develop in some other form! But behold him—a featherless, thin-skinned biped—neither beast, nor bird, nor fish; wandering, shivering, over the face of the earth, needing help from every other creature around him, yet never satisfied with anything he gets! Need I fill up the picture further, or will not every one recognise at once in this miserable animal the portrait of the superior being, MAN?"

—Well may the listeners caw! well may they wheel round and round in exulting flight. I myself grow giddy and confused. Am I then half convinced?—Yet for an imperfect being to hope to fathom the higher nature? Bah! what balderdash of folly! But hark, he has begun afresh.

"That such a degeneration is possible is therefore clear; and of the thousand difficulties cleared away by the establishment of this fact, I will offer you one more.

"You must all admit that one of the most puzzling whys in connexion with man, is, why he wears clothes? A habit which, viewing him as a perfect animal, it would be impossible to account for, but which, on the contrary, considering him as a degenerated one, is just what might be expected. He had his natural clothes once, like the rest of the animals of the earth; he has lost them now, through the disease of his deterioration, and must supply himself with the miserable make-shifts of dress.

"My friends, time does not allow me to give you now more than a few examples of my collection of proofs, the extent of which is enormous; for even after my own convictions were fixed for ever by the discoveries I have already named, I never relaxed in my researches; but being unable to be personally in more places than one at a time, I employed in active investigations several distinguished friends; I will mention particularly Mr. Raven-wing, Mr. Yellow-beak, and Mr. Grey-leg. Furnished with a complete understanding of what I believed and wished to be proved, these gentlemen have been unremitting in their efforts to procure corroborative facts; of which therefore, I will, before I conclude, mention a few of the most striking.

"Mr. Raven-wing's particular line was to find evidence of attempts on the part of man to recover the colour of the original race, namely, black; and to this end he did not shrink even from the distasteful task of approaching those vast masses of men's stone boxes, which they call cities, towns, or villages, in order that he might observe the proceedings of their inhabitants. And he came back to me absolutely overwhelmed with what he had met with. Black in all the streets struggling to overpower every other hue. Black quiescent on the pavements and walls. Black rising triumphantly into the air from the mouths of those smaller boxes, which are placed on the summit of the larger ones, apparently to raise their height—of which singular fact I shall have more to say by and by.

"Black also the usual colour of the coverings with which men protect their heads from the outer air. Black even the clumsy boots which cover their feet. Black pretty nearly everything, everywhere, Mr. Raven-wing positively declared.

"And on another occasion, in some parts of the country, he came upon whole races of men who left their homes every morning at an early hour, white, but returned to them every evening black, having accomplished this transformation during the course of the day. But by what means this significant change was effected he could not precisely ascertain; for the places to which these creatures resorted for the purpose were either deep holes in the earth, into which they descended, and soon disappeared from sight, or large dark inclosures, full of fire and heat and smoke, into which no bird could follow them and live; so that all he knew of them was that everything there being black, people became blackened who remained there long enough.

"Alas! what sufferings men endure in their struggles to become like ourselves, it is pitiful to reflect upon! And the repetition of the endurance is not the least remarkable fact of the case. For unhappily the desired result appears to last for only the period of one day. These men emerge from their stone boxes next morning, pallid as before, again to go forth to similar haunts, and undergo the same tortures, to bring back for the same short time the coveted colour of their cheeks!

"All these circumstances, gentlemen, fell under Mr. Raven-wing's personal observation, and of them, therefore, no doubt can be entertained. But it is fair to tell you also that he did, in the course of his travels, hear of another class of facts, highly corroborative of these, but of which, as depending upon hearsay evidence, I cannot so positively speak.

"That hearsay evidence went to show that there are already existing in the world, a class of men whose black colour remains with them for life—nay, who transmit it to their offspring, so effectual have been the means used by their ancestors in acquiring it! Singular and interesting as this circumstance is, if true, I do not wish to dwell upon it. Imperfect evidence is the one thing in the world on which no fair enquirer likes to build.

"On the other hand, Mr. Yellow-beak's mission was to obtain proofs of man's endeavour to resume his life in trees; and of this some very interesting instances were adduced. In the same cities or towns which were the seat of Mr. Raven-wing's investigations, Mr. Yellow-beak discovered narrow, upright, and very much elongated brick boxes, no thicker than the stems of our large trees, and in many cases strongly resembling them in formation, only destitute altogether of branches and leaves.

"And out of the tops of these Mr. Yellow-beak noticed to issue those same columns of black smoke, as he was told it was called, which Mr. Raven-wing had observed before, and which is evidently one of the many contrivances by which man is endeavouring after a restoration to the appearances of his lost primeval state.

"Indeed, my esteemed and acute friend satisfied himself that there was, at the present day, going on among men a series of systematic and unremitting efforts for a return to the lost forests and the original condition; of which efforts these stem-like buildings furnish a notable example.

"Let some ingenious plan be devised for the construction of branches on each side, and there can be no possible reason why men should not, in the course of time—but, mark me—I do say in the course of time—roost in these brick trees, as they did of yore in the natural ones. In fact, that this will eventually take place, and that men will make their homes in the branched chimneys of cities, I see no difficulty in supposing; nor that this will be one most powerful step towards a return to the common interests and hopes between ourselves and them.

"Mr. Grey-leg's information was of a miscellaneous character. He was out early one morning, near a large village, and having fixed his attention on one of those smaller boxes usually placed on the others to raise the height of the building, he all at once observed emerging from its mouth a living creature. My friends, it is a solemn and important fact that this creature was black all over.

"Black as a black feather coat could have made him. Black in his skin, black in his clothes, black in the arm which lifted itself up and waved round and round triumphantly something also black, and more like a bird's feather than anything else. The gesture was triumphant, and the voice scarcely less so—Sweep-o-oh! Sweep-oh! Sweep-oh! Some feeble attempt, we may suppose, at a return to the caw of their better days, yet, in its monotony, indicating a common origin of language.

"Mr. Grey-leg's observations were specially valuable, however, in his discovery of more than one place near great towns, in which attempts are frequently made, on the part of our poor degenerate brothers, towards bringing to perfection a substitute for the lost power of soaring in the air. Clumsy as the machine or balloon used for this purpose is, the mere fact of its invention forms one of the most valuable links in the chain of evidence of man's determination to return as soon as possible to the habits and manners of his forefathers.

"Weary of his degradation, he is, no doubt, at the very moment we are avoiding and fearing him, longing to make known to us his sense of his misery, and to obtain assistance and hope for the future. But, among other things, the total loss of our language, consequent upon a long cessation of intercourse, remains as an almost insuperable difficulty between us.

"The sounds he emits now from his bill-less mouth are, in truth, an unmeaning jargon, to which it is absolutely painful to listen. It serves his present necessities, we may presume, as orders seem to be given and taken between one individual and another; but beyond this it is mere jaw, and jaw with as little music in it as meaning.

"There is, in fact, 'neither sweetness nor sublimity, neither melody nor majesty, in the shouting, and piping, and whistling, and hissing, and barking of closely intermixed human voices and laughter.' "

—Where am I?—where am I?—what am I about? Is some mocking echo repeating my former words? But, hush once more, for the voice is speaking again:—

—"This is but the faintest outline of what will be laid before you hereafter, if, indeed, we ever meet again as now. These points meanwhile are established as facts which admit of no dispute:—man's degradation from his original brotherhood with ourselves; his yearnings for re-association; his constant efforts in that direction.

"And for my own part, I am equally satisfied of the probability of his success in those efforts. I venture confidently to anticipate futurity, and I see him mounted in his brick-roosting homes, growing wings and feathers, because they have become a necessity; while, as the long ages pass over, and his present vile habits die out from want of use, he will gradually lay aside the unmeaning jargon which he has fallen into since he ceased to be one of us, and return to the original caw of his happier state.

"Alas! my friends, that for us, personally, these bright visions cannot be realized! We shall none of us behold that glorious day! I speak it with regret. As long as we can hope to last, men will probably remain the thin-skinned, clothes-wearing creatures our grandsires remember them; still hop lop-sided on the ground, and only occasionally, and by very clumsy machines, soar into the sky.

"But I find no difficulty in looking forward through innumerable successions of ages to a time when men will again, through gradual successive developments of down and feathers, become swift-flying birds of the air; our friends, companions, brothers—rooks, in fact, like ourselves. All observations tend to show that a change in this direction is already at work, nay, has been so for a considerable length of time, and with increasing symptoms of success, as the observations of Mr. Raven-wing, Mr. Yellow-beak, and Mr. Grey-legs must have convinced you. All probability therefore is in favour of that success becoming one day complete.

"But, in the meantime, knowing the peculiar relations between their race and ours, and anticipating the day when they shall become one, should it not be our endeavour to . . ."

What silence is this, which has cut short the sentence, and which neither their caws nor the voice of the speaker break again? How is this?—where am I?—Do I wake or dream?

I peep through the hedge once more, but see nothing but a bare, deserted field. Gone, gone, all gone. The green pasture lies void and empty under the setting sun. A deathlike silence is around, or so it seems to me. Only the constant honeysuckle wearies not of breathing out its sweetness round my head. Companion, where are you? Alas! no hand is clasped in mine. Alone, then, have I been dreaming some foolish dream, or is some one in secret sympathising with me still?

—Ah! memory re-awakens by degrees. I recall the book that was lying upon my desk when I issued forth into these fields; and the thought of the first temptation of man flashes from another book upon my soul.

Woe upon us! The world grows old, and life is repeated from age to age, and the same sins are sinned. Still we desire to be as God in knowledge; still the hand writes in fire upon our walls: "Except ye become as little children, ye shall not enter into the kingdom of Heaven."

The General Thaw

"Ah! when shall all men's good
Be each man's rule, and universal Peace
Lie like a shaft of light across the land?"
    TENNYSON.

Ice, Snow, and Water—only think of such near neighbours—blood relations, so to speak, from the creation—squabbling about their rights and dignities, and which was best of the three; instead of living pleasantly together, giving and taking in turn, as the case might be.

But so it was, and the facts were these. It was a very, very hard winter that year, and the ice on the mill-dam grew so thick and strong, and was, besides, so remarkably smooth and fine, that it forgot its origin, and fancied itself a crystal floor.

Only think what nonsense! But there is no nonsense people will not be ready to believe, when they once begin to meditate upon their own perfections.

And so, fancying himself a crystal floor, the Ice got to look down upon the Water which flowed underneath him as an impertinent intruder; and considered it a piece of great familiarity, on the part of the Snow, to come dropping upon him from the sky.

In fact his head was so full of his own importance in the world, that it seemed to him everybody else ought to be full of it too, and keep at a respectful distance, and admire him. And he made some very unpleasant remarks to that effect.

For instance: "I should be much obliged to you," observed he one day to the water which ran into the dam from the stream, "if you would have the goodness to turn yourself in some other direction, when you find yourself coming near me. Over the fields to the right hand, or to the left; or into the ditches, if you please; anywhere, in fact, but just under me. You fidget me to death with your everlasting trickling and movement. Pray amuse yourself in some other way than by disturbing people in such a position as mine. I dare say you have no notion of how disagreeable you make yourself to others: you are so used to your own ways yourself. But the truth is, I can bear it no longer, and you must carry your restlessness somewhere else—it distracts my attention from my friends!"

Now the "friends" he spoke of were the skaters and sliders, who did nothing but praise his beauty as they darted along on his surface, making beautiful figures as they went.

"But I wish," answered the Water, as it kept running in, "that you would not talk nonsense, but leave me a little more elbow-room, instead of pressing so close upon me that I get thinner and thinner every day. If you don't, I shall certainly break out if I can, and be at the top myself. I've no notion of being kept down by my neighbours, however grand and polished they may be. Just take care of yourself, and look out. If the springs on the moors should get loose, and the streams fill and come in here with a rush, I should lift you up like nothing, and silly enough you would look. Turn in another direction, indeed!—into the ditches if I please—many thanks for the pleasant suggestion—and all to accommodate you! Why, I should as soon think of sinking into the ground, and I hope I know my own level better than that! Meantime I give you notice. If you won't be obliging yourself, you must expect no favour from me, and it will be good-bye to your beauty and grandeur if I can only squeeze through!"

"If!" shouted the Ice, in a mocking tone.

"If? well, if!" echoed the Water in a rage. "Stiff and strong as you are, it only wants a thaw in the hills to send a torrent our way, and the whole thing's done. But what do you know about thaws, and hills, and torrents, and the force of pent-up water, fixed in one place as you are, and never getting any information? . . .

"Now if you were to ask my advice . . . who know so much more than you do . . . and could give you a hint or two . . . upon yielding gracefully to necessity . . . it would be greatly to your advantage. . . . But . . . ."

But the but died away, and was lost; for, even while the Water was talking, some of it was freezing; and as it froze, its voice got thinner and thinner, till at last it could not be heard at all!

Meantime, the Ice got thicker and thicker, and more conceited every minute. And said he, "It cannot be worth my while to trouble myself with what is happening underneath me! There the Water is, and there he must remain, let him brag and chatter as he will; he at the bottom, and I at the top. As to making out what he means by his long talk, that's hopeless. He stuck fast in the middle of the story himself. I wish he would get out of the way; but as he won't,—well,—there he must stay, I suppose—he at the bottom, and I at the top. He's all in a muddle with his ifs and his threats. But one cannot expect firmness of mind from anything so restless as he is. It needs some solidity of character to maintain one's position in life. Rolling stones gather no moss. I sit firm. And here come my friends to do me honour, I declare!"

And come they did; and in such quantities, that the mill-dam Ice had never felt half so grand before.

It was really the prettiest sight in the world! Here were beautiful ladies in chairs, pushed along from behind by gay young men. There, other young men were skating or sliding; sometimes shooting by like stars, sometimes stooping to hit balls, which flew half across the large expanse of ice by the effort of one blow; sometimes cutting figures, which the eye could scarcely follow, so rapid and brilliant were the movements. While, in a separate corner, children were sliding and shouting, tumbling down, laughing, and getting up again, as happy as any of the others.

Really the Ice, on whom this pretty scene took place, must be excused for feeling a little vain. It seemed to him as if it was all done in compliment to himself; for, you see, he had never been at school to learn any better, and find out how insignificant everybody is to his neighbour.

"That I should be treated with such honour and distinction! that I should be the supporter of such a brilliant assembly! that I should be necessary to the happiness of such crowds!"

Such were the Ice's reflections from time to time, as his friends continued their sports. Talk he could not, for he was lost in a rapture of delight; and he felt that, as life could have nothing more to give he wished it might last on in this way for ever. Poor Ice! He thought only of himself! As to the trickling of the water underneath him, it fidgeted him no longer. "What can I or my friends care for such trifles?" was his consolatory reflection.

So it trickled away unattended to, and presently the day closed in, and the company went away home. And then, as night drew on, the wind veered to the south, and a drizzle of snow began to fall. It was very light at first—mere snow-dust, in fact, and in the darkness the Ice knew nothing of what was happening, for feel it he could not.

But by degrees the drizzle turned into flakes, which dropped with graceful delay through the air, and said to themselves as they did so, "How we shall be admired by the world when it awakes! It isn't every day in the year it's so beautifully drest. It's only now and then it has visitors from the skies. Do let us cover it well over, so that it may find itself white altogether for once!"

Which they did; and when the morning came not a bit of the mill-dam Ice was to be seen. Indeed, he might have gone on all day, fancying it was night (for everything was dark to him, as he lay underneath in the shade of the snow-fall), but that one or two luckless urchins, who wanted to slide, came and kicked some of it away with their feet.

And then he found out the truth. There he was, covered up with a great white sheet, and couldn't see out! His beauty, his friends, his glories, where were they now? He thought of yesterday, and his heart almost broke! Oh! who had dared to send those miserable Snow-flakes to disfigure him thus? Never was insolence like this! The trickling of the water below was a trifle, a mere nothing by comparison!

The Snow-flakes were amazed. "We come of ourselves, nobody sent us," murmured they, as they still kept falling gently from the sky, and dropping like eider-down on the ice; "and we have the right to come where we please. Who can hinder us, I wonder? The clouds are too heavy to carry us all, so some of us come down. My sisters and I were nearest, so here we are. We don't understand your rudeness. You ought to be flattered that we choose to come—we, who are used to be carried about by the breezes, and live in the clouds! But such a reception as this, why, it hurts the feelings, of course!"

"The feelings!" shouted the Ice, half ready to crack with vexation; "you to talk of feelings, who have flung yourselves uninvited on my face; beggarly wanderers as you are, without house or home; and have spoilt my beauty and happiness at once! . . ."

He couldn't go on; the words stuck fast as he tried.

"Beggarly wanderers!" echoed the Snow-flakes, almost losing their temper as they repeated the words: "now see what comes of being low-born, and envious, and vile. See what it is to live in the dirty hole of an earthly world! You don't know the good when it comes to you, you dreary, motionless lump of ignorant matter! Beggarly wanderers, indeed! This to us, who are carried about by the breezes, and live in the clouds of the sky! Dear us! Who would lower themselves to your level by choice? And beauty—you talk of beauty, as if we could find any here but what we bring ourselves. Fancy the beauty of dingy, dirty stuff like this earth of yours! But, of course, you know no better; and what is worse, you won't learn when you might. Oh dear, what it is to be low-born, and envious, and vile! Oh dear, what it is to belong to the winds and the skies, and to find one's self in an alien land!"

"If the winds and the skies are so fond of you, let them come and take you away," cried the Ice. "I ask only one thing—Begone! Begone with your mincing conceit and your beauty, you are not worthy that I should hold you up."

"You braggart! we should like to hide you and cover you over for ever," muttered the Snow-flakes. "And we don't intend to go for your pleasure and whim. Here we are, and here we shall stay, let you squall and bawl as you will. We at the top, and you at the bottom; and there you may remain!"

And such seemed likely to be the case; but by and by, when all the clouds had passed over, and no more snow was falling, and the sun had begun to shine, a party of skaters and sliders came and stood on the bank of the dam.

And said they one to another,—first, "What a pity!" and then, "But the snow is not very thick;" and then, "It surely might be shovelled away if we had but two or three men with shovels and brooms." So they sent for two or three men with shovels and brooms, and these swept and shovelled, and shovelled and swept, till a great space of the ice was left clear, and the snow was laid in heaps on the sides.

It was a very hard case for the snow! Such a poor, soft, delicate thing to be so ill-used,—it was really cruel work! Pushed, and flung, and dirtied, and shovelled about till she was ready to melt with self-pity.

But there is no helping one's fate, so she lay along the sides of the mill-dam, grumbling and groaning—the only satisfaction she could get.

"So inhospitable to visitors anyhow," cried she; "and so stupid to visitors like us! But this comes of leaving one's station to mix with things below. And to soil my lovely colour with their hateful besoms and brooms! And to squeeze me and throw me about with their odious shovels, as if I was dirt! Ah! we who belong to the sky should never come near the earth, that's very clear. People here don't know what it is to be delicate and refined. Oh, mercy! what comes next? . . ."

She might well exclaim. The party of sliding boys had quarrelled,—a sort of fun-quarrel among themselves. So there was just now a rush to the side of the dam, a seizing and pommelling, and squeezing of snow into lumps by a dozen active little hands; and then the balls were let fly in every direction; and some hit necks, and others faces, and others jackets, and others caps; and all got messed and broken, and thrown about. There is no knowing when the fight would have ended, if the skaters had not interfered.

The scattered, begrimed morsels could not utter a single word. But the Ice talked fast enough. "Now you have got your deserts," cried he gaily. "Now you see what it is to come and boast over your betters. Oh, you're too delicate and refined for earth, are you? Well, then, keep in the sky. Nobody wants you here—I told you that before. See, now, you have to sit in a corner, and watch how the world admires me! You wanted to hide me for ever, did you, you poor, soft, foolish thing? But my friends knew better than that, and now you've got your deserts. I shall have you all in order one of these days. You and the water below, with his fidgety spite. What a droll idea it is! Why, you both want to be at the top, if—poor dears!—you only could. And you can't see—poor blind things!—that I'm the only one fit to stand alone!"

"We will soon see to that," growled the Water from below, and surely rather louder than usual. "I feel what I feel, and you'll feel it presently, too. If I can't stand alone, I can bide my time. We both want to be at top, do you say? And who are both, if you please? Are you classing me, with my strength, and that flimsy snow together? What a judge you must be!"

"As if strength was the only merit!" murmured what still remained of flaky snow on the ice. "What a coarse, earthy notion! But it's just what one might expect; they're all alike down here, Water and Ice and all; no fit companions for us: but we've found that out too late. We lowered ourselves to come down,—the more's the pity, I'm sure!"

Were there ever three creatures so silly as the Water, the Snow, and the Ice? I dare not answer, No.

Well, before the day was over, the skaters had asked each other, as they passed and repassed, "Was there not a softness on the ice?"—"Was not the snow less crisp?" But all was perfectly safe, so people did not stop to talk then: only, as they went home, they agreed that a thaw was coming.

Which remark, the Ice, not hearing, knew nothing about. So he never suspected why the water underneath was more fussy than ever, but thought it was all out of spite to himself; so he raved and scolded away; boasting that his friends should one day help him to get rid of it, as they had done just now of the snow. "It's a great thing to have powerful friends!" cried he, triumphantly.

But the water gurgled and giggled, and made no answer.

The truth was, that one or two springs in the hills had got loose from a few hours' thaw; and a strong stream, though not a torrent, was pouring into the dam. And presently there was a cry for room.

"More room! more room! make much more room! You stiff-necked Ice, do you hear?"

And now the contest began.—"I shall not give way an inch, you noisy vagabond Water!"

—"If you don't, I shall wash you away!"

—"You shall wash the world away first. I shall maintain my position."

—"We shall see about that in a minute."

And so they went on, while the Snow-heaps whimpered at the sides, "What a coarse-minded couple they are! What it is to be low-born and vile! We are quite unfit to be here!"

Meantime, the water poured in, and kept swelling more and more; till at last there was a heaving upward—in spite of all he could do—of the crystal floor; and by and by a sharp crack rang along its surface, from one end to the other.

He could not maintain his position after all!

And now came another, and another, and these were along the sides, as the lift-up came; and at one corner in oozed the water itself. It had no chance of bragging, however; for as fast as it touched the surface it froze, and was turned to ice.

So this was all the Water could do then, for the thaw in the hills had stopped. But the Ice never rallied again, because of those horrible cracks. He was laughed at on every side—he who had boasted so much! For the Water below and the Snow above, who were ready enough to tease each other at other times, were willing to join together now in spiting a common foe. Such is the way of the world!

And when a real general thaw came in the air, and all over the country, as it soon did, and the sliders and skaters withdrew—oh, dear, those were dismal days for the poor deserted Ice!—"My friends forsake me," cried he, "and my foes rejoice! Those cracks have broken my heart! I believe it is melting away."

And it was; but the Snow-flakes were the first to disappear, and then the Ice became wet outside. And said he: "The water has squeezed through, I declare! This comes of keeping bad company; but, anyhow, the Snow-flakes are gone, and that's civil at least. They did what they were asked, and that's something."

Now the Water had not squeezed through, and the Snow-flakes had not been civil; but the cleverest people make mistakes sometimes.

And presently the Water below found the pressure upon him not quite so great. There was a little more room to move in. So said he: "Dear me! this is good. My friend the Ice is giving way. 'Better late than never,' we'll say. He's coming to reason at last."

But the Ice was not coming to reason—he was only melting away. And as he got thinner and thinner, he struggled less and less with the Water; and said he, "We shall all live to be friends and neighbours at last, I believe."

But they lived to be far more than that, for one day they found themselves brothers! For when the Ice got so thin that the water poured over the sides, it broke into a thousand fragments, and went rolling and tumbling about, dissolving away every minute. And the snow-heaps which had stuck on the sides fell in too, and they all rolled about together, Ice and Snow and Water in one. And they wept, and rolled, and tumbled, and tumbled, and rolled, and wept; and cried they, "What have we been doing? What folly have we been talking? Scolding, and thwarting, and boasting, when, my friends—my dear, dear friends—we are all of us brothers together!"

It was a long and happy embrace: it is going on still! But, oh! what a pity they did not find the truth out sooner! Let those who are brothers by nature think of this, and not wait for The General Thaw—Death.

The Light of Life

"Except the Lord build the house, their labour is but lost that build it."
—PSALM cxxvii. 1.

"What more could have been done for it than I have done!" The cry came from an afflicted heart.

It was uttered by Hans Jansen, the Hamburgh printer's only son, as he sat moaning over a dying rose-tree in the corner of a little back-yard behind his father's house.

Hans Jansen was what is commonly called not all there; that is, he could not see and comprehend the things of this life as his neighbours did. More than half of what passed around him was hidden from his eyes. He was in part, though not altogether, an idiot.

It was a great distress to his parents that this should be the case—it had been so once, however. But, being good Christians, they had reconciled themselves to it, and learned by degrees, to see comfort through the cloud. If Hans was below the rest of the world in some ways, he was above them in others.

The fear of God and the love of his neighbour had come to him almost as an instinct; at any rate without the struggles some people have to go through before their hearts are touched by either one or the other. He wouldn't have missed saying his prayers night and morning, or grace at meals, to please an emperor; and an unkind word about any one could never be got out of him.

Truly their Hans was ripening for a better state of existence, whether he had any book-learning or not. He had nothing to fear, but everything to hope for, from death.

And he had one passion—one special cause of enjoyment and delight. He doated on flowers, and was seldom seen without one in his button-hole all the summer through. But this was because his good-nature had made him many friends, who took a pleasure in seeing him pleased, and gave him a nosegay when they could. It was very well known that he had no garden of his own.

Mr. Jansen's house was a red brick one, in a row, with a square enclosure in front, covered with pebbles, and a square yard at the back, which had a pump in the middle and a dog-kennel on one side. It is true this yard was covered with soil and there were scrubby patches of grass upon it here and there; but it was used for a drying-ground and had never once been brightened by flowers since the day it was first parcelled out and the walls were built round it, across which were now stretched the lines on which the linen was hung to dry.

The fact was, Mr. Jansen had not wished for a garden. He was busy from morning to night at his printing business in the town; his wife had quite enough on her hands in household cares; and no effectual work could be expected from an idiot child.

How Hans came to be so fond of flowers was a mystery; but there are many mysteries of this sort in the world. It had been so from his baby-days, and many were the hours he had spent, unnoticed, in a corner of that back-yard, grubbing in the old black soil, "making believe" to have a garden with beds and walks like those he had seen elsewhere.

Nay, once or twice he had tried to grow mustard and cress, and even sweet-peas, a few seeds of which were given him by a neighbour's child; but somehow or other, nothing ever came of these real attempts, and he had to make himself happy with the make-believe garden at the end.

But it was no make-believe plant he was wailing over now, but a real Géant de Batailles rose-tree, which had been given him many weeks before. It was thus:—A good-natured nursery gardener, who knew his father, had let him walk through his grounds one flower-show day, before the company came; and having, by chance, noticed poor Hans sobbing from excitement at sight of the glories round him, his own heart melted; for he had an only and clever son himself, and he felt sorry for the darkness over his friend's child.

So when Hans was going away he gave him, not only a nosegay of the tulips and hyacinths, but a fine young rose-tree in a pot; "as fine a Géant de Batailles as had ever been raised," said he to Hans, as he offered it, adding that it would flower in six or eight weeks, and brighten all the place up by its rich blaze of colour.

Hans trembled as he received it, and he stood with his mouth half open, irresolute and abashed, wanting to speak, yet not daring.

"What is it, boy?" asked the nursery gardener. "Speak out."

"How do you make your flowers so beautiful?" gasped Hans, half afraid of what he had said.

"Well, well," returned the nursery gardener, with a smile, "some in one way and some in another; but we don't tell our secrets to everybody. Nevertheless, I'll tell you how to make your rose beautiful, for you'll make no bad use of anything, I'll be bound. You've a yard or a court, or some place with soil in it, eh?"

"Yes, yes," cried Hans.

"Then I'll tell you what you must do," pursued the nursery gardener. "Dig a hole in a sheltered place, pretty deep, you know, and put in a bone or two, and some hair (my son shall give you a handful) at the bottom. Then turn the plant out of the pot, not disturbing the ball of earth for the world remember; and set it right down upon the hair. Then fill up the hole neatly with soil, and say nothing about what you've done to anybody, and there's an end. Keep it sheltered, mind, and water it at first, or if you see it get very dry, and with soap-suds whenever you can get them. Soap-suds and bones and hair are the main things. There's nothing like them for bringing roses to perfection. You'll have flowers as big as a hat, and as bright as cherries, before the summer's over, if you do as I say, and look well after the plant. There! good luck to you and it! Good-bye."

And this was the plant—this, poor wizened thing—over which Hans was moaning. But how had it come to this? That was the difficulty. The gardener's son had given Hans the hair, and he had found the bones,—there were plenty by the dog-kennel; and he had dug the hole and put them at the bottom; and he had turned the plant out of the pot, and not broken the ball of earth; and he had placed it upon the hair, and filled up the hole; and watered it at first, and whenever he saw it get very dry, and with soap-suds on a wash-day; for he had only to ask and have, without question or trouble.

He had done everything, in short—surely everything! For he had put it in the most sheltered spot he could find—in the self-same corner where he had played at make-believe gardens as a child; and it seemed as if an old dream had suddenly come true. And as to looking well after it,—could a miser have watched his gold with more jealous care?

And no one had interfered; for he had told nobody, partly from some indefinite idea that the nursery gardener had ordered him not; partly because he thought it would be so nice to surprise his mother, some day before the summer was over, by the rich blaze of colour that was to brighten all the place.

The very maid who hung out the clothes in the yard didn't know of it; for to keep the secret, and make the shelter of the tree more complete, he had set up boards across the corner where it was planted, from wall to wall, and no one could see what was there. They looked upon the boards as some idle freak of the idiot mind.

It was the buds that failed first; those buds which ought to have swollen and grown larger day by day. Even his eye, sharpened now by anxious care, could detect that they rather dwindled than increased in size; and, observing this more and more as time went on, he one day summoned courage to walk to the Nursery Gardens, and tell his fears to the giver of the plant.

But he, when he found that all he had ordered had been done, only smiled.

"I tell you again," said he, "and from long experience, there's nothing like bones and hair for bringing roses to perfection. You can't go wrong with them. Give it a little more water or soap-suds. You've perhaps a light soil in your place. Give it more water. The buds will swell fast enough, I'll be bound. Indeed, I fancy you're watching it so closely you can't see true. It's easy enough to do that, I can tell you. The buds are grown, I suspect—though you don't think so. Leave it to itself. Don't fancy anything wrong. It's sure to be right with bones and hair and soap-suds. They're the finest rose-manure in the world."

Hans listened with his mouth open, nodded his head, with a "Thank-you!" at the end, and went away, hoping he had not "seen true." And he did not take the boards down nearly so often afterwards, lest his watching too closely should do harm. But every time he did take them down, he grew more and more unhappy.

The healthy green of the leaves was no longer to be seen; as for the buds, they shrivelled gradually more and more. Growth anywhere there was none. Inch by inch the plant was dying—or Hans thought so, and he rubbed his eyes for further light in vain.

And one day, when the last leaves which remained had crinkled up and turned brown, he sat down on the ground, and wailed, as I have said:—

"What more could I have done for it than I have done?"

The dream of a dream come true at last, was over. The make-believe garden was still the only one he had ever enjoyed. He must go back to it again.

He replaced the boards, for he shrank from the very sight of the dying plant, and sat down on the ground again, though he scarcely knew why.

But presently there was a barking of the dog, and an opening of the door, and a shouting of "Hans!" by his mother. The nursery gardener was passing that way, and had called to admire the roses he expected to see. Hans could not speak, but led the way to the corner of the yard, and, when they were there, he pointed to the boards before he took them down, and exclaimed, trying to smile through his tears:

"I couldn't have sheltered it more, could I? It's never been scorched, or chilled, or blown upon, even. It's had bones, and hair, and water, and all you ordered, and I've looked well after it, and yet it's dead, I know!"

As he spoke, Hans lifted down the boards, and exposed the withered tree.

The nursery gardener stared at it, and then at Hans, in genuine amazement.

"You don't mean to say you've kept it so all the time?" cried he. "Why, what have you been thinking about, man? How could you expect it to live? Why, it's had no light!"

"You said nothing about that," replied Hans, his face distorted with bewilderment and grief. "You said you made roses beautiful with bones, and hair, and soap-suds, and that I should make mine beautiful with them too."

"But not without sunshine," shouted the nursery gardener, quite excited at the idea of such a mistake.

Hans made no answer. He could not utter another word. He sat down on the ground again and hid his face in his hands.

"I must have spoken like a fool," exclaimed the nursery gardener, half to himself. "But who'd have thought of anybody fancying a plant could get on without light? Well, perhaps I ought to have thought though," added he, as his eyes fell on poor Hans' doubled-up figure. Then, laying his hand on the lad's shoulder, it came into his heart to try and explain matters.

"Look up, Hans," said he. "It's not your fault at all—it's mine. There was something I forgot to tell you. I spoke like a fool when I talked of making roses beautiful with manure and things like that, as if they could do it themselves. I didn't mean that. It is God who makes the roses, you know, and He makes them so that they can't do without the light He chooses them to live in, and that's the light from heaven—do you see?"

Here the nursery gardener paused to consider how he must go on, and Hans shuffled a bit, and then looked up at his friend. And his friend saw the light from heaven streaming on that sad, half-intelligent face, with the red eyes straining upwards for comprehension; and he proceeded.

"So they can't do without God's light, let you give them what manure you will. They're only helps, Hans, such things as those."

"A man may help or hinder what God intends, by good or bad management, it's true; but that's all, and that's all I meant. Bones, and hair, and soap-suds are the finest rose-manure in the world, that's true too, and it's a great secret; but they're all nothing—nothing, lad!—without God's secret—the light from heaven. Do you see what I mean, Hans?"

"I'm trying," said Hans.

"Hans," continued the nursery gardener, "it's been my fault, not yours; and you shall have another rose-tree, or we'll save this one yet, for if there's a bit of life left in it, God's light may bring it round. But tell me, now. You are a very good lad, you know, at times—indeed, I fancy always; but no matter, we'll call it at times. What makes you ever good?"

Hans' catechism had been short, but sound; and he answered at once, "God's grace."

"Now that's just it!" shouted the nursery gardener, in delight. "That's just what I meant. And all the schooling, and teaching, and trying in the world won't do without God's grace, will they, Hans?"

Hans nodded his negative assent.

"No, they're only manures and helps," pursued the nursery gardener, "and very good things, no doubt, the same as bones, and hair, and soap-suds for roses, and there's nobody can dispute about them. But all the helps in the world can do nothing without the main thing God chooses them to thrive by, and that's God's grace for a man, and God's light for a plant; and what one is for one, that the other is for the other, and it's my opinion it's the light of Heaven for both."

If Hans did not quite follow the thread of the nursery gardener's argument he must be excused. The nursery gardener understood what he meant himself, and that was something; and Hans added to his small stock of observations the useful truth he had bought so dearly, viz., that plants cannot live without light.

Those who are interested further in his fate will be glad to hear that the nursery gardener soon after turned one side of the old printer's back-yard into a garden, at his own expense, and gave Hans such plants and help, that both mother and son had a few bright flowers of their own the next year to delight their eyes.

But more than this. The poor lad proved so watchful and attentive; so obedient, too, to advice in his own small matters; and the rational occupation to an end seemed so evidently to clear a something from the confusion of his mind, that it struck the nursery gardener one day to trust him with some little employment on his more important premises. And the experiment was not unsuccessful. On the one subject of flowers Hans became not only trustworthy but intelligent.

And so it came to pass, that it was in the nursery garden, among the flowers—his only idea of an earthly paradise—that the poor idiot ended his days. Thence, guileless as the beautiful creatures which surrounded him, and trusting as the Highest Wisdom could have made him, did the spirit, so long pent in an imperfect earthly tabernacle, return to the great Lord of life and light and intelligence, without whom "nothing is strong, nothing is holy."

Gifts

"Now there are diversities of gifts."
—1 COR. xii. 4.

One—two—three—four—five; five neatly-raked kitchen-garden beds, four of them side by side, with a pathway between; the fifth a narrow slip, heading the others, and close to the gravel walk, as it was for succession-crops of mustard and cress, which are often wanted in a hurry for breakfast or tea.

Most people have stood by such beds in their own kitchen-gardens on soft spring mornings and evenings, and looked for the coming up of the seeds which either they or the gardener had sown.

Radishes in one, for instance, and of all three sorts—white-turnip, red-turnip, and long-tailed.

Carrots in another; and this bed had been dug very deep indeed—subsoil digging, as it were; two spades' depth, that the roots might strike freely down.

Onions in another. Beet in the fourth; both the golden and red varieties; while the narrow slip was half mustard and half cress.

Such was the plan here, however; and here, for a time, all the seeds lay sleeping, as it seemed. For, as the long smooth-raked beds stretched out dark and bare under the stars, they betrayed no symptoms of anything going on within.

Nevertheless, there was no sleeping in the case. The little seed-grains were fulfilling the law of their being, each after its kind; the grains, all but their inner germs, decaying; the germs swelling and growing, till they rose out of their cradles, and made their way, through their earthen coverlid, to the light of day.

They did not all come up quite together, of course, nor all quite alike. But as to the time, the gardener had made his arrangements so cleverly, that none was very far behind his neighbour. And as to the difference of shape in the first young leaves, what could it signify? It is true the young mustards were round and thick; the cresses oval and pointed; the carrots mere green threads; the onions sharp little blades; while the beet had an odd, stainy look. But they all woke up to the same life and enjoyment, and were all greeted with friendly welcome, as they appeared, by the dew, and light, and sunshine, and breezes, so necessary to them all, children of one mother, dependent on the same influences to bring them to perfection.

What could put comparisons, and envyings, and heart-burnings into their heads, so filling them either with conceit or melancholy misgivings? As if there was but one way of being right or doing right; as if every creature was not good after its kind, but must needs be good after somebody else's kind, or not be good at all!

It must have been some strolling half-informed grub, one would think, who had not yet come to his full senses, who started such foolish ideas.

It began with an enquiry at first, for no actual unkindness was meant.

"I find I get deeper and deeper into the soil every day," remarked the Carrot. "I shall be I don't know how long, at last. I have been going down regularly, quite straight, for weeks. Then I am tapering off to a long point at the end, in the most beautiful proportions possible. A traveller told me the other day this was perfection and I believe he was right."

(That mischievous vagabond grub, you see!)

"I know what it was to live near the surface in my young days," the Carrot went on; "but never felt solid enjoyment till I struck deeply down, where all is so rich and warm. This is really being firmly established and satisfactory to one's self, though still progressing, I hope, for I don't see why there should be a limit. Pray tell me, neighbours," added he, good-naturedly enough, "how it fares with all the rest of you. I should like to know that your roots are as long, and slim, and orange-coloured as mine; doing as well, in fact, and sinking as far down. I wish us to be all perfect alike. Perfection is the great thing to try for."

"When you are sure you are trying in the right way," sneered a voice from the neighbouring radish bed (the red and white turnip variety were always satirical). "But if the long, slim, orange-roots, striking deep into the earth, are your idea of perfection, I advise you to begin life over again. Dear me! I wish you had consulted us before. Why, we stopped going down long ago, and have been spreading out sideways and all ways, into stout, round solid balls ever since, close white flesh throughout, inside; and not orange, but red without."

"White, he means," shouted another.

"Red I call it," repeated the first. "But no matter; certainly not orange!"

And "Certainly not orange!" cried they all.

"So," continued the first speaker, "we are quite concerned to hear you ramble on about growing longer and longer, and strongly advise you to keep your own counsel, and not mention it to any one else. We are friends, you know, and can be trusted; but you really must leave off wasting your powers and energy in the dark inside of the ground, out of everybody's sight and knowledge. Come to the surface, and make the most of it, as we do, and then you'll be a credit to your friends. Never mind what travellers say. They've nothing else to do but to walk about and talk, and they tell us we are perfection too. Don't trust to them, but to what we tell you now, and alter your course at once. Roll yourself up into a firm round ball as fast as you can. You won't find it hard if you once begin. You have only to—"

"Let me put in a word first," interrupted one of the long-tailed Radishes in the same bed; "for it is of no use to go out of one extreme into another, which you are on the high road to do if you are disposed to take Mr. Roundhead's advice; who, by the way, ought to be ashamed of forcing his very peculiar views upon his neighbours. Just look at us. We always strike moderately down, so we know it's the right thing to do, and that solid round balls are the most unnatural and useless things in the world. But, on the other hand, my dear friend, we have learnt where to stop, and a great secret it is, but one I fear you know nothing about at present; so the sooner you make yourself acquainted with it the better. There's a limit to everything but folly—even to striking deep into the soil. And as to the soil being better so very far down, nobody can believe it; for why should it be? The great art is to make the most of what is at hand, as we do. Time enough to go into the depths when you have used up what is so much easier got at. The man who gathered some of us yesterday called out, 'These are just right.' So I leave you to judge whether some other people we know of must not be wrong."

"You rather overwhelm me, I own," mused the Carrot; "though it's remarkable you counsellors should not agree among yourselves. Is it possible, however, that I have been making a great mistake all my life? What lost time to look back upon! Yet a ball; no, no, not a ball! I don't think I could grow into a solid round ball were I to try for ever!"

"Not having tried, how can you tell?" whispered the Turnip-Radish persuasively. "But you never will if you listen to our old-fashioned friend next door, who has been halting between two opinions all his life:—will neither make an honest fat lump of it, as I do, nor plunge down and taper with you. But nothing can be done without an effort; certainly no change."

"That is true," murmured the Carrot, rather sadly; "but I am too old for further efforts myself. Mistake or no mistake, my fate is fixed. I am too far down to get up again, that's certain; but some of the young ones may try. Do you hear, dears? Some of you stop short, if you can, and grow out sideways and all ways, into stout, round, solid balls."

"Oh, nonsense about round balls!" cried the long-tailed Radish in disgust; "what will the world come to, if this folly goes on! Listen to me, youngsters, I beg. Go to a moderate depth, and be content; and if you want something to do, throw out a few fibres for amusement. You're firm enough without them, I know, but the employment will pass away time."

"There are strange delusions abroad just now," remarked the Onions to each other; "do you hear all this talk about shape and way of growth? and everybody in the dark on the subject, though they seem to be quite unconscious of the fact themselves. That fellow chattered about solid balls, as if there was no such thing as bulbs, growing layer upon layer, and coat over coat, at all. Of course the very long orange gentleman, with his tapering root, is the most wrong of the whole party; but I doubt if Mr. Roundhead is much wiser when he speaks of close white flesh inside, and red (of all ridiculous nonsense) without. Where are their flaky skins, I should like to know? Who is ever to peel them, I wonder? Poor things! I can't think how they got into such ways. How tough and obstinate they must be! I wish we lived nearer. We would teach them a little better than that and show them what to do."

"I have lived near you long enough," grumbled a deep-red Beet in the next bed; "and you have never taught me; neither shall you, if I can help it. A pretty instructor you would be, who think it ridiculous to be red! I suppose you can't grow red yourself, and so abuse the colour out of spite. Now I flatter myself I am red inside as well as out, so I suppose I am more ridiculous than your friend who contrives to keep himself white within, according to his own account; but I doubt the fact. There, there! it is a folly to be angry; so I say no more, except this: get red as fast as you can. You live in the same soil that I do, and ought to be able."

"Oh, don't call it red!" exclaimed a golden Beet, who was of a gentle turn of mind; "it is but a pale tint after all, and surely rather amber than red; and perhaps that was what the long-tailed orange gentleman meant."

"Perhaps it was; for perhaps he calls red orange, as you call it amber," answered the redder Beet; "anyhow he has rather more sense than our neighbour here, with his layer upon layer, and coat over coat, and flaky skin over all. Think of wasting time in such fiddle-faddle proceedings! Grow a good honest fleshy substance, and have done with it, and let people see you know what life is capable of. I always look at results. It is something to get such a body as I do out of the surrounding soil. That is living to some purpose, I consider. Nobody makes more of their opportunities than I do, I flatter myself, or has more to show for their pains; and a great future must be in store for me."

"Do you hear them? oh! do you hear them?" whispered the Cress to her neighbour the Mustard (there had been several crops, and this was one of the last); "do you hear how they all talk together of their growth, and their roots, and their bulbs, and size, and colour, and shape? It makes me quite unhappy, for I am doing nothing like that myself—nothing, nothing, though I live in the same soil! What is to be done? What do you do? Do you grow great white solid balls, or long, orange tapering roots, or thick red flesh, or bulbs with layer upon layer, and coat over coat? Some of them talked of just throwing out a few fibres as a mere amusement to pass away time; and this is all I ever do for business. There will never be a great future in store for me. Do speak to me, but whisper what you say, for I shame to be heard or thought of."

"I grow only fibres too," groaned the Mustard in reply; "but I would spread every way and all ways if I could—downwards and upwards, and sideways and all ways, like the rest. I wish I had never been sown. Better never sown and grown, than sown and grown to such trifling purpose! We are wretched indeed. But there must be injustice somewhere. The soil must give them what it refuses to us."

"Or we are weak and helpless, and cannot take in what it offers," suggested the Cress. "Alas! that we should have been sown only to be useless and unhappy!"

And they wept the evening through. But they alone were not unhappy. The Carrot had become uneasy, and could follow his natural tastes no longer in comfort, for thinking that he ought to be a solid round ball, white inside, and red without. The Onion had sore misgivings that the Beet might be right after all, and a good honest mass of red flesh be more worth labouring for, than the pale coat-within-coat growth in which he had indulged. It did seem a waste of trouble, a fiddle-faddle plan of life, he feared. Perhaps he had not gone down far enough in the soil. Some one talked of growing fibres for amusement—he had certainly not come to that; they were necessary to his support; he couldn't hold fast without them. Other people were more independent than he was, then; perhaps wiser,—alas!

And yet the Beet himself was not quite easy; for talk as he would, what he had called fiddle-faddle seemed ingenious when he thought it over, and he would like to have persuaded himself that he grew layer upon layer too. But it wouldn't do.

Perhaps, in fact, the bold little Turnip-Radishes alone, from their solid, substantial growth, were the only ones free from misgivings, and believed that everybody ought to do as they did themselves.

What a disturbance there was, to be sure! And it got worse and worse, and they called on the winds and fleeting clouds, the sun, and moon, and stars above their heads, to stay their course awhile, and declare who was right and who was wrong; who was using, who abusing his gifts and powers; who was making most, who least, of the life and opportunities they all enjoyed; whose system was the one the rest must all strive to follow—the one only right.

But they called and asked in vain; till one evening, the clouds which had been gathering over the garden for days began to come down in rain, and sank swiftly into the ground, where it had been needed for long. Whereupon there was a general cry, "Here comes a messenger; now we shall hear!" as if they thought no one could have any business in the world but to settle their disputes.

So out came all the old enquiries again:—who was right—who was wrong—who had got hold of the true secret? But the Cress made no enquiry at all, only shook with fright under the rain; for, thought she, the hour of my shame and degradation is come; poor useless creature that I am, I shall never more hold up my head!

As to the Carrot, into whose well-dug bed the rain found easiest entrance, and sank deepest, he held forth in most eloquent style upon the whole affair;—how it was started, and what he had said; how much he had once hoped; how much he now feared.

Now, the Rain-drops did not care to answer in a hurry; but as they came dropping gently down, they murmured, "Peace, peace, peace!" all over the beds. And truly they seemed to bring peace with them as they fell, so that a calm sank all around, and then the murmur proceeded:—"Poor little atoms in a boundless kingdom—each one of you bearing a part towards its fulness of perfection, each one of you endowed with gifts and powers especially your own, each one of you good after its kind—how came these cruel misgivings and heart-burnings among you? Are the tops of the mountains wrong because they cannot grow corn like valleys? Are the valleys wrong because they cannot soar into the skies? Does the brook flow in vain because it cannot spread out like the sea? Is the sea only right because its waters only are salt? Each good after its kind, each bearing a part in the full perfection of the kingdom which is boundless, the plan which is harmony—peace, peace, peace, upon all!"

And peace seemed to fall more soothingly than ever upon the ground as the shower continued to descend.

"How much more, then," resumed the murmur, "among you, to whose inner natures gifts and powers are given, each different from each; each good in its kind; each, if rightly carried out, doing service in that kingdom, which needs for its full perfection, that there shall be mountains to rise into the skies, valleys to lie low at their feet; some natures to go deep into the soil, others to rejoice on its surface; some to lie lightly upon the earth, as if scarcely claiming a home, others to grasp at it by wide-spread roots, and stretch out branches to the rivers; all good in their kind, all bearing a part in the glory of that universe whose children are countless as their natures are various—none useless, none in vain.

"Upon one, then, upon all—each wanted, each useful, each good after its kind—peace, peace, peace, peace, peace!" . . .

The murmur subsided to a whisper, the whisper into silence; and by the time the moon-shadows lay upon the garden there was peace everywhere.

Nor was it broken again; for henceforth even the Cress held up her head—she, also, good after her kind.

Only once or twice that year, when the Carrots were gathered, there came up the strangest growths—thick, distorted lumps, that had never struck properly down.

The gardener wondered, and was vexed, for he prided himself on the digging of the carrot-bed. "Anything that had had any sense might have gone down into it, he was sure," he said. And he was not far wrong; but you see the Carrot had had no sense when he began to speculate, and tried to be something he was not intended to be.

Yet the poor clumsy thing was not quite useless after all. For, just as the gardener was about to fling it angrily away, he recollected that the cook might use it for soup, though it could not be served up at table—such a shape as it was! . . .

And this was exactly what she did.

Night and Day

"The city had no need of the sun, neither of the moon to shine in it; for the glory of God did lighten it, and the Lamb is the light thereof."
—REV. xxi. 23.

In old times, long long ago, when Night and Day were young and foolish, and had not discovered how necessary they were to each other's happiness and well-being, they chased each other round the world in a state of angry disdain; each thinking that he alone was doing good, and that therefore the other, so totally unlike himself in all respects, must be doing harm, and ought to be got rid of, altogether, if possible.

Old northern tales say that they rode, each of them in a car with a horse to it; but the horse of Night had a frosty mane, while that of Day had a shiny one. Moreover, foam fell from Frosty-mane's bit as he went along, which dropped on the earth as dew, and Shiny-mane's mane was so radiant that it scattered light through the air at every step.

And thus they drove on, bringing darkness and light over the earth in turn—each pursuing and pursued; but knowing so little of this simple fact, that one of their chief causes of dispute was, which was going first. For of course if they had been able to settle that, it would have been known which was the more important of the two. But as they drove in a circle the point could not be decided, since what was first on one side was sure to be last on the other; as anybody may see who tries to draw their journey.

They never gave this a thought, however, and there were no school-masters about just then to teach them. So round and round the world they went, without even knowing that it was round, still less that there is no such thing as first and last in a circle. And they never succeeded in overtaking, so as to pass each other, though they sometimes came up very close, and then there was twilight.

Of the two, one grumbled and the other scolded the more, and it is easy to guess which did which. Night was gloomy by nature, especially when clouds hid the moon and stars, so her complaints took a serious, melancholy tone. She was really broken-hearted at the exhaustion produced all over the world by the labours and pleasures which were carried on under the light of day, and used to receive the earth back as if it was a sick child and she a nurse, who had a right to be angry with what had been done to it.

Day, on the contrary, was amazingly cheerful, particularly when the sun shone; never troubled his head about what was to happen when his fun was over: on the contrary, thought his fun ought to last for ever because it was pleasant, was quite vexed when it was put a stop to, and had no scruple in railing at his rival; whose only object, as it seemed to him, was to overshadow and put an end to all the happiness that was to be found.

"Cruel Night," he exclaimed, "what a life you lead me! How you thwart me at every turn! What trouble I have to take to keep your mischief in check. Look at the mists and shadows I must drive on one side before I can make the world bright with my beautiful light! And no sooner have I done so than I feel your cold unwholesome breath trying to come up to me behind! But you shall never overtake me if I can help it: though I know that is what you want. You want to throw your hateful black shadow over my bright and pleasant world."

"I doing mischief which you have to keep in check!" groaned Night, quite confused by the accusation. "I, whose whole time is spent in trying to repair the mischief other people do: your mischief, in fact, you wasteful consumer of life and power! Every twelve hours I get back from you a half worn-out world, and this I am expected to restore and make as good as new again, but how is it possible? Something I can do, I know. Some wear and tear I can renew and refresh, but some, alas! I cannot; and thus creep in destruction and death."

"Hear her," cried Day, in contempt, "taunting me with the damage I do, and the death and destruction I cause! I the life-giver, at whose touch the whole world awakes which else might lie asleep for ever. She, the grim likeness of the death she talks about, and bringing death's twin sister in her bosom."

"You are Day the destroyer. I Night, the restorer," persisted Night, evading the argument.

"I am Day the life-giver, you Night the desolator," replied Day, bitterly.

"I am Night the restorer, you Day the destroyer," repeated Night.

"You are to me what death is to life," shouted Day.

"Then death is a restorer as I am," exclaimed Night.

And so they went on, like all other ignorant and obstinate arguers; each full of his own one idea, and taking no heed of what the other might say. How could the truth be got at by such means? Of course it could not, and of course, therefore, they persisted in their rudeness. And there were certain seasons particularly when they became more impertinent to each other than ever.

For instance, whenever it was summer, Day's horse, Shiny-mane, got so strong and frisky that Night had much ado to keep her place at all, so closely was she pressed in the chase. Indeed, sometimes there was so little of her to be seen that people might have doubted whether she had passed by at all, had it not been for the dew Frosty-mane scattered, and which those saw who got up early enough in the morning.

Oh, the boasting of Day at these times! And really he believed what he said. He really thought it would be the greatest possible blessing if he were to go on for ever, and there were to be no Night. Perhaps he had the excuse of having heard a whisper of some old tradition to that effect: but the principal cause of the mistake was, that he thought too much about himself, and too little about his neighbour.

"Fortunate world," cried he; "it must be clear to every one, now who it is that brings blessings, and does good to you and your inhabitants. Good old earth, you become more and more lovely and fruitful, the more and more I shorten the hours of Night and lengthen my own. We can do tolerably well without her restoring power it would seem! If we could be rid of her altogether, therefore, what a Paradise there would be! Then the foliage, the flowers, the fruits, the precious crops of this my special season would last forever. Would that it could remain uninterrupted!"

"He is praying for a curse. Were it granted no life could exist," murmured Night; and Frosty-mane's dew fell in tears as she spoke. No one heard her, however, but the dew was very acceptable, for the weather was very hot.

And she had her revenge; for when it was summer on one side the globe it was winter on the other; and then it was her turn to boast, as it was in winter that Frosty-mane came out in all his glory; every now and then running his car so nearly side by side with that of Day, that he squeezed him up into the smallest possible compass, besides putting out half his light.

On which Night kept up a sort of murmuring triumph, "Good, good, very good: this is something like rest at last; now worn-out Nature is recruiting herself to some purpose. Now weary muscles may gather strength instead of giving it out. Now strained eyes may recover brightness, and worn brains energy. Now all the secret forces of Nature are at work, and exhaustion is being repaired on every side. Now trees and plants may keep their gases for themselves, and earth hold her own. Now waste and consumption cease, for the wear and tear of life have stopped. Ah, if it could but cease for ever! Then the world would be renewed, indeed, and giant races of man and beast and plant arise!"

"But never glow with the light of active life, or be seen but in the pale unmeaning moonlight," sneered the mortified Day, but he struggled in vain to make himself heard. The truth is he was in the background just then, and nobody cared to listen. Yet he made his presence known from time to time at mid-day, by the light of Shiny-mane's hair. Nothing could quite put that out, even in winter when the weather was fine; and sometimes it shone over the ice and snow so brightly that they glittered like diamonds or might almost have been taken for fireworks.

And so things went on till a check came, and it came in a very odd way. It is not always very easy to tell the exact causes of change even in one's own mind, much less in other people's, so I do not pretend to trace the whole process out in this case.

But Night and Day did grow wiser as time went on, for, as every one knows, there is no squabbling or boasting going on between them now. On the contrary, they glide after each other as gently and sweetly as possible, without any kicking of horses or rumbling of chariot wheels. And one may conclude that after the first flush of feeling cooled down, they were better able to look round them and judge dispassionately of each other.

And, lo and behold! they discovered at last that there were just two portions of the globe where each had in turn his own way as nearly as possible for six whole months at a time, viz. at the Poles: and that yet, nevertheless, the brilliant consequences which they had insisted would occur under these circumstances, never took place. On the contrary, those were the dreariest and most desolate portions of the whole globe,—barren wastes of ice and rock, where both animal and vegetable life were at the lowest possible ebb.

Nothing could be more mortifying, it must be owned. In vain did Shiny-mane drive round and round that frozen horizon with a light that was never interrupted: where was the promised Paradise which was to follow?—the foliage, the flowers, the fruits, the precious crops which should have adorned this unchecked reign of Day, where were they?

The dove would have sought in vain here for even a shrub on which to rest her foot. Scarcely a wandering seagull ever disturbed the death-like stillness of the air.

Day, the life-giver, looked down upon a kingdom without life! What wonder if he began at last to distrust himself! What wonder if he went on to suspect that there might be some truth in what Night had said after all! That she might in some way or other be Night the restorer; in some way, however mysterious and unaccountable, be necessary to his own prosperity.

—And it was the same with Night, when her turn came round. In vain did Frosty-mane distil his dews. They were useful—at least Night thought so—everywhere else; but here, what did they avail? Here was the unbroken rest which was to recruit and refresh all Nature: now her secret powers might work as they pleased: there was no waste of power now either from labour or heat, or any other destructive cause: but where were the giant races of man and beast and plant that were to arise in consequence? The wear and tear of life had stopped, but what was the Earth advantaged?

Night, the restorer, ruled, but over a kingdom where there was nothing to restore! Well might tears mingle with her dews. Well might she call to the morning stars to bring back that Day whom once she had dreaded as a rival, but now longed for as a friend. Day the life-giver, he had called himself, and Day the life-giver perhaps he was. Certainly without him she could do nothing; at any rate here, where he was not, the whole world was a blank!

They had made a terrible mistake, that was clear; and if they did not at first see that there must be other and more important powers at work, besides theirs, or the good old earth would not be what it is in most places, they must be excused. People cannot grow quite wise all at once, and they had made a very good beginning by learning to distrust themselves; that being always the first step towards doing justice to a neighbour.

"I called you Day the destroyer, bright and beautiful friend," murmured Night, in her softest tones; "you who bring light over my shadows, and make my good deeds known to all men. Day, the life-giver, forgive me, and return at the seasons appointed. Touch the earth with your glory from time to time, lest all things perish from its face, and it and I are forgotten together."

"But I mistook your friendly shadow for that of death," answered Day, with his sweetest smile, though tears trembled in his eyes as he thought of the injustice, causing the brightest of rainbows to span the landscape below: "and that was a thousand times worse! You, in whose silence and rest the very fountains of life are renewed. Ah, while earth remains what it is, an everlasting day—a day without night—would be destruction! Dear friend, forgive me, and ever and ever return."

"There is nothing to forgive," whispered Night, as she came round once more. "And death also may restore as I do," added she tenderly; for the harvest moon was shining upon long fields of golden corn, some waving still, some gathered into sheaves; and she felt particularly hopeful about everything.

"Anyhow we are friends—loving, helpful friends," sang Day.

"Friends—comforting and abiding friends," echoed Night, in return, as the weary world sank on her bosom; eyes closing, limbs relaxing, and flowers folding, as if the angel of rest had come down from heaven.

And friends they were and remain, though long ages have passed away since the time the old northern tales tell of; and though now the wise men will not allow that Night and Day drive round the world in cars with horses to them. Well, perhaps they don't.

Perhaps it is really true that the earth is a dark ball, hanging in the open space which we call the firmament of heaven, moving slowly round the shining sun, but spinning like a top all the time itself, so that first one side and then the other faces the brightness; and thus there is a constant change from light to darkness and darkness to light going on all over the world; and this makes Day and Night.

But no matter which way the changes come. Night and Day are the work of the Lord; and, like all the other "works of the Lord" which the three children in the fiery furnace called upon to praise Him, have a voice, and say many things worth listening to, especially now that they are no longer young and foolish.

And from time to time, according as we keep our ears open or shut, little streams of melody do float round us from the natural world, as musical sounds break out from the strings of an old-fashioned Æolian harp when the wind blows over it, or sweep along the wires of the electric telegraph on breezy days. Listen only, and you will hear. And which speaks you can surely guess, for they praise each other now and not themselves. One sings—

"Dear Night, whom once I dreaded as the dark end of life and enjoyment. Dear Night, whom now I know as the forerunner of life renewed. Welcome, blessed restorer; take our worn-out child to your bosom. Drop over her striving and straining your mantle of repose. All her day-labourers grow weary, for a portion of life goes from them, in the toil of limb and of muscle, in the working of eye and of brain; in all the changes that circle round an ever-changing world. Restore what thou canst and mayst, let the rest remain in hope; for the mercy thou bringest now, foreshadows a greater in store. Oh, type of the mighty change which must one day pass upon all; of the deep mysterious rest in which all things shall be renewed; of the needful, hopeful death which quickens unto life! Dear Night, my sister and friend, the twilight shades approach, and I see in thankful peace your darker shadows beyond."

And the other answers in turn.

"Dark and secret my mission; men call me Night the gloomy; but I hold in my bosom the germs of a glory full of hope; hiddenly working within, till thou, the life-giver, returnest, to break through the mists and shadows, and touch my nurslings with light. So, at the first creation, at the touch of the first young dawn, lo! gleams of life universal were lit all over the world, and Nature, amazed, awoke in songs of thanksgiving and joy.

"So come, then, Day the life-giver, ever and ever reviving the slumbering germs I nourish, the hidden life I feel. Welcome for this, but thrice welcome as type of a dayspring eternal, that shall dawn at last on the night of sin and sorrow and death; when, our secret missions accomplished, our secret workings completed, thou and I, oh, life-giving Day, shall merge our blessings in one:—when the light that never wastes, and the life that never wearies, shall be one with the rest eternal, that remaineth evermore!"

Kicking

"Rebellion is as the sin of witchcraft."
—I SAM. xv. 23.

Three years of complete liberty, and then to have to learn in three short weeks to submit entirely to the will of other people!

This sounds a hard plan of education, and perhaps is not the very best one possible. Still, thousands of young colts have turned into good horses upon it; and if there is to be a reform, it must come from above, not from below. Reforms from below savour of rebellion, and that is sure to lead to a reaction the wrong way again.

Yet people ought not to blind themselves—those above, I mean, any more than those below. Every man, therefore, ought to sit from time to time in his neighbour's chair, and look with his neighbour's eyes, from his neighbour's position, at what he himself is about. It is wonderful how much wiser, as well as kinder, people grow if they do this.

And among a man's neighbours he should not be ashamed to reckon the creatures he collects round him for his own convenience and amusement, and calls his "domestic animals." Why "domestic," but that he has taken them from their own natural homes, and brought them to his? And if so, surely it is not too much to ask that he should give them, each in his degree, the comforts of a home-citizenship, in return for the duties he exacts. If he does this honestly, a few errors of judgment on his part will not matter more than a few errors of conduct on theirs; for imperfection has not only to be struggled against, but borne in this world.

Sitting in neighbour Firefly the spirited young chestnut colt's chair, then, it is but fair to own that he may well have felt it queer, after three years' luxury of doing as he liked in large grassy pastures, to find himself suddenly cooped up in a small square stuffy place, ceiled in instead of open to the air, and surrounded by walls, to one particular part of which he was fastened by a horrible contrivance that went round his head and neck, and gave him a most unpleasant pull whenever he tried to get away.

But yesterday he was free as the wind, so far as the hedges extended—could gallop from one to the other while his breath lasted; might snort at the passengers in the road which skirted the field as much as he pleased; throw out his legs at everything and everybody; kick, plunge, bound, jump, till he was tired; whinny at his companions, whether he had anything worth saying or not; and all this at will: while now—but the contrast is too painful to dwell upon, for Firefly was now in a horse-breaker's stable, with a halter round his neck.

He had one consolation, however, and it is not a small one to most people—indeed it ought always to be a matter of thankfulness to all—he was extremely well fed. It is true the very delicious grain he had now been champing at three separate meals to his heart's content, with his nose bent over the manger, had been very dearly purchased by the loss of his freedom the morning before. The wild driving he had undergone from the field to the stable-yard, with the treacherous capture at the end, still rankled in his mind, and the cruel outrage to his young heart's nervous shyness, when hands of violent men overcame him, and the fatal noose was slipped over his head, was not to be forgotten. Still taste is taste; the food remained delicious all the same, and he was so young, he could enjoy the present, irrespective of the past or future.

But all feeds of corn come to an end at last; and at the end of the first he began to fidget, after the second he grew angrily impatient, and when he had swallowed the third, he became what is called (archaically) rampageous, for in point of fact the good corn had begun to warm his blood. It was very high living compared to the cold grass he had been used to.

Now, as was natural, one of the first things he did was to call out for his old companions of the field, and this he did in colt's fashion, of course; but what colt's fashion really is will not be known till men become good linguists, and have learnt other languages besides those of their own race.

At present they are miserably backward in that branch of learning, and have no idea even of what flies talk about, though they hear them murmuring away in the air, as soon as they themselves awake every summer morning, and for nearly all day after.

Well, in colt's fashion Firefly shouted for his companions, and after two or three attempts, each of them louder than the one before, must have made himself heard; for at last he was answered, though from what seemed a great distance, so smothered were the sounds. But this was only because they came through stone walls. In point of fact, his young friends, Whitefoot and Silverstar by name, were very near—namely, in the very next adjoining stable—both of them captives like himself; both of them with halters round their necks, one in one stall, one in another.

Conversation was difficult under such circumstances, and could not be carried on for long. What they did say, when they discovered they were near each other, amounted to about this:—

"So you are somewhere hereabouts, too, Whitefoot and Silverstar. Why don't you come where I am? Where are you?"

"We don't know where we are. Where are you? Why don't you come to us?"

"Because something twitches my head if I try to move away: so I can't."

"That's just what happens to us; so we can't."

"It's abominable!"

"It's very distressing."

"I wonder what it means! I am very angry."

"We wonder too, but it can't be helped."

Here the dialogue ended, for the colts were not the only inhabitants of the two stables. In the one, with Whitefoot and Silverstar, was a good-tempered, middle-aged, Welsh pony, known all over the country-side as good old Taffy. In the other, with Firefly, was an old, half-bred white Arabian mare, whose mother had been brought from the East.

Old people who talk to young ones should think of the young ones more than themselves. If they want to gossip and grumble, and let off vexed feelings, let them do it to each other. Life is very trying sometimes as age comes on, and those of the same age can understand the feelings of the age, and make allowance for the groanings of the natural man. But young creatures may easily be led away by a few sad or passionate words into believing all sorts of nonsense. I say, then, let old people unburden their personal feelings to each other, but never talk anything but useful sense, or pleasant nonsense, to a child.

Had the old white mare in the stable thought of this, it would have been better for Firefly—perhaps, at least, he would not have had the same encouragement to turn out unmanageable which she now gave him. For no sooner had he uttered the words, "I wonder what it means! I am very angry," to his companion next door, than she shook her own halter till the rattle roused his attention, and then observed, in a tone of melancholy which was of itself quite impressive:—"I can tell you what it means, but I am afraid when you know you will not be less angry than now, but rather more."

Firefly's quick blood ran quicker at the startling announcement.

"Oh, dear, what makes you say so? Who can you be?" cried he in excitement.

"One who ought to know something, if age and experience can instruct," answered the sorrowful old mare, adding in a lower tone still, "or if unusual opportunities in early life have not been lost upon her."

"I am almost afraid of hearing, yet suspense is intolerable," cried Firefly. "Where am I? What is going to happen?"

"You are a prisoner, at the mercy of those who shut you up," answered the old mare, to whose monotonous existence the power of lashing a young colt up to indignation was rather an amusing novelty. "It is the first time this has happened to you, I suppose?"

"It is the first time I was ever made fast in this way," groaned Firefly. "If I was ever in an enclosure before, it was loose by my mother's side. My memory is confused so far back."

"I, too, had a mother once," murmured the old mare, Egeria; and her grief in thinking how long ago made her pause.

"Tell me about her," exclaimed Firefly; "what became of her? I want to know."

"What a tone you speak in," answered Egeria. "You want to know! You forget you are a prisoner, and must learn to want nothing but what is given you."

"I shall never learn that," cried he; "and why am I a prisoner? tell me that."

"Because the people you belong to want to make you useful—useful to them, that is."

"And why must I be useful to them? Why may I not please myself as I have done before? What are they to me?"

"Ask them," said Egeria coldly. "They will tell you—masters, superiors."

"You provoke me," cried Firefly, stamping into the straw at his feet. "Tell me why I am here, as you promised. My former history is short enough, as you shall hear. I—"

"Spare yourself the trouble," interrupted Egeria. "Our histories in this country are all alike. We are left to ourselves for nearly three years, and are taught nothing; then our superiors get hold of us, by fright and force, and in three weeks make us learn everything they want."

"And then?" gasped Firefly.

"And then it depends upon the people into whose hands one falls, whether one is well or ill-used."

"And you have borne all this in patience?" asked Firefly.

"I had no heart to act otherwise," sighed Egeria. "I felt no spirit to resist."

"But I feel plenty of spirit, and shall resist," cried the young chestnut, straining against the halter as hard as he could bear, and dashing his legs against the sides of the stall, first on one side, then on the other.

"But what can you do?" whined Egeria, a little startled by his violence.

"Do?" shouted Firefly; "why, I shall kick, kick, kick!" And each time he uttered the words he struck out against the wooden partition between the stalls. Egeria began to be alarmed.

"I do not advise it," she said; "I assure you it will do no good. You had better bear it all as well as you can."

"Oh, that is all very well for those who can receive it, old lady," exclaimed Firefly: "I can't. I can't stand injustice; and what's more, I won't. Why, my blood is boiling already. Only to think of the way they drove us along before they got us here. Of course, if I had known, I should never have left the field. And the still worse fright those men gave me when they all laid hold of me and threw this horrible thing over my head! It's all treachery and injustice from beginning to end."

"Ah! if we were but in my mother's country!" sighed Egeria.

"Why, what then?" enquired Firefly.

"Oh, my poor young friend, I'm afraid it will do more harm than good to tell you," said Egeria, "yet, if you wish it so very much, I hardly know how to refuse."

The old goose, to consent to tell what she felt might do harm! But she was vain of knowing more than other people on the subject, which she really did. Besides which, she wanted to stop Firefly's kicking and plunging, by holding his attention. So said she—

"The people there—in the East, I mean—treat young colts quite differently from the people here. As soon as ever they can leave their mothers, they are brought among the tents, where the men, women, and children live, and the women take care of them, and feed them, and pet them. So they get used to their masters from the first, and there is not the fright and horror and startling change to go through which we suffer so much from at the end of our first three years; and so the halter, and teaching, and all that sort of thing, come much easier—though, of course, restraint is restraint everywhere. But, for pity's sake, don't begin to kick again," concluded Egeria, interrupting herself at the sound of renewed struggles on Firefly's part. "I have been telling you my mother's story to keep you quiet."

"Quiet!" shouted the miserable colt. "I won't be quiet, to please anybody. How can I be quiet, when I want to get away from this savage country, and go to that other one—that East you talk of—where colts are properly managed?"

"But my dear young friend, consider—it's too late," expostulated Egeria. "You can't begin life over again. You really mustn't let your feelings run away with you in this foolish way. People here don't mean badly, altogether. They are tolerably kind, on the whole; at least, some of them are. They feed you well, as you see; and after you have learnt what they teach, you will be glad, though you won't like it while it's going on."

"Then it shan't go on!" shouted Firefly. "They shan't teach me! I won't learn! I won't have their food, or their kindness! If they had brought me up properly, I could have submitted as well as anybody; but they have been unjust, and now I won't! I'll do something—I'll go to the East; and if I can't go to the East, I'll kick!"

"Oh, hush!—do, pray, hush!" said Egeria, who, to do her justice, had merely wanted to excite a sympathetic grumble, not to rouse a storm. "You go much too far, I assure you."

"You say that, because you have no spirit, you poor old creature!" exclaimed Firefly. "You know you haven't—you said so yourself just now; but that's no rule for me."

"If I have not much spirit," remarked Egeria, "I may have some sense, and I want you to have some too. You can't get away, to begin with—so the East is out of the question; and you cannot resist these people to any purpose—so, take my advice, submit and have done with it. I can tell you from long experience, that kicking is never of any use."

"Then I shall go on kicking, out of spite, because it's of no use," cried Firefly; and as he announced this grand resolution, he broke out all over into a profuse sweat from excitement.

At which moment the stable-door opened, and the horsebreaker stepped in, just to have a look at the colt; and after doing so, and observing his irritable and uneasy condition, said he to himself, "I shall have a good deal of trouble with this one, I'm afraid."

Now, in saying this, he was making a sort of comparison between Firefly and the other two; for he had just been in the next stable, and seen Whitefoot and Silverstar unusually placid and quiet—for fresh-caught colts, that is to say; nobody expects from a kitten the gravity of a cat. But what wonder? Besides that they were greys, and therefore easier-tempered by nature than was to be expected from a chestnut (for in horses, colour and disposition are apt to go together), they had been hearing nothing but good advice ever since they were shut up—and, what is more, they had actually been attending to it!

But then, good old Taffy gave his good advice in such a very pleasant way! "My dear friends," cried he, when he heard them plunging about in their stalls at first, "I do feel so sorry for you—so very, very sorry—because I know so well what you suffer. Just the same was done with me when I was your age."

"Oh, how did you bear it?" asked the colts.

"Well, well, I was very impatient just at the beginning," answered Taffy; "for my Welsh blood made me chafe at the confinement, and I was alone, and had nobody to explain the meaning of it all to me, so it was hard work; and this makes me particularly glad to be here just now to help you. I can tell you a great deal that will comfort you, and plenty more that will surprise and amuse you very much. There are two sides to everything, even to things that vex one, I assure you! But, quiet!—quiet! dear friends, I do beg," continued he, as he heard more plunging and shaking of halters, "or I shall not be able to say another word!"

"We will be quiet," cried the colts, for they liked the idea of being surprised and amused, as who does not?

Then Taffy told them they were not brought here to be teased to death, as they had perhaps supposed, but to prepare them for being taught a thousand nice things which they would never be able to do if they were not taught, and which it was immensely jolly to be able to do, when the teaching was once over; and he proceeded to hold forth on the pleasures of trotting, cantering, and galloping over the country, with a good feed of corn, a comfortable stable, and a valet to rub one down at the end; as also the delightful excitements of racing and hunting, which even he had enjoyed, though only as a looker on; but he added that they couldn't have a share in all this, without first learning to obey their masters, and love them a little bit too.

Whereupon both colts shuddered all over, for the fright of the men who had shut them up was very great, and love seemed perfectly impossible.

"Ah! you can't bear the thought of this, I see," cried Taffy. "Well, of course, if it could be, one would like to have no master but oneself—eh, my friends?"

To which both Whitefoot and Silverstar agreed, with a whinny of satisfaction.

"But what is the use of fretting oneself, by wishing for what can't be," pursued Taffy. "These men and women are, though I don't know how, or why, our masters and superiors, and I know from my own experience, that we are happiest when we submit to their wishes with a good grace; when we struggle and resist we are miserable."

"But suppose they wish something cruel and unjust?" sighed Silverstar.

"But who is to decide what is so?" asked Taffy in return. "Many things seem so that are not; your being here against your will for instance—you will be so glad about it by and by, when the teaching is finished."

"It is comfortable to hear that," murmured Silverstar. "Is the teaching itself very unpleasant?" asked Whitefoot.

"Very," cried Taffy at once, at the mere recollection of it, and the colts shuddered again. "But here I am," he continued, "none the worse, and all the better, and as happy as possible, with a man or woman, or a little child on my back three or four times a week, and a pet with all the family. Oh! you have no notion how good-natured these men very often are—bringing one tit-bits both in the stable and field—bread, or apples, or carrots, or clover, which one takes out of their hands. But for pity's sake don't begin kicking again," cried he, as he heard them flinging wildly about, at the notion of men coming so near. "Why, you surely wouldn't kick at kindness? You must meet it halfway, when it's offered, you foolish fellows, or you may live to want it before you die! But, don't alarm yourselves! You won't be able to be on these intimate terms with masters and superiors, till you've learnt to be well-mannered and obedient. But my experience tells me they are kind when we are good; and where they seem otherwise, I try to believe it is because we don't understand the meaning of what they are doing;—with superiors one can't expect that one should."

A word spoken in season, how good it is! The colts grew calmer and calmer as Taffy went on, and when, in conclusion, he told them a story about a good-natured lady, who used to bring him handfuls of oats in reward of a pretty trick he learnt of opening the stable door with his nose, they half began to believe that these men and women were not, after all, such dreadful creatures as they had supposed.

And as it was just then that the horsebreaker entered the stable to look at them, it is not to be wondered at that they bore his presence with only about half the horror they would otherwise have felt, and so kept tolerably quiet.

And thus a week went on, Taffy encouraging them by his own example and experience to bear what was coming with patience and in hope.

And he could but speak from his own experience, poor Taffy! Let us trust, then, that in these "days of advance" there are fewer and fewer exceptions to the rule, that a docile horse makes a kind master. Shame on the master if it does not!

It was at the end of the first week that the real trial began for all three colts, and a trial indeed it was! They have hard hearts who would deny it. Those heavy iron bits forced into the young tender mouths; so stiff against their teeth, so cold against their flesh, how horrible they were! And the bridles that pulled at them, forcing the poor heads to turn hither and thither, for mere whim's sake, as it seemed (for whatever reason there was for it, they could not find it out)—what a cruel contrivance! Then the long whips, which kept them at one distance all the time, so that, as they were forced to move on continually, they had no choice but to go round and round in a circle for ever—how irritating! My heart bleeds when I think of it, and imagine the two long hours of struggle on that first dreadful day. How severe the trial must have been to them,—must ever be to all!

Worse still, however, when in the course of a few days, the corners of the mouths became sore from the pressure of the iron, and there was, for a time, the pain of a raw wound, as well as a day-by-day longer time of restraint to endure.—Masters and superiors, verily, there is a great responsibility in your hands! Nevertheless, it is not for the colts to sit in judgment.

Now, then, how fared the three colts under the terrible but, at present, in some way or other, necessary training? (For even Egeria could not answer Firefly's maddened enquiries, by saying that in the East the bit and bridle and whip can be dispensed with.) Well, Whitefoot and Silverstar set out by intending to submit if possible, and therefore, though more or less cheerfully at some times than others, and with more or less pain to themselves, they contrived to manage it at last.

Firefly, on the contrary, started by a sort of resistance-on-principle plan. Wishing to resist, in fact, he always found a reason for resisting. If people treated him properly he could submit as well as any one else, he was sure; but if they ill-used him, what could they expect but that he should kick—kick—kick? And as to what proper treatment was, he made himself the sole judge. Certainly the training process just described was not proper, but on the contrary cruel and unjust, and accordingly kick, kick, kick he went, whenever it was possible.

In vain Egeria begged him to forbear, seeing too late how much mischief her folly had done.

"It is so senseless to resist when you can't help yourself," said she.

"It is so mean to yield to an unjust necessity!" cried he.

And she dared not contradict herself so far as to suggest, that it might not be so unjust as it seemed.

"Will you listen to me once more?" asked she one day.

"If you talk sense, yes," replied Firefly, "not otherwise, old lady."

Egeria sighed; for his part folly was but a stretched-out shadow of her own. Imperfect judgments; judgments formed on half-known grounds; judgments formed by the lesser intelligence concerning a greater which it cannot comprehend—what rebellion and ruin have they not caused!

"It is sense, if you have sense to find it out," cried Egeria, sharply. "It is downright wisdom. What I am going to say is truth and fact."

"I hear you; go on," said Firefly, impatiently.

"Well, if you go on kicking in this manner, every time you think you have—I beg your pardon—every time you have a reason for kicking, you know, you will get into such a habit of kicking, that you will do it whether you have a reason or not."

"Shall I!" shouted Firefly, with contempt.

"Yes, you will though!" persisted Egeria, vexed alike by his obstinacy and ridicule. "If you kick every time you can find or make an excuse, you will be very apt to kick on when you have none."

"I have never yet kicked without a reason, old lady, and I don't intend to do so," answered Firefly.

"I know, I know," replied Egeria, "so far you have always proved yourself right to yourself; what the horsebreaker thinks is another matter. But, dear friend, try and believe me,—habits are such tremendous things! If you don't get into a habit of giving way, you mayn't be able to give way when you want, that's what I am afraid of. Those who indulge themselves in kicking at all, will sometimes kick when they would give worlds to forbear."

"How can that happen to me, when I never kick without a reason?" cried Firefly.

At which moment he was fetched from the stable for a morning's lesson, and Egeria was left to fret alone. For fret she did, not being a bad creature on the whole, but such an inconsiderate old simpleton, both in her way of viewing life and talking about it to others!

And alas! there was but too much cause for fretting, when at the end of five weeks Firefly remained still untamed—still in the horsebreaker's hands! A fortnight ago both Whitefoot and Silverstar had taken leave of the place, had finished their education with respectability, and gone out into the world on their own account.

There are plenty of good masters to be found for docile, well-taught creatures, and they had been picked up at once by two neighbouring families, and often met in their rides, and talked over old times. Egeria heard this from Taffy, who, from being constantly out, learnt all the news of the country-side, and had once or twice met his friends himself; and it must be owned she regretted Firefly's conduct all the more, that she feared she had had some share in it herself.

When Firefly was led out of the stable after Egeria had spoken, he had, for a few minutes, a misgiving that there might be some truth in what she had said. But the first crack of the horsebreaker's whip made his heart as hard as ever. He had accustomed himself for so long to look upon it and him and the whole affair as a system of barbarous injustice, that he could not have rid himself of the notion without a strong effort, and there was one great difficulty to his making it—namely, that he must acknowledge himself to have been in the wrong before.

And alas! he did not make it; and so another week went on, at the end of which the horsebreaker lost patience, and told Firefly's owner he was a hopeless kicker, and a very ill-conditioned animal as to temper, though otherwise with many good points, and a valuable beast.

It was not very pleasant news to the owner, but Firefly was so handsome in appearance, and moreover, so strong and able to work, that he was undertaken at last by a very fearless young squire, who cared for little but pace and beauty, had a seat like a rock, put his faith in a strong curb, and had no scruple in using his spurs.

What Firefly underwent in his hands I do not wish to describe, though, even there, if he would but have submitted, his fate would not have been bad, for if the master loved his galloping, so did Firefly himself. But again and again he would refuse to obey the curb if it checked or turned him suddenly when his face was set elsewhere; and then like an instinct came the impulse to kick, kick, kick! and he followed it.

For an hour sometimes the two would battle together—the spur and the whip and the curb, against that insane determination to kick, kick, kick! And as to be conquered by main force and exhaustion is not to be reformed, Firefly was led away bleeding and foam-covered to his stable, as savage as when he left it, and still repeating the old strain—

"If people treat me properly, I can submit as well as any one else; but if they don't, what can they expect but that I shall kick, kick, kick?"

Like the horsebreaker's whim of driving him round in an everlasting circle, seemed the young squire's whim of checking him, and turning him round when he didn't expect it, and wanted to go straight on. He kicked, therefore, strictly on principle, and all the more when the injustice was enforced by the spur and the lash. So the squire got tired of his purchase, and Firefly was sold again.

But this time to a very knowing hand, a country doctor, who after trying different plans in turn—low feed and good feed, kindness and severity, and finding both unsuccessful, took him back to the horsebreaker. "He seems very hopeless at present," remarked he; "he kicks for nothing. But there is one more chance. Break him in for harness. Kicking-straps will perhaps bring him to his senses. At any rate try; he has many good qualities, and is a fine fellow. I hope he'll do well."

The horsebreaker shook his head, and led Firefly back to his old stable. Another colt occupied his former stall, but there were still two vacant. He was led into the middle one, and before nightfall Egeria was brought into the third.

Firefly told his story at length, and was too eager to hear Egeria's shuffles of impatience. "How unfortunate some people are!" observed she, when he ended; but there was a slight mockery in her tone.

"I have been so all along," said he; "I believe I am fated to ill-usage."

"People always are who will go nobody's way but their own," was Egeria's answer; "why don't you do what is wanted? Go the way your master pulls you, and give up fighting for your own."

"If people treat me properly, I can submit—"

"Oh, do stop!" cried Egeria, "I've heard that much too often. You never do submit."

"Because they never—"

"Oh, they, they, they! Would they be masters, if you, and not they, were to lead the way?"

"Oh, as to masters, perhaps I have my own opinion," cried Firefly; "I wonder who has been master of the two I have had! But no matter about that. I could have borne leading, but I wouldn't be dragged. It was the curb and spurs and whip of that young squire I kicked against."

"And of your last master, the doctor, when he was kind?" asked Egeria.

"He wasn't always kind," muttered Firefly.

"But when he was?" insisted the old mare.

"Fool!" murmured Firefly, between his teeth; "was I likely to go his fidgety way—stopping at one house then at another; no sooner started than having to stop; twisted down one lane and up another, never having a good run all the time; I, who had galloped over half a country-side in a morning with the squire? Kick? why who wouldn't kick at a life like that?"

"It is as I feared," exclaimed Egeria. "Anybody who wants to kick, can find a reason for it, of course." And she spoke not another word, for she did not understand the matter to the bottom, as Taffy did, and her way of argument was, therefore, not convincing.

The first thing in the morning, however, Firefly spoke to her. He had a question to ask. Did she know what kicking-straps were? Perfectly; what made him want to know.

He repeated what the doctor had said.

"Capital!" said Egeria. "If you are put into those you will never be able to kick again."

"We shall see about that," groaned Firefly, grinding his teeth as if he were champing oats. "Masters—masters—masters indeed! . . ."

In which state of mind he was taken out, two hours afterwards, put into kicking-straps, and had his first lesson of going into harness. The plan answered at first; but this was only while the shock of surprise and helplessness lasted. Still, being rather less wild, the horsebreaker returned him as "fit for harness, if driven in kicking-straps;" and Egeria twitted him when he left her, as being "fairly caught at last." "We shall see about that," muttered Firefly, fuming to himself, as the doctor drove him home. But the kicking-straps were amazingly strong, and he restrained himself. Nevertheless, the first principles of submission had not entered his head, and Egeria's folly and ridicule had done all that an unwise friend could do to confuse the truth.

The truth? Ah, we can only get at that by sitting in our neighbour's chair, and looking with his eyes. Had Firefly done this, he would have known why the kicking-straps were added to his harness, and have laid the blame on the right shoulders. As it was, he laid the blame on the doctor, and considered himself the victim of injustice.

So, one unlucky day, after a round of rather tiresome visiting, a very slight correction for impatience set his blood working; and, without thinking either of kicking-straps or consequences, he took the bit between his teeth, laid his ears down, close to his head, muttering; "Masters indeed!" to himself, and pulling madly at the reins, dashed at full speed down the narrow country lane. They stopped him at last at a turnpike-gate, and as the kicking-straps had given way soon after he started, he concluded the day's work by smashing the splashboard to pieces, his master escaping with difficulty.

So he was sent back to the market town, and resold.

It is impossible to pursue him through all his adventures; they were all, so to speak, variations upon the same set of notes—the battle of authority with one who refused to acknowledge its claims. A miserable struggle, whether of man or beast; whether against the powers ordained of God, or the God of power Himself; whether breaking out into open contest, or indulged in by inward repining.

At last, poor Firefly fell into the hands of a regular horsedealer, who forwarded him to a neighbourhood where his tricks were not known, and after some weeks of low diet and constant work, sold him (more shame for the fact) to a quiet country clergyman, for a birthday present for his daughter, just bursting into the beauty of girlhood.

Now, by this time, our friend Firefly had had experience enough to discover that his habit of opposition was constantly bringing him into trouble. And though he was not sick of the bad habit, he was decidedly sick of the trouble, and every now and then was vexed with himself for giving way to it. And now and then he recalled Egeria's words, "Those who indulge themselves in kicking at all, will sometimes kick when they would give worlds to forbear."

Still, he could not remember a single case in which he had kicked without a very good reason—as it seemed to him—so he assured himself at least, and tried to forget that Egeria had also said, "Anybody who wants to kick can find a reason for kicking, of course!"

Now at last, however, came Firefly's halcyon days. What more could heart of horse desire than to belong to a gentle young girl, who was ready to love him, not only as her servant but companion and friend? Egeria's tales of Eastern kindness came back to his mind again and again, as his new mistress brought him delicate morsels which she would fain have had him eat from her hand; and when, as was generally the case, he could not overcome his repugnance, but started back from her caresses, all she said was, the poor fellow was nervous and shy; perhaps—who knew?—he had at some time or other been harshly used.

"This is as it should be," remarked Firefly; and he began to think better than ever of himself. The few misgivings he had lately had went to sleep. "I was right, and not Egeria," thought he, as he bore his light burden over her favourite haunt, the Downs. "I was right, and Egeria wrong. I told her I had never kicked without a reason, and never should. It was nonsense about not being able to leave off."

And so he really believed, till, alas! the renewed good living brought back the impatience as well as fire into his blood, and what had he to restrain them with, who had not got the law in his heart? There followed one other week of self-confidence and enjoyment, and then . . .

... She was not in the least to blame—that beautiful young girl who had been so kind to him. He admitted this even to himself, when he saw her stretched at his feet; the eyes that had looked so kindly at him, closed; the rich black hair surrounding the white cheeks and forehead like a pall—the groom so horror-struck when he came up, that he never thought of even laying hold on Firefly's bridle.

They had been out for a morning ride on the Downs, and she had wished to canter. For a day or two past, some evil spirit (evil spirits are so ingenious) had been whispering in his ear, that to be patronised was all very well, if it were not another form of unjust restraint. Masters? had he not proved himself the master in every case yet? And so he had done here—here, where, as Egeria had prophesied, he would have given worlds to forbear.

Now rose before him the only half-valued tenderness, the anxiety for his daily comfort, the little personal sacrifices in his favour, and this as the conclusion; that because the canter had been prolonged, and she had wished to rest, and so checked him with the bridle, the old habit had proved too strong for him, and prompted him to kick, kick, kick!—and he had kicked until she was stretched at his feet. . . .

More than an hour passed, and Firefly stood by her still. Stood in the same spot, seeing the same sight, without care to go his own way, now that he might have done it at will.

And then came the trampling of feet, horses and other men, and among them all a father in the first agony of despair. But no one noticed Firefly—he was nothing to his masters then, and so he stood on there like a horse of marble, in the same old place, looking at what he had done.

But presently some one who had been touching her wrist and had sprinkled her with water whispered, "She is coming to herself!"

And it was true. Firefly's mistress had been stunned and one arm was hurt, but she awoke again to life; and when the poor father had wept out his joy on her neck, and she had looked up, she smiled to see so near them the creature who had caused this evil. Yes, there he stood, and his eye watched hers, as it first glanced at him, and then fixed on her father's face anxiously, while she murmured, "Promise me one thing, dear father. Let poor Firefly go to Rarey to be cured."

Masters?—They may well be masters and superiors, in whom the abiding spirit of forgiveness and love is triumphant! So Firefly was taken to Rarey; but what then happens to horses must be looked for in other books. This does not contain an argument on the merits of the different methods of horsebreaking; only thus much as regards Rarey's process is the turning point of the tale.

The object aimed at is the subjection of the will, not merely the control of the body,—the full and complete recognition of the mastership and superiority of man. This, and this only, is what is wanted when the legs are tied up, and struggles rendered powerless by force, so that the indignant animal is brought through exhaustion of body to submission of feeling. He has plunged, he has kicked, he has reared, for hours together, if he will have it so; but the man stands by him unscathed, unruffled, and still kind:—his master and superior—the terrible discipline proves it; but still kind—and the kindness proves it too.

All this Firefly went through; and when the Rarey-breaker "gentled" him all over his miserable frame, as he lay panting and overpowered on the sawdust, conquered and convinced at last, all his mistakes and misconceptions of other people came before him, as plainly as if Taffy himself had spoken them; so plainly, that he wondered at himself.

But remembering his old and all-too-firmly-adhered-to resolution to kick, kick, kick, whenever he was vexed, a fresh outbreak of perspiration astonished the breaker so much, that he "gentled" and soothed the troubled spirit more and more tenderly, till Firefly could think of nothing like it but the father and daughter comforting each other on the Downs, that terrible day of his guilt.

And thus at last, he learnt that it was possible for submission and love and happiness to go hand in hand together. Firefly was cured.

And then he was taken back to a home which he helped in his degree, however humble, to make what a home should be;—a circle in which animals, superior and inferior, should all work together, each after its measure and kind, for the comfort and pleasure of all.

At last, therefore, he gave a willing obedience to every touch of his dear young lady's rein: and yet he feared her no longer as before; and yet he loved her more! Which is a great mystery, but the world repeats it in a thousand forms.

Animals under man—servants under masters—children under parents—wives under husbands—men under authorities—nations under rulers—all under God,—it is the same with all:—in obedience of will is the only true peace.

Happy the colts who learn submission without a lifetime of personal struggle! Happy the men and women who find in the lesser obediences a practice-field of the greater; for assuredly the words of Egeria are true: "Those who indulge themselves in kicking at all, will sometimes kick when they would give worlds to forbear."

Imperfect Instruments

"And others' follies teach us not,
Nor much their wisdom teaches,
And most, of sterling worth, is what
Our own experience preaches."
   TENNYSON.

Over the old church-tower passed the rooks, on their way from the neighboring trees, cawing into the fresh morning air as they went. Dew hung yet upon every stone of the building,—on the bits of moss and grass which time had suffered to creep over or between them, here and there,—on the edges of the tombs below. There was no one astir at this early hour of an autumn day to speak to or interrupt the dark-eyed Geronimo, as he strode hurriedly up the pathway to the porch, the church-keys dangling from his hand, and slightly clanking against each other as he stepped.

Behind him followed a rough-haired country lad, but at a little distance, and silent. He had a stick in his hand, however, with which he began to whisk off the wet from the grass-blades of the graves on each side the path; but at one turn and glance from Geronimo, he desisted.

Soon the key was in the lock, the bolt had turned, grating, back; the heavy door was pushed open, the shock echoing through the building; and Geronimo and little Roger, the mason's son, his companion, were walking up the aisle; on one side of which, at the upper end, in a small transept, stood the organ and choir-seats.

Let me recall that lonely village, nestling in a narrow valley on the borders of Southern Wales, traversed by a rapid streamlet, which ran through it like a silver thread; rich in orchards, embosomed in ancient trees, where rooks had built their nests for generations; where the cuckoo's voice reverberated from surrounding hills.

At one extremity was the church, at the other the quiet vicarage; so that the flock were wont to watch about their doorways for the passing by of the Pastor to his sacred office, that they might follow and enter with him into the ark of the visible church on earth, he leading them on their way. It was a pretty custom and a pleasant sight; there was a tone of loyal respect and trust about it, which social progress has, it is to be feared, some tendency to disturb.

Let me recall the old Pastor himself, in his happy, scholarly simplicity; the serenity of submission on his face, for he had undergone a life's long grief. Let me recall him in the days when the time was drawing near for the silver chord to be broken, and when his visions brought him closer and closer to the day of reunion with his dearly beloved Italian wife, who had died when their only child, Geronimo, was but five years old.

And Geronimo was now his father's curate; a youth fresh from the schools; energetic, enthusiastic, determined even to self-will, a worshipper of system and order; one who had taken for his motto the words of the poet:

"—because right is right, to follow right
Were wisdom in the scorn of consequence."

The father, on the other hand, past middle-age, was old for his years; for the fire of his spirit had died out, but the power of his intellect remained unaltered, as is often the case in fine natures; and an originally widely educated judgment grew wider and gentler as the river of his life widened out to the everlasting sea.

He doubted about his son's motto, therefore, as a universal rule of life. It had to be considered, said he, whether the "right" you followed, or the "consequence" you scorned, was of the greater vital importance. There was a right and a wrong—he once added as a homely illustration—in the way of cutting a pencil; but if you have to deal with a weak-leaded one, which would not bear long shoulders without breaking, it was better to cut it with short shoulders than waste it altogether. If he had to choose a motto himself, it must be from the broader teaching of St. Paul.

Geronimo listened in impatience. He thought his father's argument a letting down of principle, the homely illustration trivial, and with regard to St. Paul, everybody knew that texts could be found to support most anything.

It stood thus, then, that the father admired the son for his strength of purpose and purity of intention, yet sometimes wondered what his future would be; but that the son never properly appreciated the father, except for his amiability to himself. He thought him a kind but feeble old man, behindhand in the lights of the day.

And it was true that while Geronimo had passed from school to college, his father had remained in the narrow valley; and while the kaleidoscope of public opinion was presenting fresh combinations of thought and feeling to the gaze and admiration of the ardent young, the old man was out of the circle of their influence, and judged of them afar off with the mind of a philosopher.

It was, perhaps, a rash arrangement that Geronimo should have come to be his father's curate; but he had made the offer, and the old man had accepted it with tears of joy. There was, in fact, between them a strong natural affection, overruling all theoretical differences of opinion, as well as a strong sense of parental and filial duty. There was also, perhaps, some hope on both sides of influencing each other for good; and there was, moreover, the unspoken bond of common interest in one grave.

The triangular white marble slab on the chancel-wall of the church bore upon it a name which to both father and son was still the dearest name upon earth, "Maria Maddalena:"—to the old man naturally so, who through so many years had lifted up weary, loving eyes to the golden letters in which it was traced, travelling in spirit to that heaven of heavens whither the taper central angle of the tablet continually pointed.

And the son had his own recollections—dim ones of old embraces from that mother who had so soon passed away—vivid ones of looking upwards to that tablet from his seat in church ever since he was a child—of gazing on the shining words, and the shining emblems above them, the palm branches, the cross, and the star, until their glitter first dazzled and then brought tears to his eyes. Had he tried, by gazing, to get nearer to the bearer of that golden name—the mother, whom every motherless child feels to want so much? Had he hoped to charm her back, he knew not whence, to comfort him, he knew not how?

He could not have answered himself. Children do and feel many things of which they can give no account, and the why, matters so little in comparison with the fact.

Enough that the long-cherished habit of love to the pure white marble slab remained as firm in Geronimo's heart, as if he had been able to reason about its propriety, and justify it by argument.

Judge, then, what he must have suffered, when, on his first coming to the place, as curate, he felt it his duty to ask permission of his father to have that tablet removed to some other part of the church!

Let us go back to that time, some nine months before that of my story, for it was the beginning of Geronimo's practical troubles.

It was a painful scene that took place; Geronimo's voice trembled as he made the request, and his father's heart-wrung "Never!" was followed by a silence equally distressing to both. Then the old man asked for reasons, and the young one gave them. The kaleidoscope had brought certain proprieties into full observation which had for some time been unnoticed—there was no doubt about that. The tablet was on a wall within the communion rails; it would have been better elsewhere. Private memorials were inappropriate there. Geronimo thought them inappropriate in the church anywhere—the father disputed this—it was the ark of the dead as well as of the living; but were the matter to be done over again, he would place the stone without the rails in preference; as it was, there was no vital principle involved—no sufficient reason, therefore, for the desecrating act of removal.

The son returned to the argument. His father had admitted the objection; was it not then clearly an act of duty to sacrifice personal feeling to the example of right—whether the right were small or great?

"Measure me the measure of right," cried the troubled father, "as compared with the impressions it will cause. You cannot drive straight lines through life without knocking over good feelings as well as bad ones, and woe to those who knock down what little there is of good in the world!"

"The right way is a narrow way," replied the son; "to trim to the prejudices of the ignorant is to sacrifice principle to man-pleasing." There was more said in the shape of argument than needs to be repeated here—let every one fight the matter out as he will. On the following day, the father had come to a resolution.

"When I am gone," said he to his son, "and my name is added to hers on the tablet, you may remove it to where you will; and even now, if, on hearing this, you remain offended, you may remove it at once. I warn you, however, that it is my belief your doing so will cause evil rather than good among those whose souls' health you are bound to consider. You cannot get them to understand your motives, and they will abominate the act. What you lose will be far more, therefore, than what you will gain. Of my personal feelings I say nothing. On that point I suspect we suffer together. Now, then, do as you please."

If the father hoped, by yielding a point so trying to himself, to set Geronimo an example of giving way, he deceived himself. Geronimo did not accept what he said as an example, but as an acknowledgment of an error that needed rectifying. About any consequences to other people he refused to think at all. Consequences were nothing in matters of duty and principle.

So he went to Roger, the village-mason, explained what he wanted, and gave his orders, announcing his intention of coming himself to assist. But the man stared in astonishment. "You ben't in earnest surely, sir?" said he. "Surely you're never going to pull down your own mother's tombstone? Why, it'll break the old gentleman's heart—and she such a woman as she was!"

"My father has given his consent," said Geronimo, annoyed, but not betraying the smallest impatience.

Roger the mason shook his head, and took up a tool he had laid down, as if intending to return to his work.

"You'll excuse me, Mr. Geronimo; you've, maybe, persuaded him to it. Young people will be young people, I know," remarked Roger; "though it's a downright miracle to me why you should want to do it—you, the lady's only son; and such a lady as she was!"

"It's out of no disrespect to my mother, I assure you," expostulated Geronimo.

"I should think not, indeed!" interrupted the mason.

"But," continued Geronimo, "we have all to sacrifice personal feelings, you know, in matters of right and wrong."

Geronimo paused; but the mason was silent—he had no idea what was meant.

"Or where there is a question of propriety in the treatment of holy places," continued the youth; but still the mason stared at him in silence.

"You don't understand me, I think," said Geronimo.

"I'm free to own I don't," answered the mason.

"Will you let me come in and explain myself?" asked the young man.

"Your father's son is welcome in my house at any time!" cried Roger, who had at last got hold of an idea he could fully understand; and leading the way along a narrow passage, he ushered his guest into a small parlour, to which he presently called his wife down, having asked permission for her to share in what Mr. Geronimo was going to say.

But let Mr. Geronimo say what he would, neither of his hearers succeeded in comprehending him, though, to do them justice, they tried. There they sat, the mason holding his cap in both hands between his knees, slightly stooping, but looking up at Geronimo from time to time; his wife bolt upright, and never taking her eyes off him for a second. And still they didn't understand!

They had two or three ideas of their own in their heads, it is true, which were adverse to Mr. Geronimo's arguments, and perhaps darkened their powers of comprehension. "The Mrs.," as they called her, had been an angel on earth, if ever there was one, and no place could be too good for her stone, they were sure, for wasn't she herself in heaven?—at least, who would ever get there if she wasn't there? And the poor dear gentleman had stood under it every Sunday ever since she was taken, and who'd have the heart to deprive him of the comfort of feeling her so near? If that stone were to be taken away, they shouldn't have him there much longer—Mr. Geronimo might depend upon that!

Roger's good woman declared she wouldn't see the poor gentleman standing there alone, as if he'd never had a wife, for all the world, if she could help it. Take down his own mother's tombstone! as if her name wasn't a credit anywhere, and a good example into the bargain—Mr. Geronimo couldn't be thinking of what he was saying! And Roger protested that if he never had another job in all his life, he wouldn't have this. But Mr. Geronimo was young, put in the wife, and hadn't come to his feelings; he would think better of it presently. They wished him a very good morning, and hoped he would call again.

Mr. Geronimo bit his lips as he left the house. Learning!—authority!—what had become of them? What had he done with them? What could he have done with them against such stolid country heads? Entirely spoilt into the bargain, thought he—the fruit of taking things easy. There was but one hope of cure—to go the way you thought right, and leave such people to get reconciled to it as they could. Explanation and reasoning!—he was ashamed of having tried them. The people had treated him like a child.

So he crossed the hills next morning, and rode ten miles, to the nearest town, where he engaged a marble-mason to come over and remove the tablet. But Sunday intervened, and as it chanced, his father was ill, and he had to stand in his place under the tablet in the chancel.

And all at once, while there, there flashed into his mind one, at any rate, of the words which Roger the mason had spoken—quite an unreasonable word, be it granted, but reason, even in the most reasoning men, is not always a match for feeling, and Geronimo was suddenly unnerved.

The Gospel for the day contained the brief, pathetic history of the widow of Nain; and crossed as all the incidents were—for he was the only son of a yet living father, and it was the mother who was dead—every word seemed to touch his case, and he had a sensation as if the Maria Maddalena of his childhood was looking down over his head from the tablet he was preparing to remove. He actually shuddered. What if his father were about to die too?

Yet, what really overwhelmed him, little as he knew it, was the contrast which made itself felt between the hardness of his own attempted system and the sympathy which breathed out of the Gospel page. The Saviour had driven the money-changers from the temple, it is true, with the hand of indignant power; but there was no question of the world's vile desecrating traffic in that still marble monument on the wall.

Geronimo did not think it all out then, nor till long afterwards, but in steeling himself to set a point of—let it be granted—ecclesiastical propriety above the much weightier matter of human sympathy, and a regard for moral results on others, he had followed the Pharisees of old, rather than Him who imposed none but necessary burdens on the tremulous human mind.

Nevertheless his resolution had received a shock, and he was up betimes next morning to meet the marble-mason on his way. He had altered his intentions, he told him, with respect to the tablet, but there was another little matter of restoration in the church which he wished him to undertake.

And now Geronimo breathed freely again, and met his father at breakfast with an easy mind. He therefore spoke quite cheerfully of the proposed restoration of a Knight Templar's tomb, which had long been in disorder, and alluded to the marble-mason from the town as being there.

A cry from his father interrupted him.

"Geronimo!—that marble-mason!—have you really had the heart to—" Here breath failed the old man, and he turned very pale.

"No, no!" cried Geronimo, passionately, for he knew what was meant.

"It is well," murmured the father. "I gave you leave, I know; but, Geronimo, I doubt if I could have borne it. One gets weaker as one gets older; and, with weak people as with ignorant ones, the grasshopper is sometimes a burden."

If Geronimo could but have recollected this! But he had seen so little of life and the world himself, that he could scarcely help being one-sided and narrow-minded; and as he would not avail himself of his father's wider knowledge, what remained but to make mistakes?

So, priding himself on an inflexible firmness in matters of "principle," however small, he confounded together things indifferent and important; did even wise ones foolishly; and attempted others which were neither wise, nor worth a hundredth part of the offence they created.

"We are to 'be hated of all men for His name's sake,' " quoted he, in justification of the course he was pursuing.

"His name's sake!" I dare not record the trivialities he dignified upon that sacred ground.

But on one or two points the father interfered authoritatively, and then domestic disagreement arose. Now Geronimo had thought scorn of Roger the mason for not yielding to his better knowledge and authoritative position, as a matter of course. Yet here, where to the counsellor was added father as well as priest, and to the knowledge of the schools the broader experiences of a long and varied life, it came quite natural to this mere lad by comparison, to think, and betray the thought, that he knew a thousand times the better of the two. Verily, if a little of the old heathen respect for the wisdom of grey hairs had been added to his theological dogmas, Geronimo's Christianity would not have suffered.

"And a man's foes shall be they of his own household," murmured the old man to himself in the bitterness of his heart, as he wondered whether it would not soon be his duty to send this his only son from his side. For how could he be justified in letting the clouds of miserable parties and party feelings gather into a storm?

But now Geronimo, too, awoke to the fact that such a storm threatened. The gossip spread on every side that father and son did not always agree, and the flock were not likely to be unanimous. The wicked natural man loves contest; the weak natural man loves excitement.

An expression of partizanship to himself, coupled with disrespect for his father, awoke Geronimo to a sense of his position, if it did not explain his mistake. And on looking further round, his tender conscience was grieved. The old confidence was broken up, the old love was failing—whether with or without a reason was not the question now. What could be the cause? What was the remedy? Perhaps he had been too busy with his plans and changes to have made himself as much a personal friend as was desirable.

He redoubled his exertions and visits, endeavoured to conciliate on all sides; but, somehow, something was wanting. If from long habit a good many still came out to follow himself and his father to church, they did so at a greater and greater distance. Only a few came up now to claim the friendly greeting, which he remembered as part of the Sunday's intercourse in the days of his childhood. Geronimo was puzzled.

Yet, if the kaleidoscope had but turned round for contemplation that crystal from the wisdom of St. Paul, "Destroy not him with thy meat for whom Christ died," he would have known the cause of estrangement, and how to apply a cure. As it was, an idea at once bright and kind struck him, and he lost no time in carrying it out with zeal.

Geronimo was musical—he had been so from childhood upwards—had introduced better music as well as greater beauty into the venerable old church; and for both these things the people were grateful, as they ought to be.

He would make use of this happily universal feeling; he would give a treat to high and low—would have a festival; they should keep holiday with singing and gladness and feasting; and the day should be his father's birthday. He would dispel the dreadful and mischievous idea that the house to which all the parish looked for example, was divided against itself!

Never was a happier thought struck out! It furnished occupation for hearts, and minds, and hands; and the old folks, who could do nothing but talk, had a harmless subject of conversation. Eh dear, then, Mr. Geronimo and his father were as friendly as ever! It had all been a mistake about their not agreeing. Eh! how pleased the old gentleman looked, to be sure, when he called, here and there, to ask them if they were going to get ready! Why, he was helping everybody to trim themselves up in their best for the grand supper there was to be at the end. And on the old gentleman's birthday, and all! It was something to think of! They were glad!"

And so they were; but so also, only more deeply so, were father and son, for they felt reunited.

And now the time drew near, and only one small contradiction had arisen. The organ was not so perfectly in tune as to please Geronimo's delicate ear; and when, nearly at the last moment, he wrote over for the one organ-builder of the distant town, he found, to his dismay, that the man was absent, and would be so till the day after the festival.

The evil was slight, and the father entreated Geronimo to be satisfied: so few would discover the imperfection. But Geronimo could not rest; his passionate love of order was offended; and it must be owned that the instinct is a good one. "In the beginning," the will of God brought an organised world out of elemental confusion. In the end, we hope He will bring harmony into the discordant world of spirits.

And in the present life men may, each one in his degree, labour to the same good end. It is both their privilege and their duty to do so. Lawyers, physicians, statesmen, men of science, and, above all, divines, undertake to do it by their very professions. Entangled claims, diseased bodies, disturbed nations, complicated physical laws and distressed souls, all need the peace that comes with being ordered aright. In Geronimo the instinct was almost a passion; but of the judicious application of means to the blessed end, he did not know a great deal more than of how to bring the organ of the village church into the desired perfection of tune.

Nevertheless, he knew something of that, for he had been present when the organ-builder had tuned the instrument before, had observed the process of widening or narrowing the mouths of the pipes in order to change their tone, and had since ventured on correcting a defective note or two himself.

What was to hinder him from tuning the whole of them now, if he could but ascertain the order in which the guiding scale of notes was made perfect? To bring all the rest into unison with that would be no difficulty, for he could perfectly trust his ear. The difficulty was, to get at the first principles of the matter. The youth who played the organ when Geronimo's duties precluded his assistance, knew nothing of the subject.

But Geronimo would not be baffled. The day before the festival he crossed the hills to the town, and called at a musical-instrument maker's shop. Could they give him, he asked, the succession of notes by which organs were tuned?

Mr. Somebody asked Mr. Somebody else, and there was a reference to an authority through a door. The shopman, who was left behind, eyed Geronimo askance. Was he in their line of business? he wondered. Presently the other man returned, and presented him with a bit of music-paper, on which twenty notes were marked down.

"These are the notes, sir," said he, rather coolly as if he, too, half suspected a rival. "The same as for a pianoforte—as, of course, you know," he added, with a half-enquiring look.

Geronimo disliked familiarity, and gave a half-impatient nod.

"Mr. —— desired me to say, with his compliments, sir," continued the messenger, "he supposed you're aware it's a difficult business, organ-tuning, to any one that hasn't practised it."

"Has your master practised it?" enquired Geronimo, with a new hope.

"Oh, no, sir," replied the man, who himself did duty as master on the other side of the door; "we're pianoforte-tuners only, sir."

"What does the fool mean?" thought Geronimo, as he walked away. "A difficult business it may be to the man without an ear, but easy enough otherwise, with the clue in his hand. Thank Heaven, there is the comfort of certainty in dealing with material things! Fixed laws, and fixed results! Not that everlasting trimming and yielding, which leaves every work one undertakes imperfect at last!"

As Geronimo mused thus, and read over the clearly-defined system by which his organ was to be brought into that harmonious order which we call "being in tune," he almost felt that an organ-builder's business was a more satisfactory one than a clergyman's.

There was still the little brass cone, used for widening or contracting the pipes, to be obtained; but this he asked for at the organ-builder's establishment—no remark passing there on what it was wanted for; and then Geronimo hurried home.

And now it will be understood what took the young curate to the church so early, on the morning of that autumn festival-day. He had begun, but not nearly completed, the tuning of the organ the evening before, having gone to it as soon as he could make an excuse to leave his father again; for the bold feat was to be kept secret till its successful accomplishment proved how wisely it had been undertaken. And now it must be finished before breakfast; for the decorations were to be brought in afterwards, and he himself had a thousand other things to do.

For two hours and upwards therefore, did he persevere in his anxious work; his greatest trouble being the special care required in the mechanical part, inasmuch as a hasty or too heavy insertion of the cone into the mouths of the pipes was liable to split the metal and do mischief. But Geronimo kept every faculty on the full stretch of attention, and his perfect ear made the bringing of the notes into correct harmony a matter of no trouble at all, but, on the contrary, of the keenest pleasure.

And the instrument was more glaringly out of order than he had supposed. His father had fancied it was only a little out of tune, and he himself had not thought the disorder very great. But now that he tested it by the scale, almost every note was wrong, and must be altered. A few of the octaves harmonised together, it is true; but all the fifths were either too flat or too sharp. That not one should have remained perfect by accident, as several of the octaves had done, puzzled him not a little; but the fact of their all being imperfect, more or less, was undeniable. What a blessing he had it in his power to remedy the evil!

Yes; for two hours and upwards did the work go on; the occasional drone of the pipes vibrating drearily through the aisles, and almost causing little Roger to fall asleep at his post of the blower. At last, however, every octave had been gone through, had been brought into perfect unison with the perfected scale of the twenty notes, and Geronimo's labours were over!

"Roger," cried he to the child, whose blowing efforts were perceptibly failing.

"Yes, sir!"

"Blow steadily and strongly now, for ten minutes more, and you shall go home to breakfast. Fill the bellows, there's a good lad."

Roger worked his arms vigorously, and the bellows were soon full.

"It's all right now, please, sir," said he.

Geronimo had his eyes on a piece of music open on the desk before him. It was Haydn's Mass in five flats—his dream of beauty among all the classical music of the world. As Roger spoke, the young curate bent forward, and struck down the full magnificent chords of the key.

But almost as he struck them, he uttered a cry, which it was well the louder organ sounds drowned, or Roger would have thought Geronimo mad—a cry of both despair and physical distress. As it was, something startled the lad, and he let go the blowing handle with a jerk. It ran up at once, and the organ notes died out in a mournful squeal.

As to Geronimo, it would be difficult to describe what he did. He was off the stool in an instant, shouting to Roger to know if he had broken the bellows; then back again to retouch the expiring notes, and see if he had been under a delusion, or if he had struck the instrument at random. But no, no, no! Then how—by what miracle—could he account for the fact that his touch upon that chord had filled the air with dissonant vibrations—horrible to the most untutored ear, but to his refined one absolutely insufferable? Chord indeed! the very word was a mockery; what he had struck was a clash of discords.

Human nature itself had never puzzled Geronimo half as much!

After the first agony was over, he examined the matter with all the calmness and care he could command—made Roger blow again—tried other chords in succession—but in all cases with the same result, in a greater or less degree. Once more, then, he got out the tuning-scale—once more ran over the guiding twenty notes: there was not a single flaw, not one; not a varying vibration could be heard; and all the others were in unison with those. And then again he struck a chord, and the chord was no chord at all.

He next examined the pipes: perhaps he had cracked all their mouths with his cone. But no, there was not a split in any one of them; he had been far too careful for that. And now time was getting on, and Roger was half starved. A knocking had already been heard at one of the doors. The decorators must be let in, and he must go home to his breakfast and his father. Geronimo's face, as he locked up the organ and put the keys in his pocket, looked ten years older than it had done before he had begun his work. He gave Roger half-a-crown, as a treat for the day, and hastened home.

It is difficult to reckon on the conduct of any one under the trial of having made a great mistake. Some people fight meanly to get out of a little fault, as if self-conceit was the leading principle of their lives, but humble themselves nobly under a great one; and this was the case with Geronimo.

He went at once to his father, and told him all he had done, blaming himself more bitterly than his father would allow he deserved. But he did more than that; he stepped into many houses that morning, both of farmers and shopkeepers, and told them they must forgive him for being the cause of what he feared would be a great disappointment. He had wanted to make the organ better, and he had, unfortunately, done something to it which had made it worse; and as he could not find out what was amiss, it couldn't be remedied. He would get the choir to make amends by singing their very best, and he would help them all he could himself. He begged that the blunder might not be allowed to spoil the pleasure of the day.

Unaccountable human race! we ought indeed to be patient, one with the other! Geronimo had not received so many smiles in all the time he had been curate as now, when he was carrying round the painful message of his own defeat.

It was wonderful! Kind words were on every lip; not a reproach was heard. It had been so good of Mr. Geronimo to try. They were sure it couldn't have been his fault, but something had gone wrong of itself. Anyhow, they didn't mind at all, and hoped he wouldn't trouble himself. They should hear him sing all the plainer for there being no music besides; and, as for that piece the old Master had talked about so much, they hoped he'd be so good as to play it to them some other day. They begged he wouldn't mind—that was all!

Geronimo felt crowned with roses, for his frankness, if not for the error he had committed; and service, feast, and festival were kept with unclouded comfort, bringing a promise of further comfort in store—a better understanding of what was meant on all sides.

And now for the explanation. Neither father nor son could unravel the mystery. The only guess even that they could make was, that the man at the music-shop might have given them a wrong scale to work by. It was not a bad idea, and it served to keep them quiet till the organ-builder, whom they sent for at once, came over. He was an odd, sententious old man, with a good deal of dry humour. So when he got into the church, and touched the fatal organ, he first chuckled and then laughed outright.

Were the bellows out of order? Were the pipes injured? Was the scale incorrect? Was the tuning imperfect? Geronimo's questions fell thick and fast.

"Nothing of the sort, young gentleman," said the organ-builder to every suggestion. "There's only one thing the matter—but it's everything—the tuning's too perfect by half!"

Both Geronimo and his father stared, to the organ-builder's great delight.

"You don't seem to have heard of this before, gentlemen," observed he; "but it's a fact, nevertheless. The scale's all right; the system's perfect: but if you stick too close to it, it sets you wrong. The organ won't bear it, that's the fact."

"Not bear being put into perfect tune?" asked Geronimo, really astonished. "How is that possible?"

"Because it's an imperfect instrument, sir," answered the organ-builder; "and that being the case, you have to make the best you can of it, and not expect to get it perfect, for that's not possible."

Here he took up the scale paper, and went on to explain that most of the fifths must be left somewhat flat, and the few others made somewhat sharp; the octaves alone being tuned in perfect unison. And this was the best plan, he assured them, of getting a harmonious whole—"not perfect, I grant, even then," added he, "but pretty fair for this present life, gentlemen, you see."

Geronimo listened in silence. A system of expediency in the material world, and in music especially, seemed to him monstrous. He sat silently by, too, while the organ-builder made his preparations for repairing the mischief that had been done. He father slipt away, as silent as himself, though possibly he made his own reflections before he went.

But Geronimo sat silently on, till at last the organ-builder began to tune the fifths, leaving each one flat in succession; and then he could contain himself no longer. He got up, but only to sit down again, and then rose once more.

"This is most trying!" he exclaimed. "As unsatisfactory to the mind as the ear! To have a perfect system to go by" (here he pointed to the scale of twenty notes) "and not be allowed to carry it perfectly out, though ear and heart rebel against the disorder! To have an evil under your very hand to be remedied, and be obliged to suffer it still. I call this dreadful!"

The organ-builder stopped his work, to listen and reply:—

"It's not very pleasant, I admit," said he, "but there's one thing worse—to find you've worked so hard for the system, that you've missed the end it was made for."

"A perfect system ought to work out a perfect end," murmured Geronimo.

But the organ-builder shook his head. "Not if the instrument isn't perfect too," persisted he; "there's sure to be a cross somewhere."

Drone went another pipe, another imperfect fifth was tuned, and the organ-builder made another pause. He was a very sententious man and liked to explain all round his subject.

"It's the same all through life," observed he; "the best rules, even, short of Gospel rules, of course, mustn't be pressed too close; neither man nor organ can bear it. If we were all up in heaven it might be different."

In spite of himself Geronimo smiled, and the smile did him good. "What a choice of evils!" said he.

"Can't be otherwise," remarked his companion, "so long as things are all imperfect together—men and organs—and perhaps even rules too, sometimes."

Geronimo shook his head, but the organ-builder did not notice it, and went back to his tuning as cheerful as if no such thing as a sad necessity existed in the world. And Geronimo went on listening to the unsatisfactory sounds, musing the while thereupon.

... Irregularity—inconsistency—contradictions even—were as rife then in the material world as in the spiritual—must be borne with—allowed for—made the best of—in the one case as in the other. The organ-builder's business was not so much more satisfactory than a clergyman's, after all! ...

"Now, sir, you may play Haydn's Mass in five flats for as long as you please," observed the organ-builder, as he concluded the tuning, striking down the full chord of the key in proof of the fact: "the organ goes sweetly enough now."

And so it did—"sweetly enough," if not as perfectly as Geronimo could have desired; but he had had his lesson, and must henceforth be contented with something short of his ideal.

"That type of Perfect in his mind,
In Nature can he nowhere find."

Nowhere in the lower nature, at least; and for the full development of the higher, he must wait in patience. But patience is the philosophy of experience: and even Geronimo attained it at last.

Cobwebs

"I cannot make this matter plain,
But I would shoot, howe'er in vain
A random arrow from the brain."
   TENNYSON.

Twinette the Spider was young, hungry, and industrious. "Weave yourself a web, my dear," said her mother, "as you know how without teaching, and catch flies for yourself; only don't weave near me in the corner here. I am old and stay in the corners; but you are young and needn't. Besides you would be in my way. Scramble along the rafters to a little distance off, and spin. But mind! just see there's nothing there—below you, I mean—before you begin. You won't catch anything to eat, if there isn't empty space about you for the flies to fly in."

Twinette was dutiful, and obeyed. She scrambled along the woodwork of the groined roof of the church—for it was there her mother lived—till she had gone what she thought might fairly be called a little distance off, and then she stopped to look round, which, considering that she had eight eyes to do it with, was not difficult. But she was not so sure of what there might be below.

"I wonder whether mother would say there was nothing here—below me, I mean—but empty space for flies to fly in?" said she.

But she might have stood wondering there for ever. So she went back to her mother, and asked what she thought.

"Oh dear, oh dear!" said her mother, "how can I think about what I don't see? There usen't to be anything there in my young days, I'm sure. But everybody must find out things for themselves. Let yourself down by the family rope, as you know how, without teaching, and see for yourself if there's anything there or not."

Twinette was a very intelligent young spider, quite worthy of the age she was born in; so she thanked her mother for her advice, and was just starting afresh, when another thought struck her. "How shall I know if there's anything there when I get there?" asked she.

"Dear me, if there's anything there, how can you help seeing it?" cried the mother, rather teased by her daughter's enquiring spirit, "you with at least eight eyes in your head!"

"Thank you. Now I quite understand," said Twinette; and scuttling back to the end of the rafter, she began to prepare for the family rope.

It was the most exquisite thing in the world—so fine, you could scarcely see it; so elastic, it could be blown about without breaking; such a perfect grey that it looked white against black things, and black against white; so manageable that Twinette could both make it, and slide down it at once; and when she wished to get back, could slip up by it, and roll it up at the same time!

It was a wonderful rope for anybody to make without teaching. But Twinette was not conceited. Rope-making came as natural to her as eating and fighting do to intelligent little boys, so she thought no more about it than we do of chewing our food.

How she did it is another question, and not one easily answered, however intelligent we may be. Thus much may be hinted:—out of four little spinning machines near the tail came four little threads, and the rope was a four-twist of these. But as each separate thread was itself a many-twist of a great many others, still finer, I do not pretend to tell the number of strands (as rope-threads are called) in Twinette's family rope. Enough, that as she made it now, it has been made from generation to generation, and there seems to be no immediate prospect of a change.

The plan was for the spinner to glue the ends to the rafter, and then start off. Then out came the threads from the spinning machines, and twist went the rope: and the further the spinner travelled, the longer the rope became.

And Twinette made ready accordingly, and turning on her back, let herself fairly off.

The glued ends held fast, the four stands twined closely together, and down went the family rope, with Twinette at the end, guiding it. Down into the middle of the chancel, where there were carved oaken screens on three sides, and carved oaken seats below, with carved oaken figures at each end of each.

Twinette was about halfway down to the stone-flagged floor, when she shut up the spinning machines, and stopped to rest and look round. Then, balancing herself at the end of her rope, with her legs crumpled up round her, she made her remarks.

"This is charming!" cried she. "One had need to travel and see the world. And all's so nice in the middle here. Nice empty space for the flies to fly about in; and a very pleasant time they must have of it! Dear me, how hungry I feel—I must go back and weave at once."

But just as she was preparing to roll up the rope and be off, a ray of sunshine, streaming through one of the chancel windows, struck in a direct line upon her suspended body, quite startling her with the dazzle of its brightness. Everything seemed in a blaze all around her, and she turned round and round in terror.

"Oh dear, oh dear, oh dear!" cried she, for she didn't know what to say, and still couldn't help calling out. Then, making a great effort, she gave one hearty spring, and, blinded though she was, shot up to the groined roof, as fast as spider could go, rolling the rope into a ball as she went. After which she stopped to complain.

But it is dull work complaining to oneself, so she soon ran back to her mother in the corner.

"Back again so soon, my dear?" asked the old lady, not over-pleased at the fresh disturbance.

"Back again at all is the wonder," whimpered Twinette. "There's something down there, after all, besides empty space."

"Why, what did you see?" asked her mother.

"Nothing; that was just it," answered Twinette, "I could see nothing for dazzle and blaze; but I did see dazzle and blaze."

"Young people of the present day are very troublesome with their observations," remarked the mother; "however, if one rule will not do, here is another. Did dazzle and blaze shove you out of your place, my dear?"

Twinette said, "Certainly not—she had come away of herself."

"Then how could they be anything?" asked her mother. "Two things could not be in one place at the same time. Let Twinette try to get into her place, while she was there herself, and see if she could."

Twinette did not try, because she knew she couldn't, but she sat very silent, wondering what dazzle and blaze could be, if they were nothing at all! a puzzle which might have lasted her for ever. Fortunately her mother interrupted her, by advising her to go and get something to do. She really couldn't afford to feed her out of her web any longer, she said.

"If dazzle and blaze kill me, you'll be sorry, mother," said Twinette, in a pet.

"Nonsense, about dazzle and blaze," cried the old spider, now thoroughly roused. "I dare say they're only a little more light than usual. There's more or less light up here in the corners even, at times. You talk nonsense, my dear."

So Twinette scuttled off in silence; for she dared not ask what light was, though she wanted to know.

But she felt too cross to begin to spin. She preferred a search after truth to her dinner, which showed she was no commonplace spider. So she resolved to go down below in another place and see if she could find a really empty space; and accordingly prepared the family rope.

When she came down, it was about a half a foot further east in the chancel, and a very prosperous journey she made. "Come! all's safe so far," said she, her good humour returning. "I do believe I've found nothing at last. How jolly it is!" As she spoke, she hung dangling at the end of her rope, back downwards, her legs tucked up round her as before, in perfect enjoyment, when, suddenly, the south door of the church was thrown open, and a strong gust set in. It was a windy evening, and the draught that poured into the chancel blew the family rope, with Twinette at the end of it, backwards and forwards through the air, till she turned quite giddy.

"Oh dear, oh dear!" cried she, puffing, "what shall I do? How could they say there was nothing here—oh dear!—but empty space for flies—oh dear!—to fly in?" But at last, in despair, she made an effort of resistance, and, in the very teeth of the wind, succeeded in coiling up the family rope, and so got back to the rafters.

It was a piece of rare good fortune for her that a lazy, half-alive fly happened to be creeping along it just at the moment. As she landed from her air-dive she pounced on the stroller, killed him, and sucked his juices before he knew where he was, as people say. Then, throwing down his carcase, she scrambled back to her mother, and told her what she thought, though not in plain words. For what she thought was that the old lady didn't know what she was saying, when she talked about empty space with nothing in it.

"Dazzle and blaze were nothing," cried she at last, "though they blinded me, because they and I were in one place together, which couldn't be if they'd been anything; and now this is nothing, though it blows me out of my place twenty times in a minute, because I can't see it. What's the use of rules one can't go by, mother? I don't believe you know a quarter of what's down below there."

The old spider's head turned as giddy with Twinette's arguments as Twinette's had done while swinging in the wind.

"I don't see what it can matter what's there," whimpered she, "if there's room for flies to fly about in. I wish you'd go back and spin."

"That's another part of the question," remarked Twinette, in answer to the first half of her mother's sentence. In answer to the second she scuttled back to the rafter, intending to be obedient and spin. But she dawdled and thought, and thought and dawdled, till the day was nearly over.

"I will take one more turn down below," said she to herself at last, "and look round me again."

And so she did, but went further down than before; then stopped to rest as usual. Presently, as she hung dangling in the air by her line, she grew venturesome. "I will sift the matter to the bottom," thought she. "I will see how far empty space goes." So saying she re-opened her spinning-machines and started afresh.

It was a wonderful rope, certainly, or it would not have gone on to such a length without breaking. In a few seconds Twinette was on the cold stone pavement. But she didn't like the feel of it at all, so took to running as fast as she could go, and luckily met with a step of woodwork on one side. Up this she hurried at once, and crept into a corner close by, where she stopped to take a breath. "One doesn't know what to expect in such queer outlandish places," observed she; "when I've rested I'll go back, but I must wait till I can see a little better."

Seeing a little better was out of the question, however, for night was coming on, and when, weary of waiting, she stepped out of her hiding-place to look round, the whole church was in darkness.

Now it is one thing to be snug in bed when it is dark, and another to be a long way from home and have lost your way, and not know what may happen to you next minute. Twinette had often been in the dark corner with her mother, and thought nothing of it. Now she shook all over with fright, and wondered what dreadful thing darkness could be.

Then she thought of her mother's rules and felt quite angry.

"I can't see anything and I don't feel anything," murmured she, "and yet here's something that frightens me out of my wits."

At last her very fright made her bold. She felt about for the family rope; it was there safe and sound, and she made a spring. Roll went the rope, and up went the owner; higher, higher, higher, through the dark night air; seeing nothing, hearing nothing, feeling nothing but the desperate fear within. By the time she touched the rafter, she was half-exhausted; and as soon as she was safely landed upon it, she fell asleep.

It must have been late next morning when she woke, for the sound of organ music was pealing through the church, and the air-vibrations swept pleasantly over her frame; rising and falling like gusts of night, swelling and sinking like waves of the sea, gathering and dispersing like vapours of the sky.

She went down by the family rope to observe, but nothing was to be seen to account for her sensations. Fresh ones, however, stole round her, as she hung suspended, for it was a harvest-festival, and large white lilies were grouped with evergreens round the slender pillars of the screens, and filled the air with their powerful odour.

Still, nothing disturbed her from her place. Sunshine streamed in through the windows—she even felt it warm on her body—but it interfered with nothing else; and, meanwhile, in such sort as spiders hear, she heard music and prayer—whether as music and prayer come to us, or as deaf men enjoy sound by touch, let those say who can!

A door opened, and a breeze caught her rope; but still she held fast. So music and prayer and sunshine and breeze and scent were all there together; and Twinette was among them, and saw flies flying about overhead.

This was enough; she went back to the rafter, chose a home and began to spin. Before evening, her web was completed, and her first prey caught and feasted on. Then she cleared the remains out of her chamber, and sat down in state to think; for Twinette was now a philosopher.

It came to her while she was spinning her web. As she crossed and twisted the threads, her ideas grew clearer and clearer, or she fancied so, which did almost as well. Each line she fastened brought its own reflections; and this was the way they went on:—

"Empty space is an old wife's tale"—she fixed that very tight. "Sight and touch are very imperfect guides"—this crossed the other at an angle. "Two or three things can easily be in one place at the very same time"—this seemed very loose till she tightened it by a second. "Sunshine and wind and scent and sound don't drive each other out of their places"—that held firm. "When one has sensations there is something to cause them, whether one sees it, or feels it, or finds it out, or not"—this was a wonderful thread, it went right round the web and was fastened down in several places. "Light and darkness, and sunshine and wind, and sound and sensation, and fright and pleasure, don't keep away flies"—the little interlacing threads looked quite pretty as she placed them. "How many things I know of that I don't know much about"—the web got thicker every minute. "And perhaps there may be ever so much more beyond—ever so much more—ever so much more—beyond."

Those were her very last words. She kept repeating them till she finished her web; and when she sat up in state, after supper, to think, she began to repeat them again; for she could think of nothing better or wiser to say. But this was no wonder, for all her thoughts put together made nothing but a cobweb after all!

And when the Turk's-head broom swept it, with others, from the roof, Twinette was no longer in the little chamber below. She had died and bequeathed her cobweb-wisdom to another generation. But as it was only cobweb-wisdom, spiders remain spiders still, and still weave their webs in the roofs of churches without fathoming the mystery of unseen presences below.

Birds in the Nest

"Safe in the hand of one disposing pow'r,
Or in the natal, or the mortal hour,
All Nature is but art, unknown to thee;
All chance, direction, which thou canst not see."
POPE'S ESSAY ON MAN.

Once upon a time there was in a wood a nest which held eight of the dearest little eggs a hen-mother ever looked upon with joy. At least this particular hen-mother thought so, and her mate rather agreed with her when they talked the matter over together. And his opinion had weight, for in his flights he sometimes saw other eggs, and would tell her about them on his return. But what could they be to her own? Nothing could be better than what was perfect, and her own were perfect in her eyes. What a fine shape they had! How beautifully rounded! How soft their tint! How tasteful the arrangement of spots! All others must needs be too light or too dark, or too something or other, to suit her particular taste. The sea-gull, who ate snails in the garden, boasted of his family egg as twenty times larger and twenty times more beautiful. "But if it be more beautiful, what can that matter to us," said the hen-mother, in conclusion, "when ours are perfect in our eyes, and we are so very happy?"

"And shall be so much happier yet," pursued her mate, who, as a travelled bird, had had experience, and knew what was in store; "when the little ones awake to a life and enjoyment of their own, and can feed and sing, and know and love us both."

"Ah, to be sure, to be sure, that will be rapture, indeed," cried the hen-mother. "Thank you so much for telling me! How silly I was, thinking I was as happy as I could possibly be! Of course I shall be happier by and by; and how very happy that will be, for I am happy enough now. I wish the day were come!"

Yet she was very happy; but most so when she forgot she was to be happier still.

And by and by the time came; and when the little ones were all hatched, and could peer about and see their father bringing food, and open their mouths and swallow it very fast, and cry for more,—

"Now then, at last the happiness is perfect," said the hen-mother; "I have nothing further to wish for."

And she watched them being fed and satisfied, and never felt hungry herself, till they had had plenty and were at ease.

"Eight darlings in one nest! What a sight to fill one's heart! There may be trouble enough, it's true, and very little room to rest; but one's own eight beautiful creatures round one, under one's wing, all chirping and alive—this is perfection of happiness indeed!"

"You cannot say so just yet," sang the mate; but he did not tell her this quite at first. He waited for a soft evening in early summer before he piped about what was in store.

"You cannot say so just yet. Our darlings are very sweet, but they are poor helpless things at present. Wait till they have grown more feathers, have learnt to take care of themselves, and fly and sing. They cannot be perfect, nor can your happiness be perfect, till then. Some of our neighbours are beforehand with us. There were fine young birds among the boughs yesterday, twitting our youngsters in their songs with being behindhand altogether."

"They will not have to twit long, I suppose," exclaimed the hen-mother rather angrily. "Of course you will bring ours forward as fast as you can. Of course they must not be behind their neighbours. Of course they must learn to take care of themselves, and fly and sing, like the rest. Dear, dear! how silly I was! But thank you so much for telling me. It's very well to be easily pleased, and the poor helpless things are very sweet, as you say; but of course it will be a much grander thing when they have grown to be fine young birds like those others; able to take care of themselves and to twit their neighbours who can't. And of course I shall be as happy again. I wish the time were come."

And it did come; but there was a great deal of trouble to be taken first. The little ones had to be nursed and fed till their feathers had grown, and then they had to be trained, by slow degrees and with much care, to use their young wings in flight.

Now the hen-mother had left her mate no rest till he began to teach; for, first, she was jealous for her children's credit; and secondly, she wanted to feel what it was to be as happy as it was possible to be. Happy enough she was, but for this wish.

But alas! for the trouble and fear that came over her when the teaching really began. The eight darlings must come out of their nest, from under her wing; she could help them no longer—they could scarcely help themselves. Yet they must spread the feeble pinion, and strain the unpractised muscle, and run a risk of failure and even life, to insure success.

Oh, poor hen-mother, what a trying change was this, though brought about by her own especial desire! No wonder that, while the teaching was going on, she would sit and shake with fright, and wish all manner of foolish things: that they were back in the nest, of course; but far more than that—even that they were back in the old baby days again, in the egg-shells of their first existence, unconscious of life and of them.

"They were all under my wing then, at any rate," said she; "my own dear little ones with me, and I with them: what more could I want?"

And, oh dear, when the youngsters were safe in the nest once more at night, how she used to gather them under her wings with joy!

"I am getting to like night better than day," said she at last to her mate, "for then my birds are in the nest again. You are training them very cleverly, I know, and I was the first to want them to be clever like other young birds, and they are getting cleverer day by day, I dare say, so I ought to be happier; but the happiness is not as pleasant as it was. How can it be, when they are away so much, and the empty nest stares me in the face? The risks are so many too, till they can really fly well, and I tremble with fear. But all is right at night, when you all come back and sing. Yes, if it wasn't for thinking of the morrow, the happiness would be perfect indeed then: if it were always evening, I mean, and they and you were always here."

"It is natural you should feel as you do," replied the mate; "but you mistake the cause. If you are not quite happy yet, it is merely because things are not quite perfect, that is all. When the young ones can fly really well, for instance, there will no longer be any risk; and when they can sing better still, our music will be pleasanter than ever; and when they are able and independent, all your cares and anxieties will be at an end. Wait a little longer, and you will be happy indeed."

The hen-mother sighed. "I suppose you must be right," said she; "I will wait. But if I could sing myself, I would sing a mother's song about the birds in the nest. It may not have been perfection, but it was a very happy time."

So she waited and did her best to be pleased. But for longer and longer intervals the empty nest stared her in the face, and she thought many things she did not dare to say—even the old foolish wish that they were all in their egg-shells again.

Still, every evening, when they came back and perched in the boughs, if not in the nest, and the singing grew sweeter and sweeter, she cheered up and rejoiced once more.

And now at last the nestlings were full-grown birds, and could fly and sing as well as their parents. Perfection had come; they were independent; nobody's young birds could twit them now. "But now, of course," said their father, "they must go out and seek their fortunes, as we did, and choose mates, and settle in life for themselves. You see the justice of this?"

The hen-mother, to whom he was speaking, answered "Yes;" but her heart was half broken. And when he added, "This is the real perfection of happiness to parents," she made no answer at all.

"It ought to be, perhaps," thought she to herself, "but it isn't so with me. I wonder why?" She sat on the edge of the empty nest and wondered still; but she couldn't find out the secret there.

Then the young ones piped to her from the woods; and at last said she: "Things are altered, I see; I will go to them!" and the very thought comforted her as she flew away.

And when she had found them, and watched them in the full enjoyment of their own young life—listened to them as they warbled merrily to each other among the trees, or sported with friends here and there, she began to understand the whole matter. She was rejoicing in their joy rather than in her own.

And time went on: and one day as she sat, so listening, on a branch in the centre of the wood, her mate by her side, said she: "It is all becoming quite clear, and I can see that you were right on the whole. This is nearer the perfection of happiness than anything else could be, but the quite perfect is not to be had. Still, this is nearest and best; whether sweetest or not, I scarcely know. But thank you for telling me! I was selfish before: wanted my own darlings to myself, under my own wing, in my own particular nest—safe, as I called it—foolish that I was! Oh, narrow, narrow thought! As if one place was safer than another, when the sun looks down everywhere, streaming warmth and comfort upon all! I see things differently now. The wood is but a larger nest, and those that live in it but a larger family. I spread out my love a little wider, and behold my happiness spreads out too! Though each in turn, for a time, must form his own little circle of joy, the whole must form one larger circle together; and who knows where it is to end?"

She ceased, and then listened again, and truly the wood was ringing with melodies: her mate by her side; her children now here, now there with the dear ones they loved. The circle grew wider and wider as time went further on.

But by and by, when age had crept over both, the mate had tender thoughts himself of old times, and tenderer still for her. She had not been wrong altogether, he whispered softly and kindly. It was not selfishness only that had filled her heart. He would sing her the song she used to wish she could have sung herself—a mother's song about the birds in the nest.

And it went to the hearts of both.

Other mothers in other nests, lift up your souls, as the circle widens from your feet. "One God and Father of all, who is above all, and through all, and in you all," has all together now in the circle of His care; yea, even though a world, or the change we call death, may seem to divide them: and He will bring His own together at last into one home—the "Father's House;"—one home, be the mansions never so many!